BALLOONS TO JETS

BALLOONS TO JETS

A Century of Aeronautics in Illinois, 1855–1955

Howard L. Scamehorn

With a New Foreword by Gene Abney

Southern Illinois University Press
Carbondale and Edwardsville

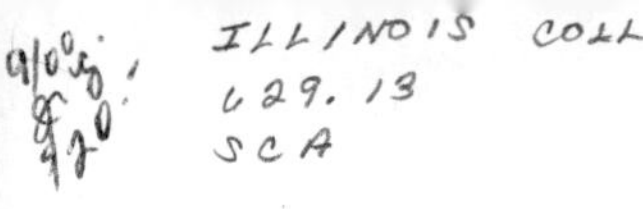

Originally published in 1957 as Illinois State Historical
Society Occasional Publication, No. 52 (General Editor, Clyde C. Walton) by
Henry Regnery Co., Chicago, Illinois
Printed in the United States of America
03 02 01 00 4 3 2 1

Library of Congress Cataloging-in-Publication Data
Scamehorn, H. Lee (Howard Lee), 1926–
Balloons to jets: a century of aeronautics in Illinois, 1855–1955 / Howard L.
Scamehorn ; with a foreword by Gene Abney.
p. cm.
Originally published: Chicago : H. Regnery Co., 1957.
Includes bibliographical references and index.
1. Aeronautics—Illinois—History—19th century. 2. Aeronautics—Illinois—
History—20th century. I. Title.

TL522.I4 S35 2000
629.13'09773—dc21
ISBN 0-8093-2336-2 (pbk. : alk. paper) 99-086254

The paper used in this publication meets the minimum requirements of American
National Standard for Information Sciences—Permanence of Paper for Printed
Library Materials, ANSI Z39.48-1992. ♾

CONTENTS

ILLUSTRATIONS

Following page 48

FOREWORD

In the early 1950s, the aviation community and the Illinois Department of Aeronautics were making preparations to celebrate the fiftieth anniversary of powered flight. Orville and Wilbur Wright had made their first flight at Kitty Hawk, North Carolina, on December 17, 1903, and there was to be a nationwide celebration in honor of this historic event. While planning the various activities to highlight this occasion, we in the department observed that no single publication provided a detailed history of aviation in Illinois. We decided to correct this omission by making it possible to bring forth a new book on the subject.

First, of course, extensive research would be required. That brought about the search for a qualified person to work on the project. Howard Lee Scamehorn, a graduate student in history at the University of Illinois, was highly recommended. Because of somewhat limited financial resources, the department offered Scamehorn a small stipend; in return, his work on this project could be used toward his dissertation for his doctorate. As it turned out, various factors precluded getting the book out in time for the fiftieth anniversary celebration. However, the fact that the effort was under way was something that could be pointed to with pride. The author was able to glean priceless information directly from many of Illinois's aviation pioneers, but this required traveling throughout the state for personal interviews, which was time-consuming. Reducing all of the collected information and writing the manuscript also took a great deal of time. The book was finally finished in 1957. By that time, Scamehorn was a professor of history at the University of Colorado.

The cost of getting the book into print caused another delay. An arrangement was made with the Illinois State Historical Society whereby the society would give the book its official approval, and its president, Clyde C. Walton, would serve as the general editor. The society would then print the book and distribute it to its members and to strategically located libraries throughout Illinois. The book was well received by both the aviation and the historical communities. The few criticisms received revolved around the somewhat abbreviated treatment of a given area or a particular activity, which was necessitated by cost considerations. Today, the original six-hundred-page manuscript is on file at the Illinois State Historical Library in Springfield.

Balloons to Jets offers a wealth of information on aviation in our state as well as on events leading up to the Wright Brothers' initial flight. In the first thirty pages of the book, Scamehorn clearly describes the aeronautical activities and experiments performed by such people as Octave Chanute, Glenn Curtiss, Thomas Scott Baldwin, Otto Lilienthal, Samuel Pierpont Langley, and others that lent support to the 1903 flight.

Members of the aviation community throughout the state of Illinois will, I am sure, join me in expressing sincere gratitude and commendations to David A. NewMyer, who serves as the chair of Southern Illinois University's Department of Aviation Management and Flight and as the editor of the series Aviation Management, for initiating the reprinting of *Balloons to Jets* and to Southern Illinois University Press for going forward with the project. This history of Illinois aviation makes for excellent reading and fills a void that has existed for many years.

GENE ABNEY

PREFACE

Aeronautics in Illinois has progressed from balloons to jets, from free, uncontrollable flight to the age of supersonics. One hundred years ago a canny Yankee from Connecticut first introduced the marvelous achievement of human flight. Today it is accepted as a natural part of life: Thousands of people travel daily on giant airliners, others use their own aircraft for business and pleasure, and to everyone aviation is a symbol of national defense.

In May, 1953, in the midst of the nation-wide observance of the fiftieth anniversary of powered flight, the Illinois Department of Aeronautics proposed that this state mark the occasion by compiling a history of flight in Illinois. For many years aviation enthusiasts have felt the need for a history of this type, and they recognized that it must be written while many of the pioneers were able to re-create from memory the events of the past. Acting on this idea, Director Joseph K. McLaughlin and Assistant Director (now Director) Arthur E. Abney decided that the Illinois Department of Aeronautics, with the aid of other interested groups and persons, should take the initiative. The late Dr. Harry E. Pratt, State Historian, suggested that the history be published by the Illinois State Historical Society. The directors of that body later concurred.

This history is little more than a survey of a vast and complex development. Although limited by time and space, the author has endeavored to present the more significant events of the past century, and to explain, wherever possible, the various factors which shaped aeronautics. Chronologically, progress is traced from the free balloon to the dirigible, then to the airplane. With the rapid improvement of airplanes after 1910, lighter-than-air craft lost their significance in Illinois, though they remained important for another twenty years elsewhere. Therefore, the story of aeronautics centers around heavier-than-air machines, the offspring of the famous Wright Flyer.

Although clearly superior to either the dirigible or the balloon, the airplane did not attain a status of respectability until given a chance to demonstrate its effectiveness under fire in World War I. After 1919, its advancement as a carrier of passengers and freight was for a time exceedingly slow and unsteady. Only the government airmail and the activities of itinerant flyers kept commercial aviation alive in the early 1920's. Then a youthful airmail pilot named Charles A. Lindbergh flew from New York to Paris—almost in a single stroke he awoke public interest in flight. Since that time, aviation has been less a matter of individual effort and more the product of groups and organized companies. In relating recent achievements, the author has treated chiefly the larger aspects—commercial air transport, the growth and expansion of ground facilities, and the broadening of state and federal regulation.

The purely scientific or technical side of aeronautics has been almost entirely avoided in order to give attention to personalities. A study of technical developments would have forced the author to sacrifice space which has been used to tell the story of man's persistent effort to advance the art of flying, whether for business or for pleasure. The technical story rightfully belongs elsewhere.

It is hoped that this survey will encourage others to make a more thorough study of the significant events which can only be sketched here.

Urbana, Illinois HOWARD L. SCAMEHORN

ACKNOWLEDGMENTS

This book could not have been written without the use of newspapers, periodicals, books, and other sources made available to the author by the co-operation of individuals and libraries throughout the United States. The author is especially indebted to the staff members of the Illinois State Historical Library, the University of Illinois Library, the Chicago Public Library, the John Crerar Library, the Missouri Historical Society (St. Louis) Library, the Rockford Public Library, and the Library of Congress. Without the aid of the staff members of these institutions the difficult task of collecting data would have been beyond the ability of a single researcher.

To the hundreds of pilots, airport operators, and aviation enthusiasts throughout Illinois who gave freely of their time and historical materials, the author is deeply grateful. Special thanks must go to the real pioneers of flight who, through their interviews, correspondence, and valuable collections of historical data, made possible the gathering of otherwise unavailable material for this book. To Eugene Brown of Peoria, Walter C. Scholl of Chicago, and Duke Schroer of Quincy, the author is grateful for much of the material which appears in the chapter devoted to lighter-than-air craft. To Charles A. Arens, Winamac, Indiana; Carl S. Bates, Chicago; Walter L. Brock, Chicago; Fred A. Hoover, San Diego, California; Frank Kastory, Bradenton, Florida; Edward A. Korn, East Orange, New Jersey; E. M. Laird, Boca Raton, Florida; James R. Mills, Chicago; Joseph M. Pallissard, Broadview, Illinois; and Gordon Thomas,

Redlands, California, the author is indebted for material which appears in the chapters devoted to aviation prior to 1917. Mrs. Constance B. Smith, Coal City, Illinois, generously supplied material concerning the activities of her father, William E. Somerville. Mrs. Harold F. Newman, Denver, Colorado, permitted the author to microfilm a scrapbook compiled by her father, Ivy Baldwin, during the height of his aeronautical career. For the recent period, the aeronautical collections, mostly scrapbooks, of Stanley Beckerman, Mt. Carmel; Fred S. Disosway and Gordon B. Snow, Sheldon; Fred E. Machesney, Rockford; Kenneth Ringel, Urbana; and Clarence K. Stewart, Elmhurst, have been of immeasurable value.

Above all, the author is deeply grateful to the staffs of the Illinois Department of Aeronautics and the Illinois State Historical Library for their always friendly co-operation. Much of the recent history can be seen in perspective only through the extensive files of the Illinois Aeronautics Commission (1931–1945) and its successor, the Illinois Department of Aeronautics. Without the aid of the clerical staff of this Department this book would not have advanced beyond the preliminary stage. For editing and typing the author is indebted to James N. Adams, Mrs. Ruth H. Lewis, and Miss Juanita Bailey. For advice, counsel, and criticism, the author is especially grateful to Professor Fred A. Shannon, who read much of the manuscript as a thesis submitted by the author to the Graduate College of the University of Illinois.

BALLOONS TO JETS

1

AERONAUTICAL DEVELOPMENT PRIOR TO POWERED FLIGHT

For many centuries man's efforts to devise a mechanical apparatus for flight proved futile. The sight of birds in the air stirred the imaginations of restless minds, turning thoughts to a search for the means of emulation. Ancient Greek and Chinese mythology indicates man's early interest in the matter. The story of Daedalus, the fashioner of wings from feathers and wax, and his son, Icarus, reveals much more than the simple moral of the consequences which result from disobedience. Disregarding Daedalus' advice, Icarus flew so near the sun that the wax holding his wings melted, causing the disobedient son to fall into the "Icarian" Sea. The wings worn by Icarus were similar to those of birds—the same design employed in the construction of ornithopters or wing-flapping machines by inventors for many centuries because of the erroneous belief that man, through his own muscular power, could raise and sustain himself in the air like a bird.

The first scientific approach to the problem of human flight resulted from the investigations of Leonardo da Vinci in the fifteenth century. He formulated the first clear idea of both the helicopter and ornithopter and invented the air screw. Although Da Vinci may be called the first successful inventor of flying machines, for his models did fly, he misled countless generations of aeronautical experimenters by perpetuating the myth that man could, by his own strength, lift himself into the air if proper supporting surfaces were attached to his legs and arms.

The search for a practical method of human flight approached success in the late seventeenth century when a Jesuit, Francesco Terzi-Lana, proposed the vague outlines of a lighter-than-air craft. In 1670 he suggested the design of a buoyant air vessel which, though based on the fallacious vacuum principle, came very close to pointing out the significance of variations in the weight of gases. His craft would not have been navigable, although his principle was theoretically sound according to his calculations of the "levity" of gases and in the suspension system of his vessel. He failed, however, to recognize that a vacuum could not be created within an object that was strong enough to withstand atmospheric pressure but light enough to be buoyant.

More than a century after Terzi-Lana's experiments, two Frenchmen demonstrated the possibility of utilizing buoyant gases as a means of performing human flight. Between 1670 and 1780, many experimenters and inventors of so-called aerial machines published erroneous, if not impossible, theories of aircraft construction and aerial navigation. Friar Bartholomeu de Gusmao's design of an airship sustained by magnets and electrified amber, and propelled by wind and manually operated bellows, was one of the many interesting but ridiculous schemes advanced in the early Eighteenth Century. The first real success was recorded in 1780, when Joseph Michel and Jacques Etienne Montgolfier, sons of a papermaker of Annonay, France, discovered variations in the densities of gases, particularly the seeming lightness of smoke as compared with air. Beginning with a consideration of the "levity" of smoke from the chimney fire, the Montgolfiers proceeded to experiment with the lifting powers of several gases. When a small paper bag of smoke, about 40-cubic-foot capacity, rose to the ceiling, the age of speculation in aeronautics ended and an era of experimentation commenced.

After several months of experimenting with smoke, the Montgolfiers gave the first public demonstration of a balloon ascension on June 5, 1783, in Annonay. Using a 23,439-cubic-foot bag of paper and linen, they sent up a balloon from the city's market place. Although this was considered a remarkable feat at the time, a scientific explanation for the phenomenon of flight based on the principle of buoyancy was unknown for several more years. For a time buoyancy was ascribed to "Montgolfiers' gas" or "l'air alkalin," as it was also called. The true cause, the fact that hot air is more rarefied (less dense) than cold air and therefore rises, was not known until the physicist Horace Benedict de Saussure called attention to the effect of temperature on the density of air in 1785.

Shortly after the Montgolfier brothers demonstrated the practicality of ascending in a smoke-filled bag, Jacques A. C. Charles proved that hydrogen gas could be more effective than hot air. Using a varnished silk bag filled with hydrogen, Charles and a companion ascended from the Tuileries in Paris on December 1, 1783, on a flight that covered 30 miles in two hours. Charles' gas balloon was described by contemporaries as a sphere 27½ feet in diameter, with the upper half enclosed in a net secured to a hoop which girded the middle of the bag. From the hoop, called an "equator," long ropes supported a highly ornamented wicker "boat" beneath. At the bottom of the bag a long narrow neck seven inches in diameter allowed inflation with hydrogen. A valve at the top, which could be opened or closed by a cord extending to the boat, permitted the aeronaut to release gas whenever necessary. Except for the fancy boat, Charles' balloon was essentially the same as that used by aeronauts in the United States for the next century and a half.

The popularity of balloons developed at a rapid pace following the demonstrations of the Montgolfiers and Charles. In Europe, and later in the United States, balloons were used primarily for sport and amusement. During the nineteenth century, they were occasionally employed for scientific and military purposes, but the majority of balloons in the United States were used by professional aeronauts to amuse and entertain the public at Fourth of July celebrations, fairs, carnivals, and festive gatherings of many types. In retrospect, the balloon and its use as entertainment appear as a transitional phase in the development of air navigation to heavier-than-air flight. Historically, the balloon is important more because it served as a constant incentive to scientists and inventors in their search for a more practical solution to the problem of human flight than because of its limited uses. The dirigible and the airplane were a direct result of that stimulus, just as public acceptance of the dirigible and airplane was conditioned by more than a century of balloon exhibitions.

The first balloon ascension in the United States was made one year after the Montgolfiers' demonstration. On June 24, 1784, near Baltimore, Maryland, a 13-year-old youth named Edward Warren performed a brief ascension in a balloon of the Montgolfier type. Ten more years passed, however, before Jean Pierre Blanchard, a celebrated French aeronaut, completed the first actual aerial voyage in the United States. Starting from Washington Prison in Philadelphia, Blanchard made a flight of 45 miles to Gloucester County, New Jersey. To Warren and Blanchard belongs the credit for introducing aeronautics into the United States; Warren's impulsive venture was of little significance other than for its novelty and daring, but Blanchard proved conclusively the feasibility of flight in a lighter-than-air craft.

Interest in aeronautics lapsed for almost two decades following Blanchard's flight but was revived as a result of exhibitions given in the larger cities of the East, in 1819, by another Frenchman. Louis-Charles Guillé completed ascensions in New York, Philadelphia, Baltimore, and other cities along the Atlantic Coast. Although his performances were exceedingly popular, they were not numerous enough to stimulate interest in aeronautics on a large scale. During the next decade other aeronauts performed in eastern cities. Among the more successful was Charles Ferson Durant, whose numerous ascensions in Castle Garden, New York's most popular amusement center, transformed ballooning into a profitable form of entertainment. More than any other person, Durant gave to aeronautics the characteristic that it retained for more than a century.

Many of the great men in this field in the nineteenth century began their careers prior to the Civil War. John Wise, who was, with the possible exception of Thaddeus Sobieski Coulincourt Lowe, the greatest balloonist of the century, performed his first ascension in Philadelphia in 1835. Lowe, the organizer of the United States Army's first Balloon Corps during the Civil War, did not take up ballooning until 1858, seven years after Samuel Archer King, a Philadelphia aeronaut, performed the first of more than 450 ascensions in his long and illustrious career. Among other aeronauts of the pre-Civil War period the names of George Elliot, Nicholas J. Ash, Samuel Wallace, William A. Woodall, and Hugh F. Walker, all of Baltimore, were well known. William Paullin and John Steiner, residents of Philadelphia, and Richard Clayton, an Englishman who settled in Cincinnati, also earned fame, if not riches, for their daring exploits with gas balloons. Their contribution to the advancement of aeronautics was unquestionably slight at the time, but through their efforts others were encouraged to take up the problem of human flight, though a practical solution remained beyond their grasp for more than half a century.

Aeronauts of the pre-Civil War period were appreciated mainly for their daring and eccentricity. The clumsy gas bags they used were of little or no practical value as a method of traveling from one city to another. In fact, the "flying professors" of the nineteenth century were at least a generation or more in advance of the time when aeronautics would assume a cloak of respectability and thrive on its entertainment value alone.

Though a familiar sight in many eastern cities as early as 1820, the balloon was unknown in Illinois until Silas M. Brooks, an extraordinary aeronaut from Burlington, Connecticut, performed in Chicago, July 4, 1855. Using the *Eclipse,* a balloon belonging to S. B. Ledgar, Brooks started his performance from a vacant lot at the corner of Peoria and Randolph streets. The flight, according to a contemporary newspaper, began with a slow, almost vertical ascent, to a height of nearly a mile before a strong wind carried the *Eclipse* toward Lake Michigan. Rather than endure the hazards of a descent into water, Brooks drew open the gas valve, hoping to lose sufficient buoyancy to make a landing near the Michigan and Southern Railroad tracks just short of the lake shore. After falling to within less than 100 feet of the ground, Brooks cast out an anchor, anticipating that its sharp hooks would catch in the prairie sod and halt the flight. However, the anchor failed to catch; the balloon "flew along at the rate of a mile a minute," heading for a single strand of telegraph wire that blocked its path toward the lake.

The first flight in Illinois ended abruptly—almost disastrously —when the *Eclipse* crashed into the wire with a terrific jolt. The initial impact severed several of the cords that held the basket to the gas bag; relentless pressure of the wind and the resulting friction of the remaining cords against the wire quickly completed the separation. As the basket fell, with the unfortunate aeronaut still inside, the balloon "mounted into the heavens like a freed bird, and sailed off into the eastern sky."

Despite the hard fall, Brooks escaped without serious injury and immediately returned to Chicago, where he posted a $50 reward for the recovery of the *Eclipse*. The balloon, valued at $800, according to contemporary reports, was the third such loss suffered by Brooks within a period of a few weeks. Even though the balloon was recovered within several days, Brooks decided to construct a new one of his own for exhibitions in the Middle West; consequently, Ledgar hired O. K. Harrison to perform with the *Eclipse*. Perhaps Brooks's decision to leave Ledgar's employ was motivated in part by the realization that the *Eclipse* was too rotten for further safe ascensions. But, whatever the reason, Brooks traveled to Rockford, Illinois, where he supervised the construction of the *Comet*, a balloon similar to the *Eclipse*.

Following the Chicago ascension, Brooks appeared in at least a dozen Illinois communities in three years. Although other aeronauts performed in Illinois prior to 1860, Brooks, more than any other one person, introduced the balloon to residents of all parts of the state. He did not perform in the state after

1858 but continued to make ascensions for more than 30 years. Altogether, Brooks completed approximately 200 performances during his career, in addition to constructing balloons for other aeronauts, many of whom he taught to handle a gas balloon in flight.

The exhibitions staged in Illinois by Brooks were extraordinary shows, combining other forms of entertainment with balloon ascensions. All of his performances were designed to draw spectators within the walls of a large pavilion constructed of canvas. The admission charge was 25 cents for children and 50 cents for adults. Unfortunately, balloon ascensions were not easily adapted to this type of audience, for spectators soon learned that the flight, once under way, could be easily viewed from outside the pavilion without paying the price of admission. In an effort to overcome the reluctance of the public to pay for the privilege of viewing the ascensions, Brooks tried to create interest in the inflation process, which was at best a dull routine. When this also failed to attract paying spectators, a fireworks display was added. For the price of a single admission ticket, the purchaser could watch the balloon ascension from within the pavilion in the afternoon and return later that night to witness a gala display of fireworks at no additional cost.

The problem of inducing spectators to pay for admission to an enclosed pavilion plagued Brooks during the three seasons he performed in Illinois. In Rockford, on August 14, 1855, nearly 12,000 people, the largest gathering in northwestern Illinois to that date, witnessed the ascension, but only about one-third of that number paid for a ticket. In later years, the proportion of paid admissions fell much lower, often resulting in an income that failed to meet expenses. The addition of music to the show in 1856 apparently attracted a larger number of paying customers, for contemporary newspapers did not call attention to nonpaying audiences during Brooks's performances in Peoria, Ottawa, and Joliet. In all three towns one Monsieur Webster's "French Sax Horn Band" presented a "discourse of sweet music with each entertainment," to accompany the afternoon balloon ascension and the evening fireworks display. At the same time, Brooks attempted to overcome the apprehensions of the meek and mild and of the fairer sex, whose delicate sensitivities might suffer from association with the generally boisterous crowds which attended balloon exhibitions. He assured them that "the most strict order & decorum will be preserved during the exhibitions, and ladies & children, will find it to be a safe and pleasant place of amusement, whether accompanied by gentlemen or not."

Despite efforts to enhance the attractiveness of balloon exhibitions, attendance must have fallen all during the 1856 season, for the next year Brooks sought employment as manager of the St. Louis Museum, a position well suited to his peculiar talents as a showman and mechanic-inventor. When Brooks returned to aeronautics in 1858, while retaining the museum position, he starred as the aeronaut for the Ericsson Hydrogen Balloon Company, presumably of St. Louis, rather than as manager-aeronaut of his own troupe. Even then, exhibitions proved unprofitable. In at least three of six performances in Illinois that season, gate receipts failed to meet expenses. In Jacksonville on July 3, Springfield on July 5, and Alton on July 10, large crowds gathered outside the canvas pavilion to watch the show, while only a small number paid for admission. The prospect of slim gate receipts for the Springfield performance induced the editor of the *Illinois State Journal* to suggest that a collection to help pay expenses of the show should be taken up "among the portion of the audience who prefer a view from outside the pavilion, to which we presume no objection will be made." The same editor hastened to point out that a large number of spectators "do not care to go into the pavilion to witness the process of inflation, which is often tedious enough, who would yet willingly contribute toward defraying the expenses incurred by the managers of the enterprise."

Other aeronauts appeared in Illinois soon after Brooks introduced the sport. Eugéne Godard, a famous French aeronaut, and John Steiner, of Philadelphia, performed one or more ascensions prior to 1860. As a member of T. S. C. Lowe's Balloon Corps in the Union Army, Steiner was also assigned to duty in General Henry W. Halleck's department at Cairo, Illinois, during several months in 1862. Godard won fame and distinction as a balloonist in Europe before coming to the United States in the late 1850's. Twice, in 1855 and 1858, he performed in the Mississippi Valley, traveling as far north as St. Louis on the first trip, and to Iowa communities on the second. In 1858, Godard was prevented by adverse weather from making an ascension in Cairo, but later, after appearing in St. Louis, he performed in Springfield. After the 1858 season, Godard returned to France, where, with his brother Louis, he served as a balloonist with the French army during the 1859 campaign against the Austrian army in northern Italy.

The Civil War produced a temporary lull in civil aeronautical activity throughout the United States, for nearly all balloonists volunteered their services as observers for the Union Army. The work of Wise, Lowe, Steiner, and other aeronauts as observers should have stirred up enthusiasm for balloons as military weapons, but neither the army nor the American public properly appreciated the potential of aeronautics as a method for observing enemy operations, or for directing artillery and mortar fire on enemy positions. In fact, officers of the Confederate forces recognized the value of balloons to the Northern armies even though many high-ranking officers of the North generally viewed them with disinterest.

During the second half of the nineteenth century, following the end of hostilities between North and South, aeronautics achieved new heights of popularity. Leading the ever increasing ranks of professional balloonists were many of the great figures of the pre-Civil War years. Wise, Lowe, King, and Steiner, to name a few, remained active for many years. Although renowned for remarkable flights and efforts to improve the safety and performance of balloons, Wise seldom appeared in Illinois, preferring to conduct his activities in the East, particularly in Philadelphia. Like Wise, Lowe and King were inventors of many aeronautical devices. King perfected rubberized balloon cloth for gas bags and first introduced into the United States the drag rope, an innovation developed by

Charles Green in England to prevent balloons from rising or landing at too rapid a rate.

In terms of popularity, Washington Harrison Donaldson was probably the greatest aeronaut of the late nineteenth century. In a four-year career packed with every thrill and feat of skill imaginable, Donaldson amassed a record of 139 ascensions on which he carried 232 passengers—better than the record of any of his contemporaries in an equal space of time. But his tremendous popularity arose not from records alone, however remarkable they were. His seemingly boundless courage and daring and his death-defying displays of acrobatic and aerial skill, invariably carried to the point of recklessness, made him the darling of audiences wherever he performed.

Between 1872 and 1875, Donaldson completed six ascensions in Illinois. On July 4, 1872, during a flight that started from Green's Garden, an amusement center north of Chicago, he drifted out over Lake Michigan, avoiding almost certain death by the narrowest margin. Three years later, as an aeronaut with P. T. Barnum's traveling Hippodrome, Donaldson returned to Chicago, where on July 15, 1875, he and Newton S. Grimwood, a reporter for the *Chicago Evening Journal*, vanished on a flight over the lake. The first clue as to the fate of the balloon and its passengers was discovered when Grimwood's body was washed ashore near Montague, Michigan, on August 17, 1875. No trace was ever found of Donaldson's body or of the balloon.

After 1870, aeronautical activity increased noticeably in response to a growing demand for exhibitions. The great boom in balloon exhibitions did not appear, however, until the late 1880's, after Thomas Scott Baldwin, of Quincy, Illinois, had developed the flexible parachute and exploited it as an entertainment medium in conjunction with the balloon ascension. The parachute drop from a balloon stimulated in turn the revival of an earlier phase of aeronautics—the use of the hot-air balloon—and nearly brought about the exclusion of gas balloons from exhibitions.

The hot air or smoke variety was better suited to exhibitions that included parachute drops. The change from gas to hot air developed for two important reasons. First, the very nature and expense of gas balloons tended to discourage their use by exhibition balloonists. Initially, Baldwin had used gas for parachute drops, but soon turned to hot-air balloons because they could be inflated more easily and at less cost. Before jumping from a gas balloon, aeronauts tied open the gas valve and hoped that the wind would not carry the balloon too far for convenient recovery. With hot air, the problem of recovering deflated bags was reduced to a minimum of inconvenience. After the aeronaut made his jump, the bag quickly lost its buoyancy as the air cooled or the bag tipped up, allowing the hot air to escape, after which the limp bag fell to the ground. Second, and increasingly important as new recruits were drawn into the ranks of the professional aeronauts, hot-air balloons were easier to operate than gas balloons. The hot-air balloonist could be a rank amateur with no real knowledge of the science of aeronautics, but the gas balloonist had to undergo a relatively complex training program in order to learn the intricacies of navigation.

By the close of the nineteenth century, balloon exhibitions had been frequently staged in almost every Illinois city and town. Holiday celebrations, fairs, carnivals, and other festive gatherings often had exhibitions by local or transient aeronauts. For a time in the late 1880's, well-known professional aeronauts, such as Baldwin, earned as much as $1,500 a performance. Most entertainers, even though not widely known as aeronauts, earned sizable fees for ascensions and parachute jumps. Inevitably, the prospect of rich rewards for exhibitions attracted many recruits to the ranks, with the result that fees fell as the supply of performers increased. By 1892, prices of exhibitions had dropped to a fraction of what they had been five years earlier; one aeronaut received only $25 for a show near Quincy. For most performers, however, the price ranged from $100 to $250, though some of the more famous ones received much more.

Soon after 1900, balloon ascensions and parachute jumps declined appreciably in popularity, though the number of exhibitions staged annually in Illinois remained at a high level.

There was clearly a public reaction against the once popular exhibitions, for the aeronaut could no longer command the attention and respect of former years. The reason for public indifference was obvious. Most important, the routine had not changed since Tom Baldwin added the parachute drop, and the balloon itself had remained essentially the same for more than a century. In plain terms, the public had grown tired of the same type of performance year after year. As long as the parachute and the balloon retained an aura of mystery and novelty, the demand for exhibitions remained fairly constant, but in time the principle of buoyancy became common knowledge, the novelty of flight in a lighter-than-air craft vanished with the repetition of unvaried performances, and the daring and skill of the aeronaut became commonplace. Public reaction also resulted to some degree from the prevalence of unscrupulous, greedy promoters and aeronauts who entered the exhibition business in large numbers solely for the purpose of making money by whatever means at their disposal. This type pretended to offer more to the public than he actually delivered, and left town with the gate receipts before action could be taken by irate citizens.

While aeronautics in the United States consisted almost entirely of balloon displays, in Europe experimenters and inventors were seeking ways of navigating with motor-driven, steerable balloons. Experimental airships, driven by hand-propelled paddle wheels, air screws, and oars, were built and discarded long before inventors looked to steam, electricity, and the internal combustion engine for motive power. A French engineer, Henri Gifford, perfected a navigable airship in 1852. Gifford's craft, a semirigid dirigible, utilized a small steam engine to turn a crude air screw or propeller. Other experimenters, particularly in France, and to some extent in England and Germany, carried on the search for a perfectly navigable airship. Progress was not always evident, however. Although Gifford's work with elongated balloons clearly indicated a practical design, if suitable motive power were devised, the impractical, often fantastic, designs perfected in the next twenty years contributed little of real value to the development of a navigable airship. Progress was again achieved in 1872, when Dupuy de Lôme, a French naval architect, utilized Gifford's design in the construction of a semirigid dirigible driven by a propeller actuated by a hand crank. The addition of a lightweight, reliable internal combustion engine to De Lôme's airship would have made it equal in appearance and performance to dirigibles constructed in Europe and the United States thirty years or more later.

In spite of the pioneering work of Gifford and Dupuy de Lôme, the first successful airship was not built until 1882. In that year two brothers, Albert and Gaston Tissandier, with financial aid from the French government, constructed an electrically powered dirigible which proved to be highly navigable. Two years later, Charles Renard and A. C. Krebs, also working in France with financial aid from the government, utilized the Tissandiers' ideas in the construction of the semirigid dirigible *La France,* the first completely navigable airship. *La France* proved conclusively the dirigibility of the elongated balloon, but its heavy electric power plant ruled out practical utility.

In the United States during the last quarter of the nineteenth century, countless inventors brought forth schemes for mechanically driven, controllable airships. But almost without exception such schemes failed to contribute to the advancement of aeronautics. Charles F. Ritchel, of Correy, Pennsylvania, perfected in 1878 a small barrel-shaped, foot-powered airship which, though more sensible than most schemes of that time, offered no real solution to the problem of aerial navigation.

A less practical invention was announced by a Chicago physician in 1884. Dr. Arthur DeBausset designed an electrically powered, vacuum-tube balloon, which he intended to use for transporting passengers and freight over vast distances at high speeds. This strange craft, as described in 1887, consisted of an airtight tube, cone-shaped at each end, constructed of thin steel sheets "to withstand the pressure of circumambient air when a vacuum has been produced by pumping all of the air out of the ship." In 1886, DeBausset and three associates, Jules Lang, G. E. Dawson, and A. Fisher, organized the Aerial Navigation Company of Chicago in order to raise $130,000 through the sale of stock for construction of a vacuum airship capable of carrying passengers and freight on intercity flights. Two years later, after an insignificant amount of stock had been subscribed, the promoters abandoned their original plans and turned to Congress with an appeal for funds. Bills appropriating $150,000 for construction of DeBausset's airship were introduced in both houses of Congress in 1888, one by Representative Ransom W. Dunham of Chicago. Although a powerful lobby gained the support of a large bloc of votes in the House, both bills failed to emerge from committees in time for consideration before the close of the session.

The merits of the vacuum-tube airship remained the subject for heated controversy among inventors and scientists for more than two decades while DeBausset tried in vain to raise enough money to build a full-sized model of his invention. As late as 1900, he claimed that, if given sufficient capital to build the airship, he could easily prove the error of his critics. The public, however, had less confidence in the scheme, especially after some of the leading aeronautical authorities in the United States, particularly Octave Chanute and Albert Francis Zahm, publicly denounced and mathematically proved the fallacy of the vacuum principle.

In 1890, another ambitious but impractical Illinois inventor announced plans for the construction of a mechanically driven, completely navigable airship. Edward Joel Pennington, a native of Racine, Wisconsin, had moved to Mt. Carmel, Illinois, where in 1890 he organized the Aeronautical Company. In January, 1891, Pennington completed a model 24 feet long and 6½ feet in diameter, which he displayed in Chicago in an effort to raise money and arouse public interest in his company.

Although capitalized at $2,000,000 (the first assessment of 10 per cent due in January, 1891), the Aeronautical Company lacked sufficient funds to do more than construct the large model and build a fence around the property it had leased in Mt. Carmel. Because of Pennington's exaggerated claims of how his invention would revolutionize transportation, the press carried on a campaign of caustic ridicule against him and the company. Statements to the effect that the Pennington airship would be able to travel nonstop from Chicago to New York at an average speed of approximately 200 miles an hour did not help the inventor's cause with the press, particularly the *Chicago Tribune*. Had Pennington been more cautious in his public statements, he might have sold sufficient stock in the company to build a full-sized airship. But, with a hostile press, the venture was doomed to failure from lack of public support.

Experiments in France and Germany in the last years of the nineteenth century provided the basis for the development of nonrigid dirigibles in the United States. Commencing in 1897, Alberto Santos-Dumont, the son of a wealthy Brazilian coffee planter, built upon the work of earlier experimenters, particularly Gifford. After conceiving the idea of adapting a lightweight internal combustion engine to an elongated balloon, he launched a series of experiments in France which led to a brief but successful flight within a year. He completed a second trial on November 13, 1899, running through a number of complex maneuvers in a short flight. After 1901, the year in which he captured the Deutsch Prize by flying seven miles, including a turn around the Eiffel Tower, in a few seconds less than thirty minutes, Santos-Dumont compiled an amazing record of flights in a number of different airships. At the same time, liberal financial aid from the French government supplied the impetus for the development of excellent military airships by Paul and Pierre Lebaudy and M. Julliot. In Germany, Major August von Parseval and Count Ferdinand von Zeppelin perfected significant improvements in airship design, the former with semirigid and the latter with rigid or Zeppelin airships, as they were popularly named.

The successes of these foreign experimenters stimulated the development of dirigibles in the United States. A veteran New York aeronaut and balloon manufacturer, A. Leo Stevens, claimed the distinction of building and flying the first motor-driven navigable airship in the United States in 1900. The next year Carl F. Myers, a balloon manufacturer from Frankfort, New York, reported initial successes with a motor-driven balloon. Others, including William Reifershied, of Streator, Illinois, conducted experiments with dirigibles between 1900 and 1904, but without appreciable success. The first practical dirigible in the United States was tested on August 4, 1904, on a flight over San Francisco Bay, with aeronaut-inventor Tom Baldwin at the controls. After experimenting for four years, searching for the right combination of elongated gas bag and lightweight, reliable gasoline engine, Baldwin built and flew the *California Arrow*, a small nonrigid dirigible which became the model for virtually every airship built in the United States during the next ten years.

The life of Tom Baldwin might have been lifted from a Horatio Alger story of rags to riches through hard work and good deeds, in the best tradition of American rugged individualism. Orphaned at an early age, Tom became an acrobat with a traveling circus when only fourteen years old and then progressed step by step to prominence as an aeronaut, inventor of a flexible parachute, builder of the first practical dirigible in the United States, and pioneer designer, builder, and flyer of airplanes. In later life "Uncle Tom" was unrivaled as a showman; as an innovator and inventor he contributed more than his share to the advancement of aeronautics over a period of nearly thirty years.

Commencing sometime in 1900, Baldwin conducted experiments with motor-driven balloons, using as a model the nonrigid airship developed by Santos-Dumont in France. After struggling nearly four years with the problem of securing a lightweight, reliable gasoline engine, Baldwin discovered the right type of engine for his elongated gas bag in the air-cooled motors designed and built by Glenn H. Curtiss, of Hammondsport, New York, for the Curtiss motorcycle. The success of the *California Arrow* was the result of a combination of the mechanical genius of Curtiss and the aeronautical knowledge of Baldwin. After 1904, Baldwin became an outstanding designer and manufacturer of dirigibles, adding this line to an extensive balloon manufacturing business. In 1908, he designed and built the United States Army Signal Corps's first aircraft, and seven years later performed a similar service for the Navy.

The success of the *California Arrow* in displays throughout the country influenced others to build dirigibles. By 1910, their apparent safety, as shown in hundreds of demonstrations, led Baldwin and other far-sighted men to advocate the creation of commercial airship passenger and freight lines between Chicago and New York and other large cities. On at least three occasions Baldwin attempted to organize intercity passenger transit. A St. Louis inventor, Albert Von Hoffman, announced plans in June, 1910, for the establishment of commercial passenger traffic between Chicago, St. Louis, and Kansas City, by way of Peoria and Springfield, Illinois. Also at that time, the Continental Aircraft Company of Chicago published notices of plans for regular passenger and freight service between Chicago and New York, using fifty-passenger airships designed by Herman Leinweber, a Chicago locksmith. Two other Chicago inventors, John A. Neustedt and Harry Jacobs, perfected a model airship which they attempted to build in 1910 for carrying passengers between Chicago and New York. Efforts to exploit small dirigibles for commercial airline use in 1910 were premature and destined from the start to failure. Not one of the schemes progressed beyond the planning stage.

Even though many efforts were made to adapt the airship to commercial transportation, the dirigible, like the balloon, remained almost entirely an amusement attraction. Prior to 1915, practically every dirigible produced in the United States was used for exhibitions. Baldwin and his protégés Lincoln Beachey and A. Roy Knabenshue, Charles K. Hamilton, Jack Dallas, Frank Gooddale, and Horace B. Wild popularized the dirigible in hundreds of performances given annually in all parts of the United States between 1905 and 1910. Between 1906 and 1912, Walter Wellman, Melvin C. Vaniman, and Joseph Bruckner, at one time editor of the *Arbeiter-Zeitung* in Chicago, tried unsuccessfully to show that the dirigible was capable of long flights under extremely hazardous conditions. Wellman and Vaniman failed in three attempts to fly over the North Pole and again in an effort to cross the Atlantic. Bruckner also planned a trans-Atlantic voyage but, unlike Wellman and Vaniman, did not actually make the start.

After 1910, interest in lighter-than-air craft was diverted to aviation, for the airplane showed greater promise than the clumsy airship. Since that time, particularly after World War I, dirigibles have frequently shown signs of extensive commercial development, but air transport with lighter-than-air craft has failed to materialize in the United States. The round-the-world flight of the *Graf Zeppelin* in 1929, followed by the inauguration of passenger service between Europe and South America with Zeppelin airships, seemed to indicate the feasibility of adapting airships to commercial air travel. However, tremendous advances in the technical development of transport airplanes in the late 1920's, accompanied by an expansion of airline facilities throughout the United States, forestalled the establishment of airship passenger service at that time. A series of unfortunate mishaps, culminating in the tragic loss of the *Hindenburg* at Lakehurst, New Jersey, in 1937, virtually precluded the development of commercial lines probably for all time.

Even before the development of a practical airplane, experimenters and inventors recognized the superiority of heavier-than-air flying machines over the lighter-than-air variety. An aircraft, if of commercial value, must navigate in all kinds of weather with a high degree of efficiency and safety. Airships employing hydrogen for lifting power were not safe. Consequently, even though they were perfected by the close of the nineteenth century, the search for a practical airplane continued. In 1903, the Wrights gave the world the airplane, ending man's search for a practical method of flight. From that date to the 1950's, the airplane retained the essential principle of the Wright flyer of 1903, though tremendous advances in design, construction, and performance have made possible a revolution in transportation since the end of World War I.

2

PRELUDE TO POWERED FLIGHT: OCTAVE CHANUTE AND THE WRIGHTS

By 1893, the study of human flight had gained a status of respectability, at least in scientific circles. A new spirit of mutual help among aeronautical researchers was leading to improvements and advances in theoretical and practical work. This development culminated a decade later in the construction of a practical flying machine.

The initial step toward co-operation, co-ordination, and free exchange of ideas among aeronautical experimenters in the United States and Europe was largely the work of one man, Octave Chanute. He provided aviation students with a comprehensive survey of all important experiments and inventions pertaining to man's search, over a period of several centuries, for a means of flight. A civil engineer of undeniable reputation and ability, Chanute was the leader of a new era of aeronautical development. His outspoken devotion, keen mind, and vast experience combined to create among engineers and scientists a deeper appreciation of the possibility of purely mechanical aviation. Simultaneously, the work of Samuel Pierpont Langley in the Smithsonian Institution, Washington, D.C., Otto Lilienthal in Germany, Louis Pierre Mouillard in Cairo, Egypt, and others contributed to a reappraisal of theories. Gradually, the idea gained wide support among scientists though the overwhelming majority of the population retained a firm conviction that flight in anything but a balloon or dirigible was impossible.

Born in Paris, February 18, 1832, Chanute spent most of his life in the United States. The son of a professor of history in the Collège Royal de France, he came to the United States in 1838, when his father accepted the vice-presidency of the College of Jefferson in Louisiana. Six years later, the family moved to New York City, where young Chanute completed his education in the public schools.

At the age of 17, he acquired his first knowledge of railroad construction, a field in which he was to earn acclaim. Starting in 1849 as an obscure surveyor's chainman on a construction gang of the Hudson River Railroad projected from New York to Albany, Chanute had an opportunity to acquire from experience the knowledge of a railroad engineer. When the line reached Albany in 1853, he moved west to take the job of surveying and constructing the Joliet and Bloomington portion of what later became the Chicago & Alton Railroad. In succeeding years he played a part in the construction of numerous railroads and bridges in the Middle West and West, built the stockyards in Chicago and Kansas City, Kansas, and served as chief engineer on the Chicago & Alton and Erie railroads. In 1888, he retired as an engineer, retaining only an interest in a railroad tie-preserving company, which he served as president during the remainder of his life.

The year after his retirement, Chanute moved from Kansas City to Chicago, where he turned his attention to aeronautics. The possibility of flight in a heavier-than-air machine had caught his imagination for the first time in the 1850's. Even then the subject "presented the attraction of an unsolved problem which did not seem as visionary as that of perpetual motion." Observation of birds indicated to Chanute the possibility of a solution, while the arguments advanced by scientists to prove it impossible seemed inconclusive. If only a lightweight engine could be obtained for motive power! Not even the history of centuries of constant failure discouraged him from investigating the possibility. Instead, the long list aroused his curiosity, giving birth to the idea that a careful scrutiny of experiments by engineers, subjecting the methods employed to scientific analysis, might provide an important clue to the eventual development of a practical flying machine. When he was about 25, Chanute had begun collecting data on the subject. This continued for a number of years, expanding from a hobby into an almost full-time job. In 1874, because his preoccupation with aeronautics interfered with his professional duties, he laid aside his voluminous notes.

After establishing a residence in Chicago, Chanute resumed the work and once more spent endless hours in the collection and analysis of aeronautical data. His letters at that time indicate that he had not formulated a definite program of research. A more active role in the promotion of flight was impractical, Chanute believed, until he had completed a study of others' experiments. A lecture which he delivered to the students and faculty of Sibley College of Engineering, Cornell University, on May 2, 1890, revealed clearly his reluctance to break with the past.

The lecture contained a review of developments in heavier- and lighter-than-air craft and the speaker's opinion of what the future held for the advancement of aerial navigation. The dominant theme was that practical flight hinged on the perfection of a machine capable of sustaining and propelling itself through the use of "aeroplanes" or wings and an air screw driven by a lightweight gasoline engine. This view was not unlike that of other students, but the manner in which Chanute predicted the flying machine would develop indicated his reluctance to abandon completely the balloon and dirigible. He emphasized the inelastic limitations of lighter-than-air craft, which doomed to failure the hopes of those who sought to perfect either the balloon or dirigible for commercial transportation. However, their shortcomings did not preclude the possibility, he thought, of employing them as the beginning point in the development of a "self-starting" and "self-landing" flying machine. By using them to launch flying machines, experimenters would have an opportunity to work out a means of maintaining stability in flight; once that problem had been solved, the balloon or dirigible could be cast aside.

Other portions of the lecture indicated the future course of his own aeronautical activities. His insistence upon experimental research on specific problems, particularly the perfection of a lightweight engine, absolute stability, initial velocity for starting, and the technique of landing safely, foreshadowed later experiments. His belief in the need for a "working association of searchers" explains at least in part why he played an important role in the movement that brought forth the Third International Conference on Aerial Navigation in Chicago three years later and why he helped to organize two aeronautical clubs before his death. Chanute was formulating the ideas that eventually led him to dedicate the last twenty years of his life to aeronautics.

In 1891, Chanute's study of aeronautical history culminated in a series of articles entitled "Progress in Flying Machines," published serially in *The Railroad and Engineering Journal* (later known as *The American Engineer and Railroad Journal*), and reprinted in book form as *Progress in Flying Machines* in 1894. This study exerted a profound influence on all persons interested in the problem of flight. Exact descriptions of unsuccessful inventions and scientific explanations for failures gave experimenters a comprehensive view of man's efforts to perfect flying machines throughout the ages. Explanations of fundamental errors, as well as correct principles, employed in earlier inventions enabled experimenters to redirect their efforts, avoiding work along lines that had been tried and found in error and concentrating on principles that showed promise of success. Aimless groping, with wasteful duplication, had heretofore characterized the work of experimenters; Chanute's study opened the way for more productive research.

A noticeable change occurred in his own outlook as a result of this study. Because he was keenly aware of the necessity for discovering a sound approach to the problem, he recognized the error most experimenters had committed. Their concentration on the obvious need for a lightweight engine had obscured the complexity of other equally important problems to be solved before a practical flying machine could be developed. He realized that the science of flight had not yet reached the point where a lightweight engine would make the difference between success and failure. An even more baffling problem was that of maintaining stability; until it was solved, motor-driven flying machines would be too hazardous to be of practical value. With this thought foremost, he began experiments with paper and cardboard models, seeking a method of balancing a machine in flight and, if possible, a mechanical means of achieving completely automatic stability. Also, about the same time, he employed C. E. Hastings, a civil engineer, to test the lifting forces of several types of wings.

While engaged in his experiments, Chanute discovered a way to encourage the exchange of information among students in all parts of the world. In May, 1892, Albert Francis Zahm, a recent graduate of Cornell University and an instructor of mathematics at Notre Dame University, proposed to Chanute that an international conference on aerial navigation be held in conjunction with the World's Columbian Exposition, scheduled to open in Chicago's Jackson Park in the summer of 1893. International conferences on aerial navigation had been held abroad, but Zahm's proposal called for one more elaborate and enlightening than any held previously. Although Chanute recognized the value of such a conference, he was not enthusiastic, possibly because he feared that it might draw only cranks and dreamers rather than scientists and engineers.

Plans for the Third International Conference on Aerial Navigation were held in check until Chanute decided to give his support. As late as September, 1892, he expressed doubts whether the time was appropriate for holding a conference. After an exchange of numerous letters, Zahm won Chanute's support, though the latter remained dubious about the outcome. Next Zahm presented his plan to other influential scientists, who, because of Chanute's prestige, agreed that a conference should be held. Finally, Zahm carried the proposal to Charles C. Bonney, president of the World's Congress Auxiliary, an organization created under the auspices of the World's Columbian Exposition for the purpose of promoting and holding various congresses during the exposition. Following a favorable response from Bonney, the Auxiliary created a Committee on Aerial Navigation, with Chanute as chairman, to draw up plans for the conference. This committee decided to hold its meetings the first four days of August, to coincide with sessions of the Engineering Congress scheduled for the same week, in order to assure the attendance of many engineers and scientists.

In December, 1892, the Committee on Aerial Navigation issued a circular outlining the program and objectives of the conference. The first three daily sessions were reserved for the reading of papers by experts on special topics—scientific principles, aviation, and balloons. The final meeting was to be devoted to discussion of topics covered in the earlier sessions. Experts on the three phases of aerial navigation were requested to submit papers. Wherever possible, the committee tried to obtain divergent views on a single subject both for the enlightenment of delegates and the stimulation of discussion in the final session.

The conference opened in Memorial Art Palace on August 1, 1893, with an address by Chanute, who presided over the first day's session. Approximately one hundred delegates from all parts of the world heard him sound the keynote of the four-day meeting: we meet, he said, to "collate and place on record the knowledge obtained on the science of flight since the last similar international congress, held in Paris in 1889, to give students . . . an opportunity of meeting and corresponding, and to promote concert of action among the various persons who take an interest in the problem." These words notified the assembled delegates and the world that the members would consider only the work of practical, serious men seeking the advancement of flight through scientific experiment.

A brief but complete summary of progress in the propulsion of balloons and the construction of flying machines filled a major portion of Chanute's address. To a prediction of the eventual development of a heavier-than-air machine, he warned: "It is well to recognize from the beginning that we have met here for a conference on an unusual subject; one in which commercial success is not yet to be discerned, and in which the general public, not knowing of the success already accomplished, has little interest and still less confidence." Caution, in this instance, was not to be misconstrued as pessimism, for Chanute continued by pointing out that, although the problem of flight remained unsolved and its students were considered eccentrics or even cranks, a measure of success was in sight with balloons, and the elements of success with flying machines had been accumulating for more than half a century.

Continuing with a reminder of the principal areas requiring the attention of experimenters, Chanute remarked that several complex enigmas had to be solved before flight in a heavier-than-air machine would be possible. He outlined seven distinct problems: the need for an efficient lightweight engine; the development of a satisfactory propelling device; the determination of the extent, texture, and construction of supporting surfaces; the maintenance of equilibrium; the development of a means of starting and stopping; the discovery of a practical method of steering; and the means of effecting safe landings. To each of these, he thought, there could be one or more solutions.

Regular conference sessions began at the close of Chanute's address. Several eminent scientists and experimenters read papers on the scientific principles of flight during the remainder of the first day. On the second day, Dr. R. H. Thurston, director of Sibley College of Engineering, presided over the session devoted to aviation. Colonel W. R. King of the United States Army served as chairman of the third session, on balloons. At the conclusion, Chanute introduced a plan for applying the knowledge thus far presented to practical experimental work: He offered $1,000 toward an experimental fund of $20,000 if nineteen others would give a similar sum. A part of his proposal called for the creation of a board of experts to distribute money to worthy projects. Though the value of the plan was obvious to many delegates, it was rejected at the final session because additional financial aid failed to materialize.

In the midst of the spectacular World's Fair, the true significance of the conference on aerial navigation was lost to all but a small group of dedicated men. However, it was a high point in the aeronautical awakening of the 1890's, producing remarkable results through its encouragement of free exchange of ideas and co-operation among the leading experimenters of the world. The proceedings, published by Chanute, emphasized technological and scientific achievements that had gone almost unnoticed until that time.

Chanute was now free to return to his experiments with model gliders. About this time he began corresponding with Otto Lilienthal, a German who had recently gained international fame for his sensational flights in gliders. He was the first to demonstrate that man could soar in the air like a turkey vulture, and, in doing so, he pointed out a method by which experimenters could eventually achieve success in their search for a practical motor-driven flying machine. Chanute recognized the value of Lilienthal's work and decided to experiment with gliders of his own design.

This decision was motivated largely by Chanute's dissatisfaction with Lilienthal's method of maintaining stability. Theoretically, stability depended upon maintaining in vertical alignment the center of pressure on the supporting surfaces and the center of gravity of the machine, the latter to be located at the point where the operator was seated or suspended, depending upon the type of glider used. As long as both these points remained in vertical alignment, the glider would remain level in flight. In actual performance, however, variations in the velocity and density of air flowing past the supporting surfaces (especially gusts of wind striking the wings at an angle to the line of flight) upset the alignment of the centers of pressure and gravity, causing the glider to plunge or dip until either the alignment was re-established or the apparatus, out of control, crashed to the ground. Both Lilienthal and Chanute sought to overcome this danger, but they disagreed as to the method to be used.

During experiments conducted in Germany between 1891 and 1896, when a gust of wind upset his glider, Lilienthal maintained stability simply by shifting the center of gravity by throwing his body and legs about. This was fairly easy, since he was suspended by his arms and shoulders, and most of his body was free for maneuvering. A movement of from one or two to as much as twelve or fifteen inches, depending upon the degree of disturbance, re-established the center of gravity. Flight then continued evenly as long as the alignment was not disturbed.

Chanute sought a more efficient mechanical balancing device; Lilienthal's contortions were adequate for his own purposes, but, if a flying machine were to be of commercial value, the operator had to have mechanical help. He could not give attention to navigating a machine while performing acrobatics. Therefore, from his savings, Chanute set up a budget of $25,000 to finance experiments (in his own gliders) intended to evolve mechanical controls.

This decision forced him to seek assistance. On March 30, 1894, he wrote to John J. Montgomery, an assistant instructor of chemistry at Santa Clara College, California, suggesting that they jointly experiment with gliders near San Diego. Chanute had met Montgomery the previous year at the Chicago conference, and, through Chanute, Montgomery's gliding experiments were first made public. Although Montgomery's experience qualified him to work out Chanute's plans, he declined the offer, preferring to work alone.

Another year passed before Chanute found a suitable assistant. In December, 1895, he secured the services of August M. Herring, an engineer who had worked with Langley in the Smithsonian Institution during the previous ten months. The two immediately began testing paper models and muslin-covered kites in search of a mechanical device for maintaining stability. In the spring of 1896, they built and flew a "ladder kite," a unique apparatus that in one position looked like a stepladder. The construction of this kite permitted the grouping of surfaces in different arrangements, to test for equilibrium. When it displayed excellent stability in gusty winds, Chanute instructed Herring to build along similar lines the first of his famous "multiple-winged" gliders, with six sets of superposed wings. During the same spring Herring also rebuilt a modified Lilienthal monoplane, which he had used two years earlier.

Chanute intended to test this before working with his own, for, with Lilienthal's data as a check, he would be proceeding from the known to the unknown, and minimizing the chance of error.

With the two gliders, Chanute carried out experiments during June and July, 1896. Aided by Herring, William A. Avery, an electrician and carpenter, and William Paul Butusov, a Russian-born sailor and glider enthusiast, Chanute established a camp on the southern shore of Lake Michigan, near Miller, Indiana. The site was well suited for the experiments. Tall, almost barren sand dunes and steady breezes permitted the men to conduct tests practically every day with a minimum of hazard. The four immediately set up a large tent to serve as quarters for themselves and shelter for the equipment and then turned to the task of assembling the gliders. Before the close of the first day Herring had put together the Lilienthal machine. The men spent most of the week testing it in about 100 glides, the longest about 116 feet, from heights of 20 to 30 feet, in winds from 12 to 17 miles an hour. Once under way, the operator had to shift weight constantly, "like a tight-rope dancer without a pole," in order to remain in level flight. Within a few days Avery learned to handle the glider, but Butusov proved less apt as a pupil, upsetting it on several occasions. In the first week the machine was broken and repaired time and again, until, on June 29, Chanute discarded it. Lilienthal's death as the result of an accident with a similar glider, less than two weeks later, proved the wisdom of this decision.

Next, the experimenters turned to the multiple-winged glider, designed to produce automatic stability through mechanical adjustment of the wings, independent of any action on the part of the operator. The principle involved was fundamentally the same as that employed by Lilienthal, but the method was different. Chanute designed the machine so that as gusts of wind disturbed its equilibrium, the wings, mounted on pivots and held by rubber restraining springs, would swing backward in a sweeping arch. The degree of wing movement was in proportion to the force of the wind. The motion of the wings thus kept a shifting center of pressure in alignment with a fixed center of gravity. As the gusts subsided, the wings returned to their normal positions, and the glider continued on level flight. The span of each set of wings was 12½ feet and the lifting area of all six sets was 177 square feet. In spite of its numerous surfaces and its size, it weighed only 37 pounds, one more than the Lilienthal machine, and contained nine square feet more of lifting area.

On the fourth day in camp, Chanute's assistants altered the original arrangement of the wings, placing four sets in the positions formerly occupied by six, and fixing the other two sets on the rear as a tail. When rigged as a kite, this glider exhibited excellent balance and ease in handling. However, no trial glides were made because the wings appeared too weak to support the weight of an operator. The next day, after the number of wings fore and aft was reversed, the glider handled more easily in flight than the Lilienthal machine and displayed greater stability than that attained with either of the two earlier wing arrangements.

Even more favorable results were obtained on July 1, when the wings were altered again, placing five sets in front and one in the rear. This model, called the *Katydid,* showed its superiority over previous ones in fine flights on July 1, 2, and 4; tests were not conducted on July 3 because of unfavorable winds. After observing the *Katydid,* Chanute decided to end the experiments temporarily in order to build a new glider embodying improvements and ideas gained during the preceding two weeks. Therefore, on July 4, he and his assistants sent their equipment and machines to Chicago by express and returned on the evening train.

The construction of new gliders kept the experimenters busy for several weeks. The old machine was dismantled, and only the wings were used in a new one. Ball-bearing sockets mounted on center posts, to which the wings were attached, replaced the crude, relatively ineffective wooden pivots. A new body frame and a short wing over the top of the old wings, to reinforce their frail construction, completed the work. The new glider consisted of four sets of forward planes, superposed vertically, plus the aerocurve, a single wing for a horizontal tail, with a vertical plane above it for a rudder. The construction introduced a new method of trussing superposed wings. From his experience as a bridge builder, Chanute conceived the idea of fastening them together in essentially the same way that strength and rigidity were obtained in bridges—with the Pratt truss, probably the first application of that method to flying machines.

In addition to the multiple-winged glider, Chanute designed one along completely different lines. This consisted of three superposed concave-bottomed wings rigidly trussed and held in a fixed position. Attached to the rear of the body, by means of an "elastic" device designed by Chanute and Herring, were vertical and horizontal planes known as a Penaud rudder. The three wings, each measuring 16 feet in length, with an opening in the center of the lower plane to provide room for the operator to cling from arm and shoulder supports, had a total lifting surface of 191 square feet. The glider weighed 31 pounds.

With financial aid from Chanute, Butusov constructed another glider, a monstrous creation of wood and muslin, similar to one he had tested some years earlier. This machine looked like a huge albatross with wings spread in flight and weighed 199 pounds. A boat-like undercarriage, formed of ribs and stanchions, could be transformed into a watertight compartment by the addition of a covering of stout oilcloth. Directly above the body, four longitudinal keels of balloon cloth acted as stabilizers, and, above them, wings 16 feet long protruded to each side.

In mid-August, the experimenters (with the addition of Dr. Howard T. Ricketts as camp cook as well as camp physician) prepared to renew tests on the southern lake shore. On the previous trip, the camp had been filled with curious spectators whose presence hindered experiments. This time Chanute hoped to keep the location a secret by transporting the party by boat to a new site five miles farther down the shore. There the dunes were higher, the location more isolated, and the path to the railroad at Dune Park more obscure than the one at the camp used earlier that summer.

Prospects for a quiet stay appeared promising at the close of the first day, for the presence of the crew was not known to residents along the lake. But all hope of remaining isolated vanished suddenly during the night in a storm that swept over the southern portion of the lake. The neat orderly camp disappeared. The tent was blown away; the gliders, removed from the protection of shipping crates, were wrecked and scattered; provisions were ruined. The damage forced Chanute to send at once to Chicago for equipment, while he and his companions sought shelter in a nearby fisherman's cottage. When the shipment arrived at Dune Park by rail the following afternoon, the presence of the camp became known; thereafter the experimenters were constantly bothered by local residents and reporters.

Following the storm, the three-surface glider, or aerocurve, as Chanute preferred to call it, was the first to be repaired and assembled. Glides completed with it on August 29 were brief in duration and distance but sufficient to indicate excessive lifting power. Therefore, Chanute instructed Herring to remove the lower surface. As a biplane it exhibited ease in handling preparatory to flight, and exceptional steadiness and control while in the air. During the remainder of the summer, Herring, Avery, Butusov, and even occasional visitors, completed hundreds of flights in the biplane, many of from 8 to 14 seconds' duration, covering from 199 to 359 feet.

Since 1896, nearly all aeronautical authorities have erroneously called Chanute the inventor of the biplane glider. In *Progress in Flying Machines*, published in 1894, Chanute had pointed out that the biplane had been used by several experimenters in Europe long before that date. But Chanute's, unlike earlier models, embodied the Pratt truss for rigidly superposing two surfaces. This was employed by nearly all experimenters and builders as long as the biplane remained in use. However, Chanute failed to realize the value of the biplane. Several years later, when designing an oscillating-wing glider, he utilized three surfaces, which he preferred.

He discarded the biplane as soon as he discovered that it did not produce completely automatic stability. During most of September, he tested the multiple-winged glider, but again the results were discouraging. In spite of the new ball-bearing sockets and other improvements, it failed to respond as its designer anticipated. The reason for this failure, Chanute insisted, was that the old wings were so "racked and distorted," they made proper balance of weight impossible.

Butusov's glider exhibited few valuable qualities but might have made a better showing had conditions been more favorable. Only two attempts were made to launch it from a trestle mounted on the north slope of the test site. The fixed position of the trestle forced the experimenters to use it only in a wind of from 18 to 25 miles an hour from the north; the prevailing winds in the summer were from the south. Chanute had foreseen this difficulty and attempted to avoid it by suggesting that the trestle be mounted on a barge which could be towed offshore and anchored in any position to permit launching the glider into the wind. However, when Butusov refused to allow the tests over water, Chanute had no alternative but to build the trestle facing north and work with the other machines while waiting for the wind to shift.

Nearly four weeks passed before the opportunity arose. On September 15, with Butusov riding in the undercarriage and with guide ropes attached to the nose, tail, and tips of each wing, it exhibited excellent balance and a fair degree of control when allowed to lift slightly above the trestle into the wind. Chanute refused to allow free flight that summer, preferring to learn more about the glider's performance as a kite before risking injury to one of his assistants. Two days later the wind shifted long enough to permit the experimenters to make a new test, with 130 pounds of sandbags for ballast. This time, after leaving the trestle, Butusov's glider flew horizontally in level flight for nearly 100 feet before slack in the front guide rope suddenly checked its forward motion and sent it crashing to the ground. On September 26, Chanute ordered Butusov to launch the glider, again with ballast, into a quartering wind from the northeast. It soared from the trestle, turned sharply to the left as the wind struck at an angle, and crashed into a tree at the far side of the normal gliding course. This incident, occurring on the morning of the final day in camp, closed experiments for 1896.

The tests of Butusov's glider precipitated a conflict whose reverberations lived on long after most of the participants had vanished from the scene. Shortly before the experiments closed, Chanute and Herring argued over the value of the machine; Herring insisted that it was too dangerous to risk testing in free flight. Even when Chanute ordered that it be tested as a kite, Herring balked and asked permission to leave the camp. Chanute readily agreed to the request. Though completing the break in the Chanute-Herring collaboration, the incident in itself was of no importance and only obscured the real reason for Herring's departure. The two men held opposite views regarding the advisability of fitting an internal combustion engine to the biplane glider. Herring wanted to attempt a flight in a motor-driven biplane in order to gain the prestige and honor success would bring; he felt that earlier tests indicated that the problem of stability had been solved sufficiently to permit the trial. Chanute disagreed. He had taken up experimental work with the one objective of seeking completely automatic stability by mechanical means. Even though he thought some improvements in that line had been gained that summer, the problem had not been solved to his satisfaction. Anything that interfered with his objective seemed of little value.

The experiments ended Chanute's active participation in aeronautics for six years. Numerous publications and speeches on the subject of flight and financial support of other experiments kept him occupied with aeronautical problems when not engaged in private business affairs. He continued to hope for progress, particularly in the all-important matter of stability, and persistently discouraged attempts to make powered flights until the problem was solved. In 1897, he declined an offer of money from a wealthy Chicagoan for the design and construction of a motor-driven machine. His belief that aeronautics had not advanced to the point where powered flight was practical was reaffirmed in October, 1898, when he went to St. Joseph, Michigan, to witness Herring's attempts to fly a compressed-air-powered biplane glider. On arriving at the camp, Chanute heard reports of a flight of 50 feet on a previous trial, but the claim seemed dubious after Herring, on October 11, failed in several attempts.

For the next few years Chanute offered aid and encouragement to experimenters who sought his assistance. His extant letter files are filled with correspondence to and from these men, many of whom thought they had invented practical flying machines. Wherever they followed logical methods, Chanute was sympathetic and helpful. To those who wasted his time with useless schemes, he was generally courteous but firm with replies intended to direct attention along more practical lines. Between 1898 and 1903, Chanute financed the work of Edward C. Huffaker, of Chuckey City, Tennessee; George A. Spratt, of Coatsville, Pennsylvania; and Charles H. Lamson, of Pasadena, California. In 1900, Herring also turned to his former employer for money to build a motor-driven flying machine, but Chanute refused. In the spring of that year a new phase in his career began with a letter from Wilbur Wright, of Dayton, Ohio, the older of two brothers who operated a small bicycle manufacturing and repair business.

The letter marked the beginning of a long friendship and set in motion a series of experiments that eventually produced a practical airplane. The writer stated that he had been "afflicted" for some time with the belief that the means for flight in a heavier-than-air machine was within the grasp of man; that he and his brother intended to devote a few months to experiments with gliders according to a plan which he elaborated. Chanute answered promptly, including information concerning suitable locations for testing gliders and giving the source of printed accounts of Percy S. Pilcher's work in England. In closing, he suggested a meeting with the Wrights to discuss problems that would be encountered in experimental work; if a meeting could not be arranged, Chanute said he would be happy to correspond further and to have a detailed account of their tests. The Wrights accepted this invitation to exchange ideas with the man then recognized as the leading authority on aeronautics in the United States.

In October and November, 1900, the Wright brothers spent several weeks in a camp at Kill Devil Hill near Kitty Hawk,

North Carolina, experimenting with a "soaring machine." During the remainder of the year they tended their bicycle business. At that time there was not the slightest hope of making money from aeronautics; therefore they had to maintain a separate business to finance their experiments. This predicament confronted all who were not independently wealthy, and few were. Chanute must have sympathized deeply with the Wrights, for earlier in the same year he had expressed the hope of conducting experiments of his own if his "business and means" would allow a heavy expenditure of time and money.

Correspondence between Chanute and the Wrights continued for more than a year before they met for the first time. There is no record of the conversation during Chanute's visit to the Wrights' home in Dayton on June 26-27, 1901; however, it is difficult to imagine that they talked for long of anything but aeronautics. It is also probable that Chanute made arrangements to have Edward Huffaker visit the brothers' camp the following month to test a glider. George Spratt, also, came to Kitty Hawk that year because of Chanute's insistence that the Wrights should have a doctor on hand in case of an accident. He agreed to pay Spratt's travel expenses if the Wrights would provide him with room and board. Although Spratt was not a doctor, he had had some medical training.

Early in August, 1901, Chanute spent a week in the Wrights' camp. His observations of their glider soon convinced him that they had improved upon his own construction. However, he did not realize that they were considering giving up experiments. In a few weeks they had learned that virtually all supposedly scientific data were grossly inaccurate and worthless. Without dependable information to use as a guide for their experiments, they felt that the task was far more formidable than originally anticipated, and possibly hopeless.

At this juncture, Chanute, without realizing the future significance of his pleas, dissuaded the Wrights from abandoning their experiments. He urged them to continue, for, in spite of imposing obstacles, they had come closer to understanding the problem of flight than had anyone else, and it would take years for another person to acquire the knowledge they already had.

This encouragement was one of Chanute's greatest contributions to aeronautics, for the Wrights listened to his advice and continued their work.

In 1901, Chanute, as president of the Western Society of Engineers, invited Wilbur Wright to address that body in Chicago on September 18. This was another valuable service. Wilbur's address, entitled "Some Aeronautical Experiments," challenged the accuracy of available data on air pressures on supporting surfaces. During Wilbur's absence, Orville's apprehension about the contents of his brother's speech led him to construct a crude wind tunnel to recheck their own figures on air pressures. The tests, conducted in a single day, indicated serious errors in existing data, but both brothers considered the results inconclusive; consequently, they built a more elaborate wind tunnel. Information obtained from further trials of miniature wings enabled them to construct an airplane capable of flight. Without these experiments, they might have spent several more years before progressing to the point where a motor could be fitted to their glider.

Before the Wrights returned to Kitty Hawk in 1902, Chanute decided to make a final test of his own machines. He hoped to reveal additional facts that would lead the brothers a step closer to their objective. Accordingly, he employed Herring to build a multiple-winged glider; the Wrights to construct a biplane; and Lamson to devise an oscillating-wing, or "rocking surfaces," machine. All three were shipped to Kitty Hawk, where Chanute and Herring helped the Wrights conduct the tests that fall.

The anticipation with which Chanute looked forward to reenacting his experiments of 1896 suffered a shattering blow. Not one of the gliders performed as he and the Wrights had expected. He discarded the multiple-winged affair after Herring failed in several attempts to complete a flight of more than 15 feet. Throughout the test period, the longest trip with any of the machines was 45 feet, a poor record in comparison with those of Chanute's earlier experiments. These performances, coupled with Orville Wright's tests of Chanute's wing sections, raised serious doubts in the brothers' minds as to the authenticity of the records of Chanute's flights of 1896. Although the data might have been exaggerated, difference in conditions between the southern slope of Lake Michigan and the North Carolina testing grounds could have been largely responsible for the poor showing. However, there is still no logical explanation for the variance in the results of Orville's tests and the earlier record.

The experiments of 1902 ended Chanute's active participation in aeronautical experiments, but he did not lose interest in flight or in the possibility of eventual success by the Wrights. During the winter of 1902–1903, he went abroad. After returning in May, he advised the Wrights to adapt a lightweight engine to their glider but discovered that they had already made that decision. After taking this step, success proved to be only a matter of a short time. On December 17, 1903, Orville flew the first practical, motor-driven, heavier-than-air flying machine 120 feet in 12 seconds. Unfortunately, Chanute was not at Kitty Hawk to witness the triumph. He had visited the camp that fall in the hope of seeing man's first flight, but the uncomfortably cold weather of early November forced him to remain indoors, and he returned to Chicago more than a month before that memorable day.

Thereafter, Chanute remained a devoted friend and adviser to the Wrights during the trying years when, harassed by interlopers seeking to rob them of their invention, they tried to protect their airplane with international patents. Until 1908, Chanute acted as unofficial spokesman for the brothers. In speeches, articles, and countless letters, with cautious regard for the rights of his friends, he informed the world of their achievements at a time when most people viewed reports of their success with suspicion. To a large degree the Wrights were responsible for this skepticism. Their almost fanatic insistence upon secrecy, in order to protect their invention until patents were issued, restricted information released to the press either by their own hands or through Chanute. Without supporting information, reports of their flights soon assumed the appearance of a grand hoax. Chanute sought to correct this false impression but could not combat it effectively as long as the Wrights refused to release the complete story of their work.

The intimate relations between the friends created an erroneous impression regarding the real inventor of the airplane. It was unfortunate, yet perhaps inevitable, that many individuals as well as widely circulated newspapers and magazines believed that Chanute was the real hero; that the Wrights had simply worked out his ideas. Had they been willing to publicize their experiments of 1900–1903, as well as their achievements in following years, rather than force Chanute to act as their spokesman, they could easily have avoided any misinterpretation. The Wrights resented the prevailing opinion but realized that Chanute was not to blame. The incident might have passed without consequence if they had not taken legal action against alleged infringers of their patent.

In January, 1910, five months after the Wrights initiated suits against Glenn Curtiss and others, Chanute, in an interview published in the *New York World* on January 17, was quoted as saying that the Wrights might gain a favorable judgment on their specific method of warping wings, but that the general principle had been used by experimenters many years earlier. They could use their time more beneficially, he said, by continuing their experiments than by fighting prolonged and useless lawsuits. After reading the interview, the Wrights were shocked and resentful of their mentor, who, according to Wilbur Wright, had stated during the experiments that the method was original with them.

It is difficult to understand why Chanute opposed the patent suits. He may have felt that a desire for wealth had overruled the Wrights' usually sound judgment and that their persistence in fighting alleged infringers in the courts would halt progress in the development of the airplane. If this was his reasoning, it does not justify his assertions that other experimenters held prior claims to the wing-warping idea. Perhaps age had clouded his memory. Whatever the cause, no one questioned Chanute's sincerity and honesty.

His relations with the Wrights were partially soothed in April, 1910, before he sailed on his last visit to France. Three days before leaving the United States, he wrote to Wilbur Wright and, after reasserting his faith in the correctness of his views, he concluded with a plea for a resumption of friendly relations. However, this was not to be, for two months later, while visiting in Paris, Chanute suffered a severe attack of pneumonia from which he did not fully recover, though he lived four months longer. He regained sufficient strength to return to Chicago in early October but remained confined to his home until his death on November 23.

3

THE AMATEUR IN AVIATION

Efforts to develop a practical heavier-than-air flying machine in Illinois antedated by more than sixty years the initial successes of Orville and Wilbur Wright. Between 1840 and 1903, twenty or more inventors attempted to build machines of various types. Until early in the twentieth century, the absence of dependable, lightweight internal combustion engines forced most inventors to depend upon movable wings, set in motion by cranks or levers.

The earliest attempt to build a flying machine was made in 1840 near Newton, a village now extinct, located six miles west of Danville, in Vermilion County. Hugh Newell, a farmer, constructed an ornithopter, or wing-flapping machine. A less determined man might have been dissuaded from the venture, for at that time, when the mere thought of human flight was beyond the imaginations of most people, interest in aeronautics was considered a sign of lunacy. Some of Newell's neighbors called him "Crazy Hugh," and others thought he was, at best, a dreamer.

After the fashion of nearly all inventors at that time, Newell based his design on observation of birds, and, before undertaking actual construction, experimented with paper and cardboard models. His "Flying Carr" or "machine" resembled a large bird. The body, from which wings extended at right angles, contained a seat for the operator and a crank to actuate the wings; at its rear a solid wooden beam, possibly a wagon tongue with "fins" on the end, acted as a tail.

In the fall of 1840, Newell obtained help for the construction of a full-sized machine. Jesse Liggate, a man of apparent wealth, furnished money for materials; Benjamin Coddington, a local blacksmith, assisted in the work. Several months before the machine was completed, the three partners drew up a formal contract defining the part each was to take in its development and in the division of anticipated profits. Newell was to furnish the "principal or Theory" and to relinquish "all right or claim to any interest, benefit or Emmolument that might arise or be gifted or donated by any Prince, Queen, King or President or Potentate of any nation except North America," except one-half of the profits from the use and sale of the invention. Liggate and Coddington were each to receive one-quarter of the profits.

On the day set for the first flight, Newell and his partners hauled the "Flying Carr" to the top of a haystack on a hill near the inventor's home. As residents of Newton watched, Newell climbed into his machine and began turning the crank to set the wings in motion. When they moved at a speed he considered adequate for flight, he signaled Liggate and Coddington to launch the machine with a shove. It moved through the air but not in the manner anticipated, for it plunged to the ground with a resounding crash. Instead of immortal fame and riches, the experimenters received stinging taunts and ridicule from the spectators.

Experiments with heavier-than-air craft apparently lagged for several decades following Newell's ill-fated venture. Extant records indicate that none occurred until 1880, when Burr Fitzwater, a blacksmith in Windsor, Shelby County, built and flew one or more gliders. In 1892, Tom Baldwin, of Quincy, built a motorless flying machine, and, about the same time, Charles Duryea, a young mechanic living near Peoria, experimented with kites and gliders. His work was successful enough that he prepared a paper on his experiments for the Third International Conference on Aerial Navigation. His excursion into aeronautics was brief, for he soon turned to the bicycle business and later to automobiles.

After 1890, interest in aeronautics increased appreciably. John A. Young, of Chicago, experimented with models as early as 1893 and continued to work with various types until 1903. Between 1897 and 1910, a New Lenox inventor named Millis Knickerbocker developed "revolving kites" which he used in the construction of several machines. His work apparently involved lighter-than-air craft and parachutes that derived "aerial support" from "electrical repulsion," a theory based on the scientific observation that two objects with like charges of electricity repel each other. Knickerbocker proved to his own satisfaction that weighted balloons charged with static electricity would "sail around for a long time when set free." Unaware that the theory was fallacious, he commenced in 1897 the construction of an aerial bicycle, an elongated craft similar to a box kite, with five flat longitudinal planes, each 10 feet long, attached to pivots in circular frames 16 feet in diameter. The mountings allowed "side gusts of wind" to pass through the planes without disturbing the balance of the machine. With enough "floating surface," the inventor claimed, manpower would be sufficient to raise and propel the flying bicycle a few feet above the ground. His later experiments followed more conventional lines, and in 1910, he built a "combination monoplane" in Chicago.

Another inventor, James B. Slinn, developed aeronautical devices between 1899 and 1910. While living in New Orleans in 1899, he designed a one-man flying machine consisting of a combination of wings and horizontal propellers. When this crude autogiro failed to fly, he invented a mechanical bird, which he hoped to sell to raise money for further experiments. In 1904, Slinn sold the toy during the St. Louis World's Fair, earning enough to build the following year an airplane with superposed wings and an "explosion" engine.

After moving to Chillicothe, Illinois, Slinn designed and constructed at least one airplane. In 1910, he built for Eugene Brown, a Peoria real estate dealer and president of the local aircraft club, a unique biplane with a new longitudinal control.

Slinn disposed of the front horizontal rudder, then a feature of all successful models, incorporating its function into the top main plane, which the operator could raise or depress along the trailing edge to control pitch. In place of wing warping, he used ailerons built into the trailing edges of the lower main plane, similar to the method employed by many foreign builders of monoplanes. Named the *Falcon*, this airplane completed a single flight that ended with an accident and its total destruction.

A Chicago inventor of streetcar "bumpers" turned to the investigation of aeronautics in 1893. Ira P. Clark designed and built an apparatus with movable wings, but he was unable to purchase a lightweight engine for motive power. Nine years later he began construction of an airship, a combination of an elongated gas bag and wings with a total lifting area of 4,000 square feet. While engaged in this work, he sought a suitable means of propulsion, preferably a small steam engine, and financial help; since there is no record of the ship's completion, he apparently failed to find one or both.

The flights of the Wright brothers in 1903 had little immediate influence upon aeronautical activity. Because of their secrecy, other inventors had to search for five more years for a practical method of controlling equilibrium in a flying machine. In 1908, another practical airplane, fully the equal of the Wright biplane in performance, became the model for most builders of homemade machines. The Aerial Experiment Association of Hammondsport, New York, composed of Dr. Alexander Graham Bell, F. A. Baldwin, J. A. D. McCurdy, Glenn Curtiss, and Lieutenant Thomas Selfridge, of the United States Army, built and flew a number of biplanes using ailerons to maintain lateral balance. Known as the Curtiss machine, this plane was not protected by patents and consequently was widely copied during the next five years.

In Chicago, William Avery and William Paul Butusov, who had formerly worked with Chanute, continued to experiment with gliders but did not attempt to adapt motive power to them until 1910. Silas J. Conyne designed an "aeroplane" as early as 1901, as did Alexander P. Criswell two years later, but they did not construct full-sized machines. Avery and Butusov, unlike Herring, who remained active in aeronautics for nearly twenty years, seldom devoted more than a few weeks a year to glider tests. Butusov, with financial aid from Chanute, built at least one glider in 1900 and thereafter remained relatively inactive until 1910, when he built two or more biplanes.

Following the 1896 experiments, Avery returned to carpentry for a livelihood, but he retained a strong interest in aeronautics. In 1904, when Chanute decided to enter a glider in the St. Louis World's Fair Aeronautical Meet in competition for prizes totaling $200,000, he hired Avery to rebuild a weather-beaten biplane. During August, Avery replaced broken or rotten pieces of the frame and re-covered the wings and then shipped the plane to St. Louis, where, between September 23 and October 26, he completed 46 flights with it. On all but three, he used a car mounted on rails, propelled by a cable attached to a drum turned by a 19-horsepower electric motor, to launch the glider. It was thus able to reach a maximum height of 70 feet and distances of 300 to 400 feet. In spite of this excellence Chanute terminated the glider's performance sooner than expected because the judges of the meet repeatedly delayed official trials for prizes. The expense—reportedly $1,400—and the difficulties encountered in St. Louis prompted Chanute to cancel plans for sending Avery on an exhibition tour of the United States with the glider. After that date Avery apparently lost interest in aeronautics until September, 1910, when he constructed for an unnamed Chicago "syndicate" a "warped wing" parabolic biplane with automatic pendulum traverse control.

Unlike Chanute's former assistants, few other experimenters possessed either the training or experience that qualified them to cope with the technicalities of airplane design and construction. None of the twelve Illinois men who obtained patents on aeronautical devices between 1900 and 1910 had the skills or formal training necessary to develop their inventions for commercial exploitation; consequently, none of them indicated that he really understood the principles of flight. Only one inventor, Carl S. Bates, a mechanical engineer of Chicago, produced a practical airplane, which, he claimed, flew on several occasions.

In 1898, at the age of 14, Bates constructed a man-carrying kite on a farm near Cedar Lake, Iowa. Despite objections from his parents, he built and flew a Chanute biplane glider the following year. Experiments with other devices heightened his interest and in 1903 he moved to Chicago so that he could enroll in Armour Institute of Technology and conduct experiments under the guidance of Chanute. By attending night classes, Bates was able to operate a small shop during the day. A sign over the entrance reading "Aeroplanes Built to Order" soon attracted a customer, who paid for the construction of a ten-winged ornithopter, a curious machine consisting of two sets of five wings that moved simultaneously up and down in opposite directions. Bates could not find a small engine for the machine, but he nevertheless insisted that it was not airworthy; the designer was of an opposite view. After discovering the need for efficient, reliable motive power, Bates began designing and building his own gasoline engines, and eventually established the Bates Aero Motor Company of Chicago, manufacturer of some of the finest water- and air-cooled motors in the United States.

In 1908, Bates constructed an airplane of his own. Although smaller than the Curtiss design, Bates's followed that model in almost every detail. A short span and two planes rigidly trussed, front horizontal and rear vertical rudders, and ailerons between the wings near their extremities constituted the principal features of both makes. Even their tricycle landing gears were similar, though Bates mounted the front wheel of his plane to a swivel fixed to the chassis in order to facilitate maneuvering on the ground. All of his struts and exposed parts were "fish-shaped cross section," an early example of streamlining. A 10-horsepower, two-cylinder air-cooled engine designed by Bates was the most controversial feature. Critics, of whom there were many, charged that the small power plant could not support the combined weight of the airplane and a pilot. The inventor countered with claims of flights, which he failed to corroborate with statements from witnesses.

Early in December, 1908, he tried to fly for the first time. On a level area of the golf course in Washington Park, he completed a series of short jumps before his makeshift ignition system failed. Because he had little money and was unable to buy a magneto, he had wired the engine directly to a battery, an expedient that worked satisfactorily only as long as the battery remained at full strength. News of the failure reached Chanute, who bought a new magneto, which Bates wired to his engine. Next, Bates transported the machine to White City Amusement Park, at South Park Avenue and 63rd Street, where Joseph Beifeld, the principal owner, paid for leveling enough ground for a renewal of the tests. Shortly before the close of the month, after waiting several days for a wind of the proper velocity, Bates claimed that he flew easily.

In order to continue flying that winter, he moved to Florida. In March, he exhibited his biplane during the annual automobile races at Ormond-Daytona Beach, but even there adverse weather delayed tests for more than a week. While waiting for favorable weather, race fans milled about Bates's tent-hangar and speculated on the ability of the seemingly underpowered airplane to fly. A majority of those who saw the machine concluded that it was not airworthy—for a time they seemed correct. On March 27, the final day of the races, Bates tried to fly, but a balky engine restricted his performance to a series of dashes along the sandy beach.

After failing in several attempts, Bates returned to the hangar and carefully tuned the engine in preparation for another trial. Before dawn he returned to make a final check. As the sun rose, he opened the engine to full throttle and raced down the beach. Several minutes later, after covering 460 yards at an average height of from 10 to 12 feet, the flywheel broke loose from the engine, shattering the ribs and main structure of the wings. Despite the mishap, he landed without additional damage. Although given national recognition for the flight, he failed to produce witnesses.

In April, he returned to Chicago to become the leader of a small group of inventors who were building machines of many types. Bates, James F. Scott, Horace B. Wild, and Edward E. Harbert worked together on problems common to all but pursued entirely independent experiments. Ray Harroun worked with Bates, assisting him with the construction of new airplanes. Other inventors designed various types of flying apparatus, though they did not actually build them: George H. Benedict, August E. Mueller, and Sidney S. Williams developed plans for "aeroplanes," and Ewald E. Steinhaus devised a "dirigible flying machine."

About 1905, Scott, a scenic artist, began experimenting with aeronautical devices, and in the next five years he built at least three machines. First, he designed a multiplane, an apparatus with three or more sets of wings. In January, 1908, in response to an advertisement by the War Department for bids on a heavier-than-air flying machine, Scott hurriedly submitted, at almost the last minute, specifications for a multiplane, which he agreed to build for $1,000 and deliver to Fort Myer, Virginia, for tests within 185 days after the award of a contract. He realized that the price would cover only a small part of the construction costs, but he could not ask more because of the requirement that a 10 per cent deposit must accompany each bid. He had been unable to raise more than $100 on such short notice. When accepted from 41 applicants, among whom were the Wright brothers and Herring, Scott confidently expected to raise the needed funds and hoped to offset his loss through the sale of additional machines. However, a month later, he had to ask that the contract be canceled.

Although unable to fill the contract, Scott built a multiplane, possibly the one he had designed for the Army. In a shop near Lawrenceburg, Indiana, he constructed it as an experiment for "working out the proposition of assembling into a controllable apparatus the fundamentals of mechanical flight, power, weight, and the area of carrying surfaces." When completed in April, 1909, this machine consisted of five sets of wings, two sets in the front and three sets as a tail. The front ones were divided into several separate sections, each "independently deflectable." The rear ones were designed to enable the operator to adjust them to a wide range of angles of incidence. The complete machine weighed 650 pounds and contained 558 square feet of lifting surface. A two-bladed "screw fan" driven by a 40-horsepower engine supplied the motive power. Whether

Scott flew this machine is not a matter of record. Its lack of stabilizing devices and frail construction, however, would have made flight dangerous if not impossible.

Later the same year Scott moved to Utah. In August, he was reportedly constructing a multiplane on a "testing ground" between Salt Lake City and Saltair Beach. Although he did not release an exact description of the machine, he did state that it contained a multiplicity of planes and various propellers "set along the fore and aft line . . . rather than along the front face." Again the results of his work are unknown.

In the summer of 1910, he came back in Chicago and built a helicopter with sixteen disks. When moved up and down by a lightweight engine, the disks were supposed to lift and sustain the machine in the air. A full-sized craft completed in September failed to fly though it had been patterned after a model which did "all sorts of stunts." One observer caustically remarked that Scott's helicopter would at least take first prize as the most fantastic flying machine in Chicago at that time.

A balloonist of more than 20 years' experience, Horace B. Wild built and flew dirigibles and experimented with airplanes. In May, 1907, as a charter member of the newly formed Aero Club of Chicago, Wild boasted of having performed flights in an airplane employing "gyroscopes revolving at the rate of 6,000 revolutions per minute." The accuracy of the statement is questionable, for he had a habit of exaggerating or fabricating stories about his own achievements. However, by October, 1908, according to a reputable authority, he was actually building an airplane, and the following month he joined Bates, Harroun, Harbert, and Scott, who, with the aid of influential newspapers, secured permission from the South Park Board to use portions of Washington Park for testing machines. Less than two years later, Wild apparently owned an airplane, for he announced that he was planning to fly to Louisville, Kentucky, in conjunction with exhibitions at that place by Curtiss and other aviators. However, Wild's flight was later canceled after he reported a bad accident while making a final test in preparation for the trip.

Ray Harroun was well known as an automobile racer before

THE GLORIOUS FOURTH of JULY
IN JACKSONVILLE.
Grand, sublime and Novle Exhibition

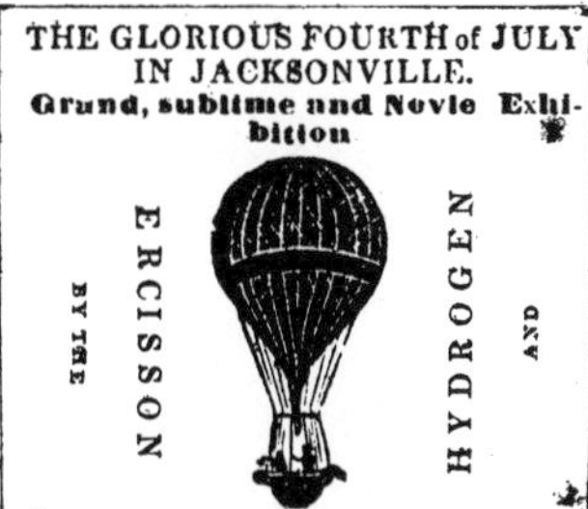

BALLOON COMP'NY
Will exhibit at Jacksonville on Saturday
July 3d, 1858.
IN THEIR MAMMOTH WALL PAVILION,
POSITIVELY FOR ONE DAY ONLY.

CIRCUSES!! MENAGERIES!!!
AND ALL OTHER EXHIBITIONS.
THROWN IN THE SHADE!
BY THE
THRILLING SUBLIMITY!
OF THE
MOST STUPENDOUS BALLOON EXHIBITIONS
IN THE WORLD!!

TWO UNRIVALLED ÆRONAUTS WITH THIS
COMPANY.

PROF. S. M. BROOKS,
(Manager of the St. Louis museum)
The Greatest of American Æronauts.
AND
MONS. LE WHITE.
The Great, Daring, Foreign, Equiliptic Æronaut.
Have been engaged by this Company, at an immense expense, to visit the princial cities and towns of the United States for the purpose of making a variety of their unrivalled and magnificent
BALLOON ASCENSIONS.

The company will distribute at each place where the Ascension takes place
$1,000 WORTH OF PRESENTS!
TO THE AUDIENCE.
Consisting of Handsome
GOLD AND SILVER WATCHES!
MAGNIFICENT GOLD JEWELRY!
Beautiful Gold and Silver Pencils!
And admission tickets to Prof. Pyrington's
GRAND FIREWORKS EXHIBITI'N

Admission tickets to the Balloon Exhibition,
ONLY FIFTY CENTS.
Each one admitting the holder, and entitling them to one of the presents.

For full particulars, see small and descriptive bills.
Pit tickets, without a present, 25cts.
MAJOR BURNELL, Agent.

Left: Advertisement from the *Jacksonville Sentinel*, July 2, 1858, announcing a future performance of Silas M. Brooks, aeronaut for the Ericsson and Hydrogen Balloon Company. Below: Farmer Atchison sighting Brooks' stray balloon which carried off Martha Anne and David Harvey, September 17, 1858. (*Frank Leslie's Illustrated Newspaper*, October 23, 1858.)

A hot air balloon inflated and ready for an ascension in Springfield, Illinois, 1890. (*Illinois State Historical Library*)

Above left: The gas balloon "Buffalo" used by Samuel Archer King to perform for P. T. Barnum's Hippodrome in 1875. (*Walter C. Scholl*) Above right: Crew members of the "America" on its ill-fated voyage to Europe, October 1910. Left to right: Walter Wellman, Chicago, Albert Louis Loud (standing), Springfield, and Fred Aubert. (*Mrs. A. L. Loud*) Below: Nonrigid dirigible "Comet" used by Horace B. Wild, Chicago, to perform exhibitions throughout the United States, 1907–1910. (*Walter C. Scholl*)

Above: A. Roy Knabenshue piloting Thomas Scott Baldwin's "California Arrow" at the start of a flight from St. Louis, 1904. (*Technical World*) Below: Dirigible SC-1, the United States Army's first aircraft, built by Thomas Scott Baldwin. (*Mrs. Mabel Baldwin*)

Above: A hot air balloon manufactured by James L. Case, Chicago, Illinois, ready for an ascension by Walter C. Scholl in Canton, Illinois, October, 1923. (*Walter C. Scholl*) Below: A. Roy Knabenshue's dirigible "White City" in flight over Chicago, 1914. (*Charles A. Arens*)

Left: Octave Chanute (1832–1910), Chicago, Illinois, engineer and aeronautical experimenter. (*Library of Congress*)

Right: John Wise, Lancaster, Pennsylvania, the leading aeronaut of the nineteenth century. (*Walter C. Scholl*)

Above: Octave Chanute's three-winged glider in flight, Dune Park, Indiana, 1896. Left: Chanute's multiple-winged glider, Dune Park, Indiana, 1896. (*Library of Congress*)

AEROPLANING FOR CHICAGO

THIS IS FOR YOU, MR. OR MRS. OR MISS CHICAGOAN, WHO MAY HAVE OVERLOOKED SOMETHING IN YOUR OWN CITY

No City in the World has Anything Bigger in Aviation than Chicago Has Now.
No City in the World Has Many of the Things in Aviation, Chicago has in Plenty.

And Where, In Chicago, Are These Things?

THE AERO CLUB OF ILLINOIS

FLYING FIELD IN CICERO

Douglas Park Branch, 50TH AVENUE, Metropolitan Elevated Station.

- DAILY AERIAL TAXICAB SERVICE
- LEARN TO OPERATE ANY STANDARD MAKE OF AEROPLANE
- SEE TYPES OF AEROPLANES UNLIKE ANYTHING ELSE IN THE WORLD
- WATCH MEN TESTING NEW IDEAS WITH MODELS
- ILLINOIS MODEL AERO CLUB HAS WEEKLY CONTESTS
- EXPERIMENTS WITH MOTORLESS AEROPLANES
- TAKE A RIDE WITH A SAFE OPERATOR ANY HEIGHT YOU WISH
- MEN BUILDING NEW AND OLD TYPES OF AEROPLANES
- SCHOOLS INSTRUCTING PUPILS TO BUILD MACHINES, AND THEN HOW TO FLY THEM
- FASTEST TYPE OF AEROPLANE IN THE WORLD
- LARGEST MONOPLANE IN AMERICA
- LARGEST AEROPLANE IN AMERICA
- MOST CONVENIENT AND COMPLETE AERODROME IN THE WORLD
- FACTORY, WHERE MODEL AEROPLANES AND MOTORS ARE MADE
- MEMBERS' CLUBHOUSE OFFICE AND DIRECTOR'S OFFICE ON GROUNDS
- LICENSED PILOT ENGAGED BY CLUB AS FIELD DIRECTOR IN CHARGE.
- APPOINTMENTS CAN BE MADE WITH CLUB ENGINEERS TO GIVE ADVICE ON ANY ORIGINAL DESIGN

Aviators' International Licenses granted under Observation of National Officials.

CHICAGO GETS BIGGEST PLUMS IN AVIATION

¶World's Championship—Gordon Bennett International Aviation Race, September Ninth.
¶Start and Finish of American Grand Circuit Aeroplane Race of 1800 Miles.

These are the greatest events in sports since man raised himself into the air in mechanical flight.

How Can You Get In Touch With This?

The Club's Office is in the Auditorium Hotel.
Its Field is at the 50th Ave. Station, Douglas Park Branch of the Met. Elev. Ry.

BY AUTO—West on Twelfth Street to Ogden Avenue; southwest on Ogden to 48th Avenue, north on 48th just across Metropolitan tracks, to automobile entrance to field.
West on Jackson Boulevard to Ashland Avenue; south on Ashland to Twelfth; thence to field as before

TELEPHONES:

HARRISON 5006 . . . . . . At Cicero
HARRISON 3289 . . . . . . Flying Field
HARRISON 7022 . . . . . . Morton Park 41

EXHIBITION FLYING, INSTRUCTION AND PASSENGER-CARRYING EVERY SATURDAY AND SUNDAY

Aerial Age, Vol. I (June, 1912)

Above left: Carl S. Bates, Chicago, in an early biplane of his own design and manufacture. (*Carl S. Bates*) Above right: Emile Gustafson of Joliet with his Curtiss-type biplane at Cicero Field, 1913. (*Joseph M. Pallissard*) Below: Aerial view of Cicero Flying Field, maintained by the Aero Club of Illinois in Cicero, Illinois, between 1911–1915. (*Walter C. Scholl*)

Above: Malcolm G. Adams seated at controls of a tail-less monoplane which he built in Villa Grove, Illinois, in 1911. (*The Villa Grove News*) Below: Lester E. Holt of Springfield in Bertraud's Curtiss-type biplane, built in Essex and flown in Kankakee, Illinois, 1913. (*Joseph M. Pallissard*)

Above: The "Falcon" biplane built by James B. Slinn, Chillecothe, Illinois, for Eugene Brown, Peoria. F. W. Baldwin is seated at the controls. (*Eugene Brown)* Below: Curtis Prichart in William Selleck's Nieuport monoplane, Cicero Field, 1915. (*Joseph M. Pallissard*)

Above: "Baby" biplane built and flown by E. M. "Matty" Laird, Chicago, 1915–1916. Below: Small biplane built by Charles A. Arens, Chicago, and flown at Ashburn Field, 1916–1917. (*Charles A. Arens*)

Above: William E. Somerville (1908–1912), Coal City, Illinois, pioneer designer and builder of airplanes. (Mrs. *Constance B. Smith*) Right: Charles Dickinson, seed magnate and patron of early aviation in Chicago. (*Charles A. Arens*)

Above: Walter R. Brookins' Wright biplane after reaching the State Fairgrounds in Springfield on a 176-mile flight from Washington Park in Chicago on September 29, 1910. (*James T. Hickey*) Below: The Curtiss biplane used by Charles F. Willard to perform exhibition flights in Decatur, Illinois, July 16-17, 1910. Willard is standing in the center, in front of the pilot's seat, adjusting the control mechanism. (*Loren N. Hodge*)

Above: A view of Grant Park as an aviation field for Walter R. Brookins' exhibition flights along Chicago's lake front, September 27-28, 1910. The tent is a temporary hangar for Brookins' Wright biplane. Below: Wilbur Wright (left) and Walter R. Brookins beside a Wright biplane during Brookins' exhibitions. (*Mrs. Walter R. Brookins*)

Above: Lincoln Beachey performing during an exhibition at Hawthorne Race Track, Chicago, in 1913. Below: Glenn H. Curtiss (left) and Charles F. Willard standing in front of a Curtiss pusher-type biplane at Hawthorne Race Track, Chicago, October, 1910. (*Joseph M. Pallissard*)

he entered aeronautics in 1908. While living in Chicago that year, he worked with Bates and built at least one machine. After winning the Indianapolis speed classic in 1910, he retired as a racer and organized the Ray Harroun Company of Indianapolis, manufacturers of monoplanes similar to the Antoinette built by Hubert Latham in France.

Prior to 1910, several other inventors designed and attempted to build flying machines. Frank M. Mahan, president of the Lindgren-Mahan Fire Apparatus Works of Chicago, planned a combination dirigible and airplane in 1905 and built one four years later. In September, 1909, he announced a flight from Chicago to Washington, D.C., where he expected to take President William Howard Taft for a ride over the capital. This machine, described in a patent issued July 23, 1907, consisted of a buoyant body and "propelling and lifting wings" designed to produce upward force through the expansion and contraction of a flexible covering. There is no record that Mahan actually flew this unorthodox apparatus. Perhaps he recognized the futility of a trial and chose not to risk his life in a useless invention.

Another Chicagoan, Robert A. Moore, sought to avoid the hazards of a long flight by constructing the component parts of an airplane at home and shipping them to Fort Myer, to be assembled at the scene of proposed trials. This machine, which Moore hoped to sell to the United States Navy, had "double" wings, a cabin for a pilot and one passenger, and three propellers driven by a single engine. According to the inventor, the craft was capable of traveling at a speed of approximately 100 miles an hour and featured numerous safety devices. Gas chambers built into the wings were designed to keep it afloat if a landing was made in water. In the event of an engine failure, an auxiliary compressed-air motor was capable of driving the machine about 10 miles.

Two brothers, George and Robert Anderson, Chicago coal dealers, developed an amphibian airplane. In May, 1909, after nearly 18 months of work, they announced the completion of their machine. Because of the proximity of Lake Michigan, they fitted their craft with a hull and wheels. Otherwise, the design followed closely that of the Blériot monoplane.

Outside the Chicago area there was comparatively little aeronautical activity prior to 1910. As early as 1902, Charles E. Van Deventer, of Springfield, designed a flying machine utilizing an expansible circular wing for lifting power. He obtained a patent on this invention but apparently did not build a full-sized machine. Three years later another equally obscure inventor, Leroy Haines, of Colchester, applied for a patent on an airship consisting of "a parachute shaped propeller having blades drooping about a common center, and the means for varying the inclination of said blades." C. T. Pritchett, of Springfield, built an airplane and engine of unknown design in October, 1909, but there is no evidence to indicate that it flew. More successful experiments were started in 1908 by William E. Somerville in Coal City and J. Nick Sparling in East St. Louis; both men built several very fine airplanes after 1910.

Illinois experimenters and inventors received a needed boost in October, 1909, when Glenn Curtiss performed the first recorded flights in the state. During a three-day exhibition at Hawthorne Race Course in Chicago, he completed three flights, which were little more than short hops. Though inferior to flights elsewhere, they dispelled much of the local skepticism toward airplanes and created new interest in their construction. Curtiss' pusher biplane offered inventors, for the first time, a glimpse of a machine of proven design and became the model for most of those built in the state during the next few years.

Among the more than 100 flying machines built in Chicago in 1910, not one was capable of sustained flight. From nearly every occupation and trade, recruits were drawn into aviation; among their ranks were businessmen, engineers, carpenters, students, salesmen, and teachers. Aeronautics usually occupied the evenings and week ends of men regularly employed, but some sacrificed steady employment in the hope of gaining fame and riches with flying machines. Faced with innumerable hardships and lacking the requisite training or experience, most inventors lost interest in their work within a few weeks or months and turned to other occupations.

All builders had to sacrifice enormous amounts of money and time, and some their lives, for aviation. The cost alone was beyond the means of most, unless they had large reserves of capital to draw upon. Homemade machines cost at least $4,500, and some as much as $5,000, or even $8,000. Custom-built airplanes, of which the Wright and Curtiss designs were the best, cost from $3,000 to $5,000; shelter, tools, and replacement parts required $1,000 more. Added to the initial expense, the risk of damage during trials placed the expense of aviation too high for the average builder. Many who attempted to construct machines had to abandon unfinished projects because of insufficient funds.

Flying machines produced in 1910 were of many types. A large number were copies of the Wright, Curtiss, and foreign airplanes; others were products of fanciful imagination and even dreams. A lack of understanding of the basic principles of flight led some inventors to pattern their models after the features of birds, a logical if not fruitful course to follow for those who knew nothing of the complexities of the problem. Some builders created machines without wings, preferring to use revolving disks or blades. One Chicago resident designed an apparatus embodying "principles of respiration," with lift achieved through the rapid intake and discharge of air by three pneumatic pumps operated by a windlass.

In the Chicago area alone approximately 100 inventors, and in the rest of the state possibly 30 more, built flying machines of several varieties. There was, however, a definite trend toward standardization even as early as 1910. Among 46 products of Chicagoans, 5 monoplanes and 24 biplanes followed proven designs of either American or foreign manufacturers. Others possessed a vague resemblance to standard types. Prominent builders included Avery, Bates, Butusov, Scott, Wild, and others who had been active in aeronautics during the previous decade or before. The majority, however, were newcomers. Three of the younger builders—James J. Ward, St. Croix Johnstone, and Victor Lougheed—eventually made aviation a profession, the first two as exhibition flyers, the last as a writer and designer. But for every success there were scores of failures.

Although interesting, the products of most inventors contributed nothing of value to the advancement of aeronautics. Those machines that were not copies, at least in part, of successful models, seldom proved airworthy, if completed. H. H. Dailey, an automobile dealer, built a "center-drop" biplane with inverted dihedral wings similar to those of a sea gull. De Bert Hartley, a 60-year-old inventor of "almost everything under the sun," built a "safety" monoplane with "self-balancing and self-steering" devices of unknown make. Charles F. Lewiston, a printer, constructed a "French type monoplane with new arrangement of ailerons." Max K. Kasmar, a former roller skate manufacturer and secretary of the Aeronautical Society of Chicago, built a "collapsible" biplane, which he later sold to C. W. Curzon. Ludwig Fahrenwald, Mark Mikkelson, and Fred W. Kreck developed triplanes; Kreck's invention contained a "warped wing" and a "triple shutter control." Monoplanes appeared in several varieties: F. Gottwald, a machinist, created one "dispensing with propeller drive"; H. Bertsen, a sculptor, completed a self-balancing tandem design; and Edward Bjork, a building contractor, constructed a "double" model. Other products included winged dirigibles, movable disk helicopters, and a rotary wing "gyropter."

As to activities in other communities: in Freeport, Fred Heegle and J. H. Mapes constructed biplanes, and W. J. Martin completed a monoplane of original design. In May, 1910, Daniel A. Kreamer purchased a Curtiss biplane built by Everette K. Barnes and Harold H. Havens, of Rockford. In the following year, two other Rockford residents, R. Frank Coleman, a professional wrestler, and Willard Broling, produced biplanes. In Aurora, Alexander Kopesa, a former Hungarian army officer, invented a "flying device . . . [to] travel on land or water as well as in the air." In July, 1911, August Hendrian, of Decatur, performed several flights in a small monoplane resembling the French Demoiselle, and Usher Rausch, of Palestine, built a similar model. In Villa Grove, Malcolm G. Adams, a mechanic in the local railroad shops, smashed a tailless monoplane on its first trial. In Tom Benoist's airplane factory in St. Louis, Fred Morlan, of Fairfield, built a Curtiss machine that he flew several times. Robert Haller, of Lincoln, also constructed one but demolished it on the first flight. A dozen or more airplanes were built in other cities, including Bloomington, Edwardsville, Effingham, Elgin, Joliet, Peoria, and Springfield, but, according to available records, they all failed to fly. The less conventional designs, such as an ornithopter constructed in 1910 by R. H. and W. A. McNair, of Peoria, were destined to failure before they were started.

The formation of clubs and societies devoted to the promotion of aviation introduced a degree of order into the field of construction. The Illinois Aeroplane Club of Chicago, organized in January, 1910, by Edward E. Harbert, Oscar Newstrom, and John A. Montgomery, encouraged co-operation and exchange of ideas among local builders during the two years it remained active. The Aero Club of Illinois, created in February, 1910, drew together outstanding inventors and experimenters and prominent businessmen who were willing to support the work. Chanute served as the first president until his death. Other officers were James E. Plew, Harold F. McCormick, Charles E. Bartley, Robert M. Cutting, and Victor Lougheed.

For three years the Aero Club of Illinois remained under the direction of Plew and McCormick, the first and second vice presidents, respectively, at the time of its organization. After 1912, Charles Dickinson, a Chicago seed magnate, assumed a larger part of the leadership, gaining in 1915 the office of president, a post he retained until his death twenty years later. Until 1913, McCormick financed nearly all activities, including the operation of Cicero Field and the sponsorship of three spectacular aviation programs. Dickinson paid the bills for nearly all activities after that date. In 1915, he purchased and turned over to the club a tract of land that became Ashburn Field, and thereafter made up from his personal funds its annual operating deficit. Through the generosity of these and other wealthy members, the club was able to promote effectively the growth of aviation in the Middle West.

As a patron of aviation, McCormick was interested in the development of new designs. In three years he spent approximately $100,000 on two experimental airplanes that proved to be complete failures. Beginning in 1910, he financed the work of William S. Romme, a New York inventor of an unorthodox machine called the "Umbrella-plane" because of the shape of its supporting surface. Before abandoning that project in 1912, the McCormick-Romme Company spent $50,000 in an effort to make the craft airworthy. As soon as this was demonstrated with a series of short flights, it was dumped into Lake Michigan. In the same year McCormick put up $50,000 to develop a monoplane designed by Sidney V. James and built by C. Milton Vought. Known as the "Mustard Plaster" because of its dingy yellow color, this machine featured a novel wing with greater width than length. In spite of McCormick's failures, he contributed $25,000 to the creation of a laboratory at Cicero Field, for the use of local experimenters without charge.

In 1911 and 1912, inventors made this spot the center of local aeronautical activity. During July, 1911, the first month of operation, all but one of 13 machines there were owned by amateur builders—Otto W. Brodie's big Farman was the single exception, and the only airplane capable of actual flight. Hangars along the edge of the field contained machines owned by Bates, S. D. Dixon, Ole Flottop, a local propeller manufacturer, Charles A. Hibbard, Dan Kreamer, Willie Lenert, McCormick, William A. Mattery, a veteran balloonist, A. Steinhaus, and Claude L. Young. During the balance of the flying season only three machines achieved sustained flights, three others completed short hops, and the rest were wrecked or abandoned.

In 1913 thirty-five machines, besides those owned by transient flyers, were at the field. Fourteen belonging to local club members were untried experimental craft of unorthodox design; the remainder were mostly copies of the Curtiss and foreign airplanes. Newcomers to amateur ranks that year were J. D. B. Blayney, Thomas Preston Brooke, Charles Curtiss, G. W. Davis, Perry David, R. D. Dwight, G. M. Ellis, Joseph L. Mix, Walter O. Runcie, K. G. Sandell, Grover F. Sexton, and John W. Smith, all of Chicago. Brooke, a noted bandmaster, formed in 1912 the Brooke Aircraft Company of Chicago, manufacturer of biplanes and "non-gyro" engines. Two engineers, R. D.

Dwight and J. B. Lund, built a "quadraplane" consisting of eight surfaces in tandem, and a 50-horsepower engine. Smith, known familiarly as "Six-Cylinder Smith," because of his success with radial engines, developed a remarkable monoplane with a streamlined, molded fuselage composed of pressed wood fiber.

After 1912, a large number of experimental machines were sometimes present, but the principal activity of Cicero Field was provided by exhibition flyers, who tested their machines for weekend engagements or extended tours in adjacent states. Lured by the prospect of gain and public approbation, many Illinois residents took up aviation as a profession and made their headquarters at Cicero. With the growth of a professional class of builders and flyers, the amateurs gradually disappeared. The decrease in their numbers was especially noticeable after 1912 though a few remained active until 1916.

Between 1913 and 1916, Chicago inventors produced 14 airworthy machines, mostly copies of successful models. In 1913, James Colovos, Fred Hartman, and Frank Pontowski built replicas of the Curtiss biplane. Colovos equipped his with a Wright control. The next year Pontowski and John Lickorsik constructed a tractor biplane designed by Vought. Other successful builders in 1914 were Emil M. Laird, G. LeGaucier, W. C. Miller, Robert Neal, Yves Rolland, R. Selleck, James S. Stephens, Otto A. Timm, and G. Viks. Rolland developed a monoplane of steel construction throughout, with an automatic stabilizer and a "double propelling system actuated by gears and shafting." In May, 1915, Neal piloted his small biplane from Chicago to a point within 20 miles of Kansas City, Missouri, before an overheated engine forced him down. In 1916, Walter L. Brock and Charles A. Arens constructed biplanes that were used for exhibitions during at least two seasons.

Outside the vicinity of Chicago, there was also an appreciable decrease after 1912 in the number of homemade airplanes. Obstacles confronting amateurs in downstate localities were usually greater than those experienced in Chicago, which abounded with technical advice on design and construction. There was also the problem of acquiring proper materials, for mail-order supply houses were not always trustworthy and there were no local outlets. In an effort to overcome these and other difficulties, builders outside Chicago generally copied standard models for which blueprints and parts could be ordered by mail. Biplanes of the Curtiss design were built in 1913 by J. H. Mapes, of Freeport, and Art Bertrand, of Kankakee. Harry Younts, of Decatur, constructed and flew a monoplane similar to the French Nieuport. In 1914, Herbert Kellogg, of Kewanee, developed a double monoplane, and Stanford Wright, of Dwight, produced a machine of unknown type.

The amateur builder and flyer contributed little of value to the technical advancement of aviation, but his enthusiasm and faith in the future of the airplane encouraged others to take up the art. He created interest in flight, and, though seldom successful, his homemade machine was all that was known of the subject in some communities for many years. Too often, his work was forgotten in the midst of praise for professional exhibition flyers. Though ridiculed by friends and acquaintances and called unflattering names, later events proved that the amateur's vision of air travel was not a dream.

4

GROWTH OF THE AVIATION INDUSTRY, 1910–1916

The early aviation industry existed primarily as a form of entertainment. Aside from ineffective efforts to organize a military air service in 1908, the first use of airplanes in large numbers was in exhibitions. Considered for many years an impossibility, the airplane naturally became an object of curiosity. In almost every community people wanted to see one in flight; exhibitions seemed a logical means for showing it to the public. Charles F. Willard, one of the first flyers trained by Curtiss, suggested the idea after Tom Baldwin assured him of favorable public reception. Curtiss began giving exhibitions in the fall of 1909 in an effort to influence sentiment against the Wrights. The following year, exhibitions on a large scale marked the beginning of an aviation industry, for the business of designing, constructing, and flying for public performances quickly became a job for trained professionals rather than amateurs.

The airplane gained rapidly in popularity in 1910 after the formation of three exhibition companies. The Wright company was the first to create a troupe of performers. Under the tutelage of Wilbur and Orville Wright, three flyers were trained and turned over to A. Roy Knabenshue, who directed the nation-wide activities of the Wright Exhibition Company. A short time later, the Curtiss Aeroplane Company formed a subsidiary, the Curtiss Exhibition Company, under the direction of Jerome Fanciulli, a former member of the Associated Press staff in Washington, D.C. Both companies employed outstanding aviators. Walter R. Brookins, Arch Hoxsey, and Ralph Johnstone were the original members of the Wright team. Curtiss' performers included Lincoln Beachey, Eugene Ely, J. C. Mars, and Willard. In December of that year, Alfred W. and John B. Moisant organized the Moisant International Aviators, a group of talented flyers, mostly foreigners.

This company, formed for the purpose of manufacturing airplanes and giving exhibitions, employed three Frenchmen, Rene Barrier, Rolland Garros, and Rene Simon; one Italian, Oresces Farrara; and two Americans, St. Croix Johnstone and John J. Frisbie. Until his death in an airplane accident while performing in New Orleans on December 31, 1910, John Moisant was the most skillful pilot in the group. Johnstone, a resident of Oak Park, Illinois, did not join the company until the spring of 1911, after he had been graduated from Blériot's flight schools in London and Paris.

The Moisants were born in Chicago and spent most of their lives in foreign countries, particularly Central America and France. As young men they settled in San Salvador, where they prospered as bankers and businessmen. Despite numerous myths about their filibustering adventures, they were as respectable as they were succesful. About 1908, John Moisant became interested in aeronautics and, although he had never seen an airplane, designed a metal monoplane. The following year he went to France to enroll in the Blériot flying school near Paris, from which he was graduated after three brief flights. On August 24, 1910, with a new Blériot monoplane, Moisant flew from Paris to a point within six miles of London before engine trouble interrupted the first attempt to link the two capitals by air. After completing the trip on September 6, he returned to the United States to take part in the Gordon-Bennett Aviation Cup Race and the International Meet held in October at Belmont Park, New York, under the auspices of the Aero Club of America.

In 1910 and 1911, the Wright, Curtiss, and Moisant companies presented practically all of the exhibitions staged in Illinois. They completed at least 31 engagements, including one or more flights on each of 83 days. In 1910, the Curtiss flyers gave 6 of the 13 exhibitions in the state. Willard made 5 flights in Decatur on July 16 and 17, of which only one, a 5-mile, cross-country trip, extended beyond the limits of the local driving park. Elsewhere, Ely completed one flight in Quincy on August 20; Beachey performed twice in Rock Island on September 24; and Willard appeared in Streator on October 15. Curtiss' aviators performed twice in Chicago: in a meet held at Hawthorne Race Course, July 3-5, under the sponsorship of the Colonial Aero Club; and at the same place, on October 2-8, in a preliminary event for the Chicago-New York airplane race.

The Wright company completed three exhibitions in 1910. On July 5 and 7, Arthur L. Walsh flew as a feature of the Aurora homecoming program commemorating the opening of the Aurora & DeKalb Electric Railway. Mechanical failures and high winds prevented him from performing as scheduled on July 2-4, but he remained in the city until he was able to fulfill the terms of his contract.

The most spectacular exhibition of the year occurred on September 27-29, when Brookins performed along Chicago's lake front and then made a record-breaking flight to Springfield. The first two days he flew along Michigan Avenue and Grant Park at noon and five o'clock in the evening for the entertainment of approximately 200,000 watchers at each performance. On one flight he carried Grover F. Sexton, giving Chicagoans their first view of an airplane with pilot and passenger. After the last show, Brookins and Wilbur Wright checked the biplane carefully before towing it to Washington Park, the starting place for the flight to the state capital the next morning.

Several weeks earlier the finance committee of the State Board of Agriculture had proposed a race between an airplane and a passenger train as a promotion stunt for the forthcoming State Fair, if funds could be raised to pay for the scheme. At first, there appeared to be no chance of holding the race, but in mid-September H. H. Kolhsaat, publisher of the *Chicago*

Record-Herald, offered $10,000 for a flight from Chicago to Springfield. The Agriculture Board and the Wright company immediately announced that the race would take place on the day before the fair opened. Originally, Wilbur Wright gave the assignment to Hoxsey, for Brookins and Johnstone had received earlier opportunities to earn fame. However, Hoxsey was later replaced by Brookins as a reprimand for having taken unnecessary risks, in violation of orders, during an exhibition in Detroit.

At a few minutes past nine o'clock, Brookins started as 30,000 spectators looked on. Seven hours and 20 minutes later, following brief stops in Gilman and Mt. Pulaski, he landed on the infield of the State Fairgrounds race track. American records for total distance and nonstop flight fell as a result of this 175¾-mile flight. In other respects Brookins' performance was not especially impressive. Because of a ten-mile-an-hour headwind his average speed of 30.4 miles an hour was below that recorded earlier in the same machine.

Hoxsey performed flights daily, except Sunday, during the fair and on the last day flew to Kinloch, Missouri. On October 8, after winning a five-mile race against Barney Oldfield, he refueled and checked his biplane thoroughly and set out on a flight to St. Louis following the Chicago & Alton Railroad. En route he circled over Staunton, his birthplace 26 years earlier. After crossing the Mississippi River below Alton, he became lost in the smoke over St. Louis and landed near Clayton for gasoline and directions. He then flew on to Kinloch, a distance of 10 miles. There 60,000 spectators of an aviation meet sponsored by the Aero Club of St. Louis anxiously awaited his arrival. Three days later, he made front-page news by taking former President Theodore Roosevelt on a flight over St. Louis.

Only two of the four exhibitions scheduled by Illinois pilots in 1910 were successful. Horace B. Wild and Otto W. Brodie, aviators employed by James E. Plew of Chicago, were unable to stage the series of flights in a Curtiss biplane that had been billed as a special attraction by the University of Illinois Athletic Association, on May 20-21, during the annual interscholastic events in Urbana. Brodie wrecked the machine on the first trial. However, the Association then agreed to pay half the original price for a single flight, and the aviators made plans to put the repaired plane in the air. Before a crowd of about 3,000 persons, assembled on the golf course on the south campus, they took turns in trying to coax the airplane into the air. The best performance of the day was turned in by Brodie, who managed on one occasion to lift the wheels a few inches off the ground. Despite the poor performance in Urbana, Brodie made a number of successful flights with the biplane during June and July, and James J. Ward used it to perform in Galesburg on September 29 and 30. Another Chicagoan, Charles W. Miller, a former bicycle-racing champion, failed in Monmouth on July 4 with a biplane of his own design. Two East St. Louis aviators, Hillery Beachey, brother of the star of the Curtiss flyers, and J. Nick Sparling, scheduled flights in Carlinville on July 19 during that city's celebration of the last payment on the million-dollar debt on its 40-year-old courthouse. Sparling appeared with a monoplane of his own and a biplane constructed by Howard W. Gill, who later became an outstanding pilot with the Wright Exhibition Company. Sparling completed one brief flight in Gill's airplane.

During the 1911 season, the Wright company filled only four contracts in Illinois: Brookins appeared in Quincy and Peoria in June and July; Gill flew in Quincy in June; and Cliff Turpin performed at the State Fair in October. The Curtiss company, using Lincoln Beachey, Beckwith Havens, J. C. Mars, Robinson, Arthur Walsh, James Ward, and Charles Willard, completed seven exhibitions. In addition to performances in Cairo on July 3 and 4, Robinson flew from Minneapolis to Rock Island in a hydroairplane on October 17-21, a flight originally planned to continue on to New Orleans. The Moisant International Aviators, composed of Barrier, Simon, and Frisbie, presented five exhibitions in Illinois, with three- and four-day programs in Galesburg, Joliet, Freeport, Kankakee, and Danville. Members of the Wright, Curtiss, and Moisant troupes also appeared in the International Aviation Meet held in Chicago's Grant Park on August 12-20.

A newcomer, the Benoist Aircraft Company and Flying

School of St. Louis, Missouri, captured a large share of the exhibition business in central and southern Illinois in 1911, and for the next three years ranked as one of the leaders in the field. Owned and operated by Tom Benoist, the company also gained an enviable reputation as a builder of tractor biplanes and flying boats; its school for aviators at Kinloch, Missouri, was one of the finest in the Middle West. Although not active until September, 1911, Tom Benoist, John D. Cooper, and Horace Kearney completed eight exhibitions that year. The following year W. H. Bleakley, Anthony Jannus, Edward A. Korn, F. N. Bell, and J. A. Woodlies gave 15 exhibitions in Illinois and many more in Ohio, Indiana, Kentucky, Missouri, and Iowa. In 1913 and 1914, the company moved to Chicago and then to Sandusky, Ohio, where Benoist concentrated on the manufacture of flying boats and seldom returned to exhibitions.

The emergence of an aviation industry in Chicago increased exhibition activity in Illinois and adjacent states. Almost without exception, manufacturing and exhibition companies were one and the same. Even flying schools relied upon public performances for a regular income. Those who did not soon went out of business. Some manufacturers devoted their entire production to equipping their own pilots, but even then, because of the high accident rate, they had difficulty maintaining enough machines in flying order to fill all engagements.

In 1909, two companies were organized to manufacture aircraft. According to the broad terms of their certificates of incorporation, they were authorized to engage in a number of other activities. The Horgan Flying Machine Company of Chicago, organized by Jacob Winnen, John C. Benthall, William C. Horgan, and Carl Stover, in March, proposed to "manufacture, operate, sell and lease flying machines; to develop and exploit inventions and patents; and to conduct a general manufacturing business, and to do all things incidental thereto." Typically for that time, Horgan received $99,990 of the $100,000 capital stock in return for all rights, patterns, models, and other property pertaining to an invention known as the "Horgan Flying Machine." E. M. Strangland and Benthall, of Chicago, and Winnen, of Melrose Park, served as officers of the company during its brief existence. The second firm, the Black Crow Manufacturing Company, formed by Isaac Fulton, of Babylon, with a reported capitalization of $35,000, failed to produce a single airship. There is no evidence that the company ever existed except on paper.

In 1910, at least six airplane manufacturing companies were created and three other firms were building planes, although principally engaged in other activities. The Bates Aero Motor Company of Chicago, owned and operated by Carl S. Bates, manufactured airplanes in addition to several types of aero engines. In South Chicago James L. Case, an awning, tent, and balloon maker, built at least one airplane. Eddie Hearne, with aid from Claude L. Young, used the facilities of the Hearne Motor Company of Chicago to construct one airplane described as "a novel apparatus."

Only two of the six manufacturing companies actually produced airplanes. Four others—the Illinois Aviation Company, the Swedish-American Aerial Club, and the Aerocraft Company, all of Chicago, and the Sparling-McClintock Company, of Grafton—failed to conduct the businesses for which they were created. The two producers were the Chicago Aero Works and Max Stupar, both of which built airplanes and accessories for many years. In 1915, Herbert S. and Antonio Renton, owners of the Chicago Aero Works, merged with Stupar to form the Chicago Aero Works, Inc., which remained in business until the early 1920's.

Manufacturers might have prospered in 1910 had they been able to produce machines suitable for exhibitions. Until the war in Europe provided the impetus for expansion and consolidation on a large scale, the majority of airplanes flown in Illinois were built by individuals and small companies, who also engaged in exhibitions. A succession of firms appeared in Chicago during the years 1911–1916, but few continued in business for more than a year, and many disappeared without actually constructing a machine. The Mills Aviators, the National Aeroplane Manufacturing Company, and the American Aeroplane Manufacturing Company were typical of those that played an active part in the advancement of aviation for a year or two; others remained in operation too short a time to affect the development of the fledgling industry.

Two brothers, George P. and James R. Mills, of Chicago, were active in aviation for nearly three years. In June, 1911, James Mills announced completion of a new type of biplane fitted with a gyroscopic stabilizer, which he intended to enter in the International Aviation Meet in Chicago the following August. Earlier the same month, he had placed on sale a pamphlet entitled *How Flight Is Possible,* purporting to explain the facts of airplane construction to novices for the nominal fee of $1.00. At that time he was also selling blueprints of Curtiss, Blériot, Farman, and Antoinette airplanes to amateur builders. The drawings sold much faster than the pamphlets.

Early in July, 1911, the brothers organized the Mills and Mills Aviators' Exchange, a booking agency for exhibition engagements. At first they did business only with owners of airplanes, but, in 1912, following the organization of Mills Aviators, manufacturers of a biplane designed by George Mills, the company retained a number of skilled pilots to fly its own machines. In order to raise funds for the continued manufacture of airplanes and experimentation with new designs, the Mills company had to expand its exhibition business in 1912 and 1913. If there had been a market for machines, this company, like many others, would have preferred to limit its activities solely to manufacturing. A few biplanes were sold, in Iowa and Montana, but not enough to support the company's extensive operations. Therefore, a subsidiary, the Mills Exhibition Company, with Nels J. Nelson, Art Smith, E. G. Vedder, Fred A. Hoover, and Diddier Masson as pilots, performed throughout Illinois and in other parts of the country.

The Mills team was especially active in the Middle West. Nelson, a native of New Britain, Connecticut, was the leading member of the troupe. After performing with Jimmy Ward in Little Rock, Arkansas, in March, Nelson returned to Chicago to test a new flying boat from the Mills factory before returning to exhibitions six weeks later. He performed in Galesburg, Illinois, and Clinton, Iowa, in May; in Janesville and Ashland,

Wisconsin, in July; in Jackson and Eaton Rapids, Michigan, in August; and in Clinton and Monroe, Wisconsin, in September. Art Smith, the stunt flyer, joined the Mills team in April, and appeared in Sterling, Illinois, in May; in Hillsdale, Michigan, with teammate Hoover, in mid-June; in Deadwood, South Dakota, in July; in his home town—Fort Wayne, Indiana—and in Bogard, Missouri, Havelock, Nebraska, and Clifton and Rush Center, Kansas, in August; in Chilton, Wisconsin, in September; and again in Fort Wayne in October. Hoover joined the company in March for a single season, and appeared in Quincy and Jacksonville, Illinois, and Lansing and Hillsdale, Michigan, as well as in communities in other states. Masson, a mechanic who had accompanied Louis Paulhan to the United States in 1910, began flying that year and joined the Mills company in the spring of 1912. During May and June he appeared in Galesburg and Quincy, Illinois, and Burlington, Iowa. In July, while in Frankfort, Indiana, he suffered an attack of pneumonia that ended his association with the Mills Aviators, though he later returned to France, where in 1915 he became one of the original members of the famous Lafayette Escadrille.

Exhibition flying was not an easy job. The partial list of engagements filled by Nelson, Smith, Hoover, and Masson points out the problems of traveling long distances, packing and unpacking, and assembling and disassembling machines during the brief but busy flying season. Furthermore, the alarming death rate among exhibition pilots attests to the hazards of flying biplanes from ball parks, race tracks, and other makeshift landing fields. During 1912, Art Smith smashed machines with such regularity that his colleagues gave him the nickname "Smashup Kid." However, not all the hazards of exhibition flying were encountered in the air. On one occasion, when rains caused a cancellation of Smith's flights in Bay City, Texas, he and his mechanics found it necessary to have sheriff's deputies escort them to the railroad station from which they were to leave for their next engagement, since a demonstration by disappointed spectators seemed imminent. Later they learned that the crowd had mistaken the word "Honeybug" stenciled on the crate of the airplane—a pet name for the girl Smith later married—for the word "humbug." This they interpreted as a taunt from the jubilant flyer who, they felt, had swindled the local promoters out of the guarantee for appearing for the exhibition.

The National Aeroplane Manufacturing Company of Chicago carried on an extensive manufacturing and exhibition business in 1911 and 1912. This company was the successor to the International Aeroplane Company, founded in May, 1911, for the purpose of manufacturing airplanes and conducting a flying school. In the first year Lester V. Bratton, chief construction engineer, built four biplanes and rebuilt seven others after they were wrecked in exhibitions. In spite of a large output and extensive business, the company soon foundered in financial difficulty. Dr. E. W. Spates eventually took over management of the company and worked out a reorganization. A new name was adopted, and control of the firm was given to him and to Howard and W. S. Linn.

During the seven months the International Aeroplane Company had remained in operation, exhibitions were conducted throughout the Middle West. Two early graduates of its flying school, Harry Powers and Allan Lougheed, of Chicago, flew in several Illinois communities in July, 1911. Ignace Semeniouk, John W. Rosenbaum, and Vannie Ludvik joined the company later that summer. In September, Rosenbaum, a Chicago aviator, lost his life in a crash at De Witt, Iowa.

The company also used machines from its downtown factory to conduct a flying school at Cicero Field. During the winter of 1911–1912, the National Aeroplane Company moved the school to Galveston, Texas, where J. H. Worden, Paul Studensky, and Mart McCormack began new classes in January. Bratton, Rudolph Sestak, and F. G. Joytz completed the staff. Until late April, student training in handling water and land craft continued at a rapid pace, but with the advent of warmer weather in Chicago the school returned to establish headquarters in the two largest hangars at Cicero Field.

In 1912, the National company expanded its school and exhibition business. An important addition in May was a monoplane, an Anzani-powered Nieuport, which made possible the first regular training program for that type of craft. Marcel Tournier, a graduate of the French Nieuport school, joined the staff at that time. A. C. Beech, chief construction engineer, built two large Beech-National biplanes, which were added to the school fleet and used by him and Studensky for instruction and exhibitions. Tournier and W. C. Robinson, a mechanic in Max Lillie's school, used the Nieuport for exhibitions during the summer and fall. Other than flights by Studensky in Bushnell and Rushville in August, all performances took place outside of Illinois.

The Chicago School of Aviation and its successor, the American Aeroplane Manufacturing Company and School of Aviation, remained in business little more than a year. The original company opened a training school on the grounds of the Franco-American Aviation Company near West Pullman in April, 1911, and later moved to Hawthorne Race Course. Within a few months, a reorganization of the company produced the new firm, with a capitalization of $1,000,000, of which only a small part was subscribed. In an attempt to acquire new prestige and customers, the company named J. C. Mars field captain and chief instructor of a new school at West Pullman. However, he resigned in January, 1912, and Andrew Drew, a former St. Louis aeronaut and a graduate of the Wrights' school in Dayton, took charge of the school until the company went bankrupt the following May.

Nearly all of the aviation industry was located in or near Chicago, where Cicero Field was the only permanent landing field in the state. There were, however, several attempts to establish manufacturing and flying centers in other cities. In workshops in Washington Park, East St. Louis, J. Nick Sparling and C. W. Curzon built machines, principally for their flying schools and for exhibitions. The Crescent Aeroplane Company of Moline built one airplane during the summer of 1911. The Illinois Aero Construction Company of Coal City might have succeeded in marketing its highly stable products if its plant and equipment had not been destroyed by fire in December, 1912.

Two years before the first practical airplane performed in

Illinois, William E. Somerville, mayor of Coal City, turned his attention from the manufacture of wire rope to aeronautics. Experiments with scale models and the study of birds in flight led, in 1910, to the construction of a biplane and monoplane, but nearly nine more months passed before either actually flew. On June 11, 1911, Somerville completed a short flight in the biplane. To witnesses the plane seemed satisfactory, but Somerville was disappointed with its stability. Therefore, he built a tractor biplane, which Edward Korn tested in June, 1912. This time the results were all that the inventor had anticipated; with a number of friends he formed the Illinois Aero Construction Company to produce and sell airplanes, conduct a flying school, and present exhibitions. Earl S. Daugherty, of Long Beach, California, became chief pilot and construction engineer for the company. During the remainder of the season he performed in Chicago, Joliet, and Odell, in addition to making numerous flights at the Coal City field.

After the destruction of the plant, Somerville remained active as a builder and exhibitor of airplanes. In January, 1913, he purchased and rebuilt the Morane-Borel monoplane that George Mestach had wrecked the previous September during the International Aviation Meet in Chicago. Daugherty, Mestach, and Lester E. Holt flew it in exhibitions for the Western Vaudeville Managers' Association, with whom Somerville had closed a contract the previous year.

He might have abandoned aviation in July, 1913, had the Kopesa Air Navigation Company of Aurora fulfilled a contract for the purchase of the monoplane. When the sale failed to materialize, Mestach used the ship to perform in a number of western states, closing the season in October with a five-day engagement in Albuquerque. After a slow start the following year, Somerville sold the monoplane to Daugherty, who used it in exhibitions in Illinois and Michigan.

The few companies that managed to stay in business after 1912 catered almost entirely to the needs of exhibition flyers and wealthy sportsmen. Between 1913 and 1917, several manufacturers produced airplanes in the hangars and shops of Cicero and Ashburn fields. The Partridge-Keller Company, owned by Elmer Partridge and Henry Keller, built biplanes, mostly for professional pilots, until 1917, when they closed their plant temporarily while serving as civilian instructors for the Signal Corps. In 1914, Emil M. "Matty" Laird, a 14-year-old bank messenger, built a small airplane, which he used for exhibitions. During the next two years he built three more, and, after serving as a civilian instructor, he returned to Chicago in 1918 to establish the E. M. Laird Airplane Company at Ashburn, the forerunner of the E. M. Laird Company of Wichita, Kansas, producers of the Swallow, the first postwar commercial airplane.

The oldest airplane manufacturing firm in Illinois, the E. B. Heath Aerial Vehicle Company of Chicago, remained in business without interruption from 1909 to 1931. A native of Brooklyn, New York, Edward B. Heath experimented with gliders in 1904 and built his first airplane four years later in Antlers, New York. In 1909, he organized a company in Chicago to manufacture airplane parts and accessories, which he sold mostly by mail order to builders of homemade machines. After buying out Carl S. Bates in 1912, Heath produced complete aircraft. Following World War I, the company became the Heath Airplane Company, manufacturers of several types of machines for private and commercial pilots.

The Aero Club's fields served as the midwestern headquarters for exhibition flyers from April until late October of each year. Members of this group included flyers associated with local flying schools and manufacturing concerns, plus many independent pilots, of whom the most familiar were Frank Kastory, C. N. Sinclair, Harry Crewdson, Louis Gertson, Joseph M. Pallissard, Charles A. Arens, and Matty Laird. Visitors and temporary residents included, some time or another, practically every well-known flyer in the United States.

Though crude by modern standards, Cicero Field was one of the most elaborate airports in operation between 1911 and 1915. Occupying a small tract bounded by 16th and 22nd streets and 48th and 52nd avenues, it offered aviators a turf landing field, sheet metal and wooden hangars, and adequate facilities for maintenance and service of airplanes. A board fence, six feet high, topped by a single strand of barbed wire, assured pilots a reasonable degree of freedom from curious spectators. During the regular flying season, the field buzzed with activity on week days as flyers tested their machines for week-end engagements.

Much of the activity at Cicero and Ashburn fields consisted of flying instruction for young men who were lured into aviation by the prospect of profits from public performances. Twenty or more schools were located at Cicero Field; few lasted more than a single season. Practically every manufacturer conducted flying schools, whose tuition fees, ranging from $200 to $350, usually included courses in airplane construction.

In 1912 and 1913, the Lillie Flying School, one of the best in Chicago, trained many students who became leading flyers and promoters of aviation. Principal owner and chief instructor Max Lillie (born Maximilian Liljestrand in Stockholm, Sweden, in 1882) came to the United States in 1903. After learning to fly in 1911 at Kinloch, Missouri, Lillie operated a school at Moncrief Park, Florida, and performed exhibitions throughout the South before moving to Cicero Field in the spring of 1912. In the next two seasons he trained approximately 30 students, of whom the most outstanding were DeLloyd Thompson, later an instructor for Lillie, C. Milton Vought, and Katherine Stinson.

In 1912, Lillie expanded his activities, opening schools in Kinloch, Missouri, and San Antonio, Texas, for the winter. Both were closed in the spring of 1913 when Lillie enlarged his Cicero school, establishing a branch at the Columbia Yacht Club in Grant Park for flying-boat instruction. His interest along this line had led to the formation of the Weckler-Armstrong-Lillie Company of Chicago, manufacturers of the Welco Craft flying boat. Lillie's career ended in a fatal accident in Galesburg in September, 1913. Thompson tried to keep the school in operation but soon gave it up to enter the exhibition business.

William C. Robinson, of Grinnell, Iowa, joined the Lillie school in 1912 as a mechanic. He learned to fly Wright and

Nieuport airplanes and the following year, when Marcel Tournier returned to France, Robinson took charge of the National Aeroplane Manufacturing Company's Nieuport. He used it for instruction and exhibitions until it was purchased in May, 1914, by Hans W. Buddecke, a German flyer.

Buddecke went back to Germany in August, but by that date Robinson had returned to his home where he was organizing the Grinnell Aeroplane Company to manufacture a parasol monoplane of his own design. An airplane crash in March, 1916, ended Robinson's life and brought about the dissolution of the company.

Women also played an important role in the exhibition business. Katherine and Marjorie Stinson, Bessica Faith Raiche, Julia Clark, and Ruth Bancroft Law were as skillful and as active as many of their male contemporaries. Because they were the "darlings" of the public, they were effective popularizers of aviation. Wherever they appeared, great crowds turned out to witness their performances, for women flyers were rare and almost a curiosity in themselves.

The famous flying Stinson family was familiar to Chicago residents for nearly twenty years. Four members—Katherine, Marjorie, Eddie, and John—became well-known pilots, though the two women were the stars of the group until they retired in 1918. The men became manufacturers of airplanes during the 1920's, and Eddie, until he crashed in Washington Park in 1931, was, at one time or another, holder of practically every record for piloting skill and endurance.

In March, 1912, Katherine came to Chicago from Jackson, Mississippi, to enroll in the Lillie school. Small and frail in appearance, she seemed unsuited to be an aviatrix; in fact, the Mills Aviators had rejected her application for admittance to their school, and, for a time, Lillie threatened to do the same. Even though she became the favorite of the field, veteran pilots insisted that she would not be able to handle the controls of a Wright biplane on windy days. However, after three weeks, she easily passed the complicated tests for the Aero Club of America pilot's license, becoming the first woman to accomplish that feat in a Wright machine, and set out on a spectacular career as an exhibition flyer and instructor, unequaled by many of the aviators who had doubted her ability to handle an airplane.

Marjorie, encouraged by her sister's success, entered the Wright school in Dayton in 1914 but did not begin flying professionally until the following year. In 1916, the year Eddie learned to fly, Marjorie piloted small biplanes built by Walter Brock, Matty Laird, and Charles Arens of Chicago. Meanwhile, Katherine performed throughout the United States. Her popularity soared to a new high in July, 1915, when she executed three consecutive inside loops; Ruth Law claimed the honor of being the first woman to perform a loop, but, in all probability, she and Katherine Stinson performed it at about the same time. After a triumphant tour of Japan and China in the winter of 1916–1917, Katherine joined Marjorie, Eddie, and John in the operation of a training school for Royal Canadian Air Force pilots at San Antonio. The brothers later served as instructors in the United States Air Service, and Katherine, after being turned down for military service, played an active role in Liberty Bond drives and other wartime activities on the home front.

Bessica Raiche organized the first flight instruction class exclusively for women in 1912 while she was an instructor for the Standard School of Aviation in Chicago. A native of Wisconsin, she was graduated from Tufts Medical School in Boston and practiced as a physician before taking up aviation. For a short time in the spring of 1912, she and her husband, François, were employed by the Chicago company.

A Chicago stenographer, Julia Clark, was the first woman to be graduated by Curtiss' training school at San Diego. In the spring of 1912, she joined the International Flying Circus, a team of exhibition flyers organized by William H. Pickens from former Curtiss students, including Horace Kearney, Lanny Callan, Farnum Fish, Mohan Singh, and Motohisa Kondo. After performing in several states, this troupe broke up in June, 1912, following Miss Clark's death in an accident which occurred while she was testing her airplane in preparation for a show in Springfield, Illinois.

A young woman from Lynn, Massachusetts, Ruth Bancroft Law, became a regular visitor at Chicago's fields because of her many appearances in the Middle West. She captured newspaper headlines and the hearts of the American public during the years she vied with Katherine Stinson for honors as the nation's leading aviatrix. Although active as early as 1912, she did not gain much recognition until November, 1916, when she shattered the American nonstop flight record, piloting a Curtiss pusher biplane 666 miles. Miss Law was married several years before her retirement to Charles Oliver, who had long been her manager, and in 1922 she left exhibition work after having earned nearly $100,000.

Wartime expansion of the aviation industry in 1917 to meet the anticipated demand for military airplanes led to the formation of many new companies in Illinois. These new companies were to be disappointed, however, for none built airplanes for the government. Though 331 firms received contracts to supply the War Department with "aeronautical materials," only one tenth of these were contracts that totaled more than $10,000. Disappointed manufacturers included the American Aviation Company, the Bates Aeroplane Company, the Brooke Aircraft Company, and the Lawrence Lewis Aeroplane Company, all of Chicago.

5

AVIATION CONTESTS AND MEETS

Between 1910 and 1912, numerous contests and flights were held to stimulate interest in design and construction, to encourage the use of improved types of airplanes, and to focus attention on air travel as a method of transportation. Progress depended upon public understanding, confidence, and acceptance, for the early pusher biplanes had many shortcomings. Above all, a strong, financially stable industry depended upon sales, either to exhibition flyers or to sportsmen. Competitive programs and long cross-country trips contributed significantly to a better understanding of aviation's capacity for advancement and concentrated attention on aeronautical achievements, slight as they sometimes appeared to be when interpreted by the press.

Cash prizes, some as much as $50,000 for a single event, produced a series of remarkable records for speed, altitude, distance, and other types of performances. Aviation events in the years 1909–1912 cost promoters more than one million dollars; but without the inducement of prize money, many aeronautical records and achievements would not have been attained for several more years. Unfortunately, contests degenerated into extravagant shows, and promoters and flyers, motivated by lust for prizes and public approbation, lost sight of the fact that aviation must prove itself as a method of transportation if it was to prosper. The great show era came to a close after the 1912 season, for the appearance of improved machines made performances once unique and marvelous now ordinary and uninteresting. Thereafter, attention was concentrated on cross-country flights.

In May, 1910, aviation received a tremendous impetus from Curtiss' flight down the Hudson River from Albany to New York, for which he won $10,000 from the *New York World*—the first substantial prize awarded in the United States. This, following his victory the previous fall in the first Gordon-Bennett Aviation Cup Race at Rheims, France, electrified imaginations. Americans began to realize that an airplane could do much more than hover above the ground or fly in short circles over a landing field.

In the midst of the excitement, Charles K. Hamilton suggested an even greater challenge, a thousand-mile race from New York to Chicago. He offered to give $2,000 toward an award for the winner. Joseph Pulitzer's *New York World* and *St. Louis Post-Dispatch* also announced a prize of $30,000 for the first aviator to fly betweer St. Louis and New York; William Randolph Hearst offered $50,000 for the first coast-to-coast flight; and the *New York Times* posted $10,000 for a round trip between New York and Philadelphia.

On May 31, J. C. Shaffer, editor and publisher of the *Chicago Evening Post,* added $1,000 to the purse for a flight from New York to Chicago and announced that his newspaper would accept additional contributions. On that same day, he opened negotiations with the *New York Times* for promoting the race as a joint publicity venture. The two agreed to sponsor the contest and to guarantee one-half of the purse of $25,000; the remainder, other than contributions already obtained, was to be put up by communities along the route.

In the formative stage, rules governing the race stipulated that entrance applications must be filed no later than August 1, 1910, and that the event must take place sometime between that date and October 15. Both men and women were eligible if they had machines, including lighter-than-air craft, which demonstrated ability to perform a flight of one hour's duration.

The inclusion of dirigibles was probably the result of pressure from the Aeronautique Club of Chicago. Later they were excluded.

The official rules, released by Shaffer on July 5, contained provisions which, in retrospect, seemed to assure the failure of the race. In final form they showed little resemblance to the tentative regulations formulated a month earlier. Besides a change in the direction of the race, the contest was to be a mass flight. In order for the contest to be officially recognized, at least three entrants had to start from Chicago on October 8 and land within the corporate limits of New York in not more than 168 hours of elapsed time. In order to qualify, a contestant had to be in Chicago before October 1, prepared to make daily flights as evidence of his flying skill and the airworthiness of his machine. One of the trial flights was required to be of an hour's duration. Experienced flyers with machines of proved ability were to be automatically qualified; others had to qualify between October 3 and 8. In the final race the aviator who covered the entire distance in the shortest elapsed time, within the specified period, was to receive the entire purse of $25,000.

On June 2, the contest received the approval of Orville Wright and Glenn Curtiss, who stated that they would each enter one or more airplanes. As a result, the race appeared certain to attract most of the well-known flyers in the United States. James E. Plew, speaking for the Aero Club of Illinois, urged the promoters to extend invitations to outstanding foreign aviators.

Because the plans for the New York to Chicago race had been drastically altered, Chicago leaped into the spotlight. The direction had been reversed after many experienced flyers, among them Curtiss and Wilbur Wright, pointed out that contestants in an east-to-west flight would have the disadvantage of flying against the prevailing winds. The logic of the argument was clear, but the full result was not immediately discernible. This simple change gave Chicago the position of prominence in aviation in 1910, and the sustained public interest resulting from the contest produced the initial impulse for a remarkable era of flight development in the Middle West.

Immediately following the announcement of the rules, activity in the Chicago area proceeded at an accelerated tempo. The first local flyer to submit an application was George M. Dunlap, who claimed he had completed two flights near Wheaton in a copy of the Curtiss biplane. Confident of winning, he ordered a new machine from the Curtiss Aeroplane Company. On July 7, Carl S. Bates announced plans to enter. In the next four days, two other Chicagoans made similar statements: Charles W. Miller, with a biplane of his own design, constructed by C. A. Wittemann of New York; and John A. Neustedt, an inventor of a combination dirigible and airplane.

Throughout the summer, preparations continued amid expressions of confidence in the skills of the entrants and the capabilities of their machines. Hamilton stated publicly that aviators with large airplanes and plenty of gasoline could easily fly from Chicago to New York. No less an authority than Clifford B. Harmon, president of the Aero Club of America, expressed the opinion that Hamilton, Curtiss, Baldwin, and Walter R. Brookins could navigate the entire course. Confronted with these and similar assurances, the public naturally expected great achievements. Few people outside of aviation fully appreciated the true immaturity of its development: the fragile machines, unreliable engines, and the lack of experience among even the best pilots. Privately, every contestant must have realized the futility of the race. However, public statements of skilled flyers contained not a hint of the insurmountable obstacles lying along the uncharted 900-mile route.

Applications poured into the offices of the promoters during July. In addition to local aviators, Hamilton, Baldwin, J. C. Mars, and a dozen others entered the lists. Invitations issued to foreign aviators, following action by the United States Court of Appeals vacating the Wright company's temporary injunction against Curtiss, produced favorable responses from Louis Paulhan of France, and James Radley of England.

In order to stage an aviation meet while at the same time allowing contestants to increase their earnings as they completed the required qualifying and trial flights, the promoters suggested that the week prior to the start of the contest be scheduled as "Exhibition Week." Daily flights, they thought, would attract thousands of Chicagoans to the Hawthorne race track, and a profit-sharing plan would partially compensate for the expenses of those who failed to win a share of the prize. An agreement with the contestants provided for a seven-day event from October 2 to 8, inclusive.

Brookins' flight to Springfield roused public interest in the forthcoming intercity race, for it seemed to indicate the feasibility of the greater contest. However, experienced flyers, recognizing the hazards, dropped out one by one. By October 2, only three of them remained. The promoters hoped that Radley would reach Chicago in time to enter his Blériot, and Curtiss consented to participate if necessary to complete the required number of contestants.

During the seven-day program, Eugene Ely, J. A. D. McCurdy, and Charles F. Willard presented spectacular flights. Curtiss joined them on the first two days, before leaving for Cleveland, ostensibly to make arrangements for the big race. Blanche Stuart Scott and August M. Post, students in Curtiss' school at Hammondsport, took part but restricted their efforts to "grass cutting" maneuvers across the infield. The three veterans, however, performed every trick they knew for the enthusiastic crowds. On the final day, Willard closed the meet with a breath-taking, five-mile race against W. H. Pearce in a Folcar racing automobile.

Two days before the start of the race, rumors prompted the *Chicago Evening Post* to assert publicly that it would begin October 9 as planned, and that only Ely, McCurdy, and Willard were to participate. This notice contained a hint that the flyers and the promoters were not in complete agreement, for it stated emphatically that the rules would not be modified. Actually, the contestants had asked that only one of them start the race, in order to allow the other two to use their efforts and equipment to assure his success. When turned down, they threatened to withdraw. Faced with the possibility of complete failure, the promoters sent an urgent telegram to Curtiss requesting that he return immediately to break the deadlock.

Meanwhile, the three decided to make a definite stand. In a

conference in Ely's rooms in the Blackstone Hotel early on the morning of October 8, Ely contended that they had expected a truly competitive event; instead, they now faced the prospect of competing among themselves. Only one could hope to win, but two others were forced to risk their lives and machines. If all took part, the chance of one's winning would be very remote. The argument proved effective, for within twelve hours the promoters agreed to allow a single contestant. They further held that the other entrants could use their equipment to assist the contestant. Lots were drawn to determine who would make the flight. The assignment fell to Ely. In an effort to conform to the rules, McCurdy and Willard agreed to make a pretense of starting. They would then return to the field, where their machines would be dismantled and crated for shipment to points along the route.

The start took place on October 9 at Hawthorne Race Course. Ely guided his Curtiss biplane across the infield and into the air on the first stage of the flight while McCurdy and Willard circled above the field. Ten minutes later, Ely landed near Honore Avenue and 85th Street, nine miles away, to free a clogged fuel line. In starting again, he smashed the front wheel of the landing gear. A telephone call brought Curtiss to the scene of the accident with a replacement, but, by the time repairs were completed, darkness forced Ely to delay until the following morning.

In the next two days he experienced a series of unfortunate accidents. One minute after starting, he landed in a ditch three blocks away. Repairs took several hours, but in the mid-afternoon he set out for South Bend, Indiana. Thirty minutes later, motor trouble necessitated another emergency landing, this time in a slough adjacent to Stieglitz Park in East Chicago. By then he had covered 20 miles.

After mechanics worked through the night, Ely set out again. By this time the machine showed the effects of rough landings, but even with numerous makeshift repairs, he made a fine start. Soon disaster struck again. As he flew along the southern lake shore, the motor suddenly stopped, forcing him to glide from an altitude of 2,000 feet to a crash landing 19 miles east of

East Chicago, Indiana. At this point he gave up all hope of reaching New York within the time limit. Leaving the machine to be dismantled and shipped East for repairs, he boarded a train at East Chicago to rejoin the Curtiss exhibition team in Cleveland.

In the midst of excited talk about contests, cross-country flights, and large cash prizes, an unusual meet was held in East St. Louis. Participation was restricted to flyers who had never performed for profit or earned prizes worth more than $250. The "First Aviation Meeting for Novices," sponsored by the Aero Club of St. Louis, took place from July 11 to 17 in Washington Park. Originally scheduled for St. Louis in the latter part of June, it had been postponed until the sponsor found a larger field which would accommodate the number of entrants expected to compete for prizes totaling $300. Prospective contestants for the event were W. Thomas, Hammondsport, New York; William C. Robinson, Grinnell, Iowa; C. W. Curzon and Eric Bergstrom, Chicago; Howard W. Gill, Baltimore; J. Nick Sparling, East St. Louis; Hugh A. Robinson and William F. S. Zehler, St. Louis; Charles Kuhno and Claude Harris, whose home towns are unknown. Bergstrom and W. C. Robinson were disqualified when they failed to appear on the grounds within the stipulated time.

Only two of the eight airplanes that were entered actually performed. On the first day, Gill crashed into a ditch while attempting to land at the close of a trial. On the following day, he crashed again, causing irreparable damage to the machine and seriously injuring himself. While Gill remained in a local hospital, Curzon captured all the prizes, including two awards for the best daily performance and one for distance. Flights on July 14 and 16 netted two prizes of $100 each, and another run of 322 yards on July 14 brought $100. Although the officials extended the program one day, high winds prevented another performance. Two monoplanes, Hugh Robinson's Blériot and Zehler's plane of unorthodox design, maneuvered over the grounds, to the delight of the spectators, but lacked sufficient power for flight. Sparling's Curtiss biplane and Kuhno's monoplane were displayed during the meet.

In August, 1911, the Aero Club of Illinois, with the co-operation and support of a Chicago syndicate of prominent businessmen, presented the first of two spectacular aviation programs. This event, the largest to be held in the United States up to that time, grew out of Harold F. McCormick's desire to hold a contest that would attract the best aviators and airplanes available. Early in April, McCormick and James E. Plew had discussed plans for an event the following July but refrained from making definite plans until the matter could be presented to the membership of the club at its next regular meeting. Meanwhile, Albert B. Lambert, of the Aero Club of St. Louis, and Carl G. Fisher, aeronautical enthusiast and principal owner of the Indianapolis Speedway, approached McCormick with a plan for contests in their respective cities. After waiting several days for assurances that a series could be arranged, McCormick decided to proceed with the original plan. He formed the International Aviation Meet Association for the purpose of raising $100,000 for a program scheduled to take place in Grant Park under the direction of the Aero Club of Illinois. The Association, with McCormick as principal backer, guaranteed the operating expenses and prize money.

The nine-day International Aviation Meet drew to Chicago nearly all the well-known American aviators and five celebrated foreign flyers who were performing in the United States that summer. A novel plan for distributing a large part of the prize money according to flying time (in addition to cash awards for specific events) made it especially attractive to skilled flyers. Adopted by the sponsors in an effort to encourage as much flying as possible, this plan guaranteed contestants two dollars for each minute they were in the air during official hours. The program also included a variety of contests: duration, speed, altitude, and cross-country races, in addition to passenger-carrying and trick-flying events.

The prospect of large prizes induced flyers to enter despite the refusal of the sponsors to give guarantees. Until that time, aviators had insisted upon being paid for their appearance, even if they failed to fly. They were considered temperamental artists who had to be cajoled and flattered before risking a haz-arduous flight. Because the guarantee usually covered expenses and left so little for profit, some flyers refused to perform unless conditions were perfect—which they invariably were not. Aviation suffered because of the "horror and dread" built up by such practices, which might have continued for many more years had not 32 aviators forgotten the foolishness about the "terrible risk" to earn two dollars a minute in weather once considered too dangerous for performances.

A remarkable record of 206 hours of flying time established among all contestants, between the hours of 3:30 and 7:00 P.M., in nine consecutive days, proved that airplanes could fly—a somewhat doubtful assumption until that time. The officials boasted that the participants recorded twice as much flying as ever before logged in an equal period of time. The accuracy of the statement may be questioned, but the significance of the event cannot be denied.

Star performers of the Wright, Curtiss, and Moisant teams competed with one another and with independent pilots for shares of the $100,000 prize money. Brookins, Leonard W. Bonney, Frank T. Coffyn, Gill, Philip O. Parmalee, Cliff Turpin, and Arthur L. Walsh, seven of the most skillful flyers in the country, entered under the sponsorship of the Wright Exhibition Company. Led by the "incomparable" Beachey, the Curtiss team included Ely, Robinson, Ward, and Charles C. Witmer. Robinson flew two machines, a standard biplane and a hydroairplane. Calbraith P. Rodgers, George W. Beatty, T. O. M. Sopwith of England, and Andrew Drew flew Wright biplanes, which cost each $100 a day for a license. The Moisant International Aviators entered Simon, Frisbie, and Johnstone. Illness prevented Barrier from participating. Other familiar names on the roster were Tom Baldwin, Lee Hammond, J. C. Mars, and William R. Badger, all pilots of Baldwin's "Red Devil" biplanes. James V. Martin, J. A. D. McCurdy, and Earle R. Ovington entered copies of the Curtiss biplane. Eight used monoplanes: Sopwith (who also had a Wright biplane), Simon, Ovington, and James Cummings flew Gnome-powered Blériots; Johnstone used a Moisant; and Arthur Stone and Laddie Lewkowicz employed Gnome-powered Queen machines, American copies of the Blériot. George Mestach's Morane-Borel was the first of that design ever seen in Chicago.

For nine days the elite of the professional flyers competed for records and prizes. Top honors in the speed contests went to Sopwith, Beachey, and Ovington. Sopwith and Ovington fought for awards in the monoplane and free-for-all races, while Beachey consistently captured high prizes in the biplane events. Sopwith's record included seven first-, two second-, and one third-place awards for speed, besides honors in such special events as accurate-landing and quick-starting contests. Prizes from speed contests netted the flashy Englishman about $10,000, his best effort occurring on August 18 when he captured three first-place awards worth a total of $1,850, in addition to duration money. Beachey won five first-, two second-, and three third-place awards, as well as prizes in altitude, climbing, and daily duration contests. His altitude mark of 11,642 feet, established on the final day of the meet, remained the official American record until surpassed by DeLloyd Thompson in Kansas City three years later.

Honors for total duration went to Rodgers, a comparatively unknown pilot. Using a slow but reliable Wright biplane, he remained in the air more than three hours on each of eight days, "lolling in his seat each afternoon, legs crossed and dangling, a cigar in the long holder he held in his mouth." At the close of the meet, his total record was 27 hours and 16 seconds, of a possible 31½. For this he earned $2.00 a minute and half of the $16,000 prize for total duration. To the original $10,000 prize, the promoters had added $6,000 in unearned prizes, which was divided among the leaders in the duration event.

Two deaths and numerous accidents marred an otherwise spectacular display of flying skill. The first fatality occurred on the afternoon of August 15 when the wings of Badger's biplane crumpled during a high-speed stunt and trick-flying exhibition over a sunken portion of Grant Park. He was trying to duplicate Beachey's trick of dipping into the hollow, but the strain proved too much for the wings of his machine. While the crowd remained stunned at the sight of Badger's tragic accident, Johnstone plunged into the lake about a mile offshore from 12th

Street. The impact of the machine apparently caused him to become entangled in the heavy wires used to brace the wings, and he sank with the wreckage. Robinson, who was over the lake in his hydroairplane, raced to the scene but failed to locate Johnstone, though he circled over the spot until rescue and salvage boats arrived. A series of minor accidents plagued Baldwin's machines, disabling all but one of the four he entered. Badger demolished one; Hammond dropped one into the lake and later wrecked another. Mars did all of his flying in an old Curtiss biplane owned by Baldwin. Pilots of the Queen monoplanes also experienced bad luck: Stone fell into the lake but escaped uninjured, and Lewkowicz, hampered by mechanical failures, had only one opportunity to fly, a short hop that lasted 18 seconds. Ovington used Cummings' Blériot on three successive days while his own was undergoing repairs after being damaged in a collision.

The highlight of the program occurred on August 14 when Harry N. Atwood, piloting a Burgess-Wright biplane, landed after a 283-mile trip from St. Louis. It was the first phase of a flight to New York for $10,000 offered by Victor J. Evans, a Washington, D.C., patent attorney. On the trip, Atwood followed the Chicago & Alton Railroad, landing in Springfield and Pontiac for brief celebrations in his honor. As he came down in Grant Park, thousands of cheering spectators, who had followed his progress by telegraph dispatches, swept aside guards along the edge of the landing area. As the machine came to a stop, the surging throng rushed forward, lifted Atwood from his seat, and carried him triumphantly to the officials' box. Even there, the milling crowd had to be restrained by a police guard.

On the next afternoon, he renewed the air journey that ended 11 days later on Governors Island in New York. From Chicago he flew to Elkhart, Indiana; then by successive stages he pushed on to Toledo and Cleveland, Ohio; Swanville, Pennsylvania; Buffalo, Lyons, Belle Island, Fort Plain, Castleton, and Nyack, New York, traveling 1,295 miles in 28 hours and 53 minutes of actual flying time. His 1,155 miles, by straight-line measure from town to town, exceeded by 82 miles the world's distance record, set earlier the same year in the *Circuit of Europe.*

CONTESTANTS IN THE CHICAGO INTERNATIONAL AVIATION MEET, AUGUST, 1911, SHOWING MAKE OF AIRPLANE, TOTAL DURATION, AND TOTAL EARNINGS

Name	*Airplane*	*Duration*	*Total Earnings*
Atwood, Harry N.	Burgess-Wright		$ 1,000.00
Badger, William R. *	Baldwin	2:28:00	900.00
Baldwin, Thomas Scott	Baldwin	28:02	556.07
Beachey, Lincoln	Curtiss	14:33:05	11,667.00
Beatty, George W.	Wright	24:21:58	7,125.00
Beck, Paul	Curtiss	1:03:53	900.00
Bonney, Leonard W.	Wright	9:19	518.63
Brindley, A. Oscar	Wright	23:44:54	3,351.00
Brookins, Walter R.	Wright	2:38:11	816.37
Coffyn, Frank T.	Wright	58:56	650.00
Cummings, James	Blériot		
Drew, Andrew	Wright	17:13	650.00
Ely, Eugene	Curtiss	7:28:13	4,672.00
Frisbie, John J.	Curtiss-type	2:49:43	2,000.00
Gill, Howard W.	Wright	3:45:17	2,450.00
Hammond, Lee	Baldwin	1:51:46	1,050.00
Johnstone, St. Croix *	Moisant	4:56:36	1,093.20
Lewkowicz, Laddie	Queen	18	250.60
McCurdy, J. A. D.	McCurdy	2:55:55	2,400.00
Mars, J. C.	Baldwin	2:44:08	828.27
Martin, James V.	Burgess	2:03:43	750.00
Mestach, George	Morane-Borel	3:53:48	967.60
Ovington, Earle R.	Curtiss & Blériot	5:04:49	5,900.00
Parmelee, Phillip O.	Wright	5:04:08	4,451.00
Robinson, Hugh A.	Curtiss	55:51	611.70
Rodgers, Calbraith P.	Wright	27:00:16	11,285.00
Simon, Rene	Blériot	9:55:47	5,050.00
Sopwith, T. O. M.	Wright & Blériot	9:14:56	14,020.00
Stone, Arthur	Queen	1:01:28	622.93
Turpin, J. Clifford	Wright	4:21:07	1,022.23
Ward, James J.	Curtiss	20:36:34	3,413.00
Welsh, Arthur L.	Wright	19:49:46	6,121.00
Witmer, Charles C.	Curtiss	13:38	527.27
Curtiss hydroairplane			3,500.00
Total		206:31:18	$101,119.87

* Killed August 15, 1911.

Atwood's achievement was surpassed within less than three months. Between September 17 and November 5, Cal Rodgers piloted a Wright biplane from New York to Pasadena, California, 5,393 miles along a route that extended west to Chicago, diagonally across Illinois into Missouri, south into Texas, and across New Mexico and Arizona to California. Altogether, he spent 82 hours and 4 minutes in the air, and stopped in 67 cities and towns, including five in Illinois. He reached Chicago on October 8 but continued on to Denwood Park, near Joliet, before stopping for the night. The next day he flew to Springfield, stopping en route in Peoria. On October 10, he proceeded to Marshall, Missouri, making stops in Nebo, Illinois, and Thompson, Missouri.

Although the flight was primarily an advertising "stunt" to promote a soft drink known as "Vin Fizz," Rodgers hoped to win the $50,000 prize offered by Hearst. This prize had been offered as early as May, 1910, but Rodgers was the first to try for it. According to Rodgers' plans, he had 30 days to make the trip. However, the offer expired on October 10. He did not reach the Pacific Ocean until December 10, landing on the beach at Long Beach, California. Two months later he plunged to his death in a power dive near the same spot.

The Hearst prize prompted two other aviators to attempt transcontinental flights in competition with each other. Jimmy Ward started from New York City and proceeded as far as Rathbone, in the same state, where, on September 22, 1911, he smashed his biplane and withdrew from the contest. Robert G. Fowler left San Francisco for Jacksonville, Florida, on September 11. After reaching the lofty Sierra Nevada mountains near Alta, California, he had several accidents, which delayed him so that he could not reach Jacksonville within 30 days; therefore, he canceled the trip and immediately began preparations for a new attempt from Pasadena. After many postponements, he started on October 20 and reached the Atlantic Ocean at San Pablo Beach, near Jacksonville, on February 17, 1912.

The Aero Club of Illinois, encouraged by the success of the International Aviation Meet of 1911, planned a more elaborate program for 1912. It scheduled three new events in addition to a contest similar to the earlier event. The Gordon-Bennett Aviation Cup Race for the international speed championship was to be held in or near Chicago on September 9, three days before the start of four days of contests. Another race, the American Grand Circuit, covering approximately 1,800 miles, was to start from Chicago on September 16, immediately following an open-air "aviation warplay," featuring airplanes in support of military ground forces in maneuvers. Failure to raise the necessary funds forced the club to cancel the last two programs, but the contests were extended five days.

The announcement in April of the Gordon-Bennett program stirred up interest in retaining the trophy in the United States. In 1909 and 1911, Americans had won the speed classic, but monoplanes developed by French manufacturers seemed sure of capturing it in 1912. Three American companies announced intentions of entering special racers, but by midsummer not one seemed capable of matching speed with France's fast Deperdussin racers. In order to challenge the French entries, an American racer would have to average more than 100 miles an hour over the 124-mile course established at Clearing, Illinois. A group of prominent Chicago businessmen and aviation enthusiasts, led by Charles Dickinson, formed the American Cup Defender Syndicate for the purpose of raising $15,000 to purchase a 160-horsepower Gnome engine and a speedy monoplane designed and built by A. Starling Burgess of the Burgess-Curtiss Aeroplane Company, Marblehead, Massachusetts. Syndicate members, in addition to Dickinson, were Norman Prince, a lawyer, and Robert J. McGann, a businessman.

Unfortunately, the syndicate did not have time to complete its work. When the *Chicago Cup Defender* arrived in Chicago late in August, its many new features required exhaustive tests and adjustments. Realizing the need for haste, Glenn L. Martin volunteered to finish the monoplane. With the aid of a staff of engineers, he attempted to increase the speed of the racer above 121 miles an hour, the mark achieved by Jules Verdrines in one of the French entries. However, on September 7, when the contest committee of the Aero Club of America met in Chicago to designate the United States representatives in the race, Dickinson withdrew rather than permit DeLloyd Thompson to risk his life in an untested racer.

The race turned out to be an all-French affair. Flying a powerful Gnome-driven Deperdussin monoplane, Verdrines outdistanced Maurice Prevost and André Frey. The only American entry, a Columbia monoplane flown by Paul Beck, was withdrawn prior to the start because of a faulty magneto. The Belgian contestant, Charles Frank van der Nerrsche, better known in the United States as Charles Norok, died of typhoid fever in Brooklyn less than two weeks before the race. Airplanes from England, the Netherlands, and Switzerland were withdrawn because of their inability to match the speeds of the French.

Verdrines and Prevost flew almost identical airplanes. But a powerful 140-horsepower engine gave Verdrines an advantage over Prevost's 100-horsepower model. The winner circled the 124-mile course at an average speed of 105 miles an hour, while the runner-up recorded a creditable 102 miles an hour. Frey completed 23 circuits in a Hanriot monoplane at an average of 92 miles an hour. Before the event ended, Max Lillie, who was not an official participant, went aloft in his Wright biplane, completing three circuits while the faster monoplanes passed him several times. Later, in a statement about his impressions of the event, Lillie said: "The best I can say is that I was in sight most of the time of the French drivers. I had a hard time telling whether I was ahead or behind them in any certain lap. I can say that I was above them though, for I flew higher."

Three days later at Cicero Field, the International Meet Association and the Aero Club of Illinois opened their second and last program. The first four days were filled with daily events: races, bomb- and mail-throwing, accurate-landing, and similar contests designed to test the skills of pilots and the capabilities of their machines. In order to devote the last four days to events in which flying boats and hydroairplanes could take part, the scene shifted on September 16 to Grant Park.

On opening day at Cicero Field the lack of enthusiasm among participants and spectators was readily noticeable. In part, the contestants reacted to the tragic death of Paul Beck on the previous day. Beck had been killed while testing his Columbia monoplane. Unaccustomed to the small racing wings fitted to the machine for the Gordon-Bennett race, he had lost control of the plane while descending in a tight spiral. Four days later, the death of Howard Gill, whose machine crashed after colliding with Mestach's, nearly ended all flying at the meet, for the contestants bitterly denounced the officials as incompetent, arrogant, and incapable of showing respect or appreciation for the peculiarly hazardous activities of the flyers. Gill's accident had occurred when the officials called for the start of a race at a late hour while contestants from the previous race were still in the air. Though reluctant, Mestach had agreed to race against Tony Jannus, who was in a speedy Blériot biplane. After circling the course twice, Mestach overtook Gill without seeing the slower biplane ahead and below his line of flight. Just as he started to pass, Gill must have become aware of the monoplane. To avoid a collision, he dipped his biplane, raising its tail directly into the path of Mestach's landing gear. The impact tore away the rear structure of the Wright, sending it spinning earthward. Unable to regain control, Mestach also crashed but escaped without serious injury though his machine was demolished.

On September 17, the contestants met to draw up rules to govern their actions during the remainder of the program. All agreed not to fly when conditions were unfavorable, as they were in adverse weather and in contests at dusk. Hostility toward the officials continued, but it did not flare up again until September 20, after an announcement that Beachey and a Mlle. Clarise Lavaseur would perform in a special program on the following Sunday (September 22). The flyers insisted that, because of the star performers, additional money should be added to the duration awards for that day. The officials refused, pointing out that unused money from September 17 and 18, when all events were canceled because of rain, had been added to the duration fund, together with all other unused prizes. Realizing that the officials were determined to make no further concessions, the contestants grudgingly decided to fly in the program.

They were partially mollified by an award of slightly more than $3.00 a minute for duration.

Top money winners during the meet were Glenn L. Martin and Anthony Jannus. Each won more than $4,000 in prizes. Two prominent local flyers, Max Lillie and DeLloyd Thompson, and Beckwith Havens, of the Curtiss exhibition team, each won more than $2,000. In the biplane races, Martin, Jannus, Lillie, and Horace Kearney were the principal winners; in the monoplane events, Mestach's speedy Morane-Borel easily outdistanced Maurice Prevost's Deperdussin and Roman J. Montero's Blériot. Most of the events demanding exceptional skill went to Martin, followed closely by Lillie, Thompson, and Prevost. Farnum, Fish, and Kearney might have challenged Martin's apparent superiority had they reached Cicero in time to compete during the first three days.

When the site shifted to Grant Park on September 16, Fish, Jannus, Kearney, Lillie, Martin, and Thompson flew from Cicero to the lake front, using a roundabout route because an ordinance prohibited flights over residential and business areas. Two others—Charles A. Wiggins and A. C. Beech—did not make the flight as scheduled because of engine trouble, but both completed it the following day.

Five flying boats and hydroairplanes were the attractions of the second portion of the contests. Jannus, Martin, and Havens dominated the water events: The first two converted their biplanes to hydroairplanes by attaching pontoons in place of landing gears; Havens performed with a Curtiss flying boat. Contests for land craft supplemented the water events. In addition to the contestants from Cicero, others entered the program. Albert J. Engle and Ignace Semeniouk participated with a flying boat and hydroairplane, respectively. On September 17, Engle lost his way on a flight from Clarendon Beach to Grant Park, flying several miles offshore before landing. In order to prevent his craft from sinking in the rough water, he inverted it and held on to the hull until rescued by a passing sand scow. Water damage kept him out of competition four days. On September 19, Semeniouk, a Russian aviator, crashed into the lake.

As the craft struck the water, an explosion of the radiator showered him with scalding water, inflicting severe burns.

CONTESTANTS IN THE CHICAGO INTERNATIONAL AVIATION MEET, SEPTEMBER, 1912, SHOWING MAKE OF AIRPLANE, TOTAL DURATION, AND TOTAL EARNINGS

Name	*Airplane*	*Duration*	*Total Earnings*
Beech, A. C.	National	1:26:45	$ 441.39
Daugherty, Earl S.	Somerville	38:15	114.03
Engle, Albert J.	Curtiss		188.24
Fish, Farnum T.	Wright	5:15:25	1,558.17
Gill, Howard W.*	Wright EX	1:49:00	382.94
Havens, Beckwith	Curtiss		2,170.59
Jannus, Anthony	Benoist	3:08:15	4,003.73
Kearney, Horace	Curtiss	6:46:10	1,959.41
Lillie, Max	Wright	9:18:40	2,811.57
Mars, J. C.	Curtiss	5:05	15.67
Martin, Glenn L.	Martin	5:35:45	4,854.24
Mestach, George	Morane-Borel	1:46:00	930.99
Montero, Ramon J.	Blériot	1:24:10	358.94
Prevost, Maurice	Deperdussin	40:15	368.18
Robinson, William C.	Wright	1:37:35	300.33
Semeniouk, Ignace	International		
Sjolander, Carl	Curtiss-type	45:00	197.94
Thompson, DeLloyd	Wright	7:01:16	2,057.31
Tournier, Marcel	Nieuport	1:47:00	329.31
Wiggins, Charles A.	Wright	5:19:20	956.96
Total		54:23:56	$23,999.94

* Killed September 16, 1912.

Although originally scheduled to end on September 21, the program was extended one day to compensate for the two days on which rain had canceled all contests. In addition to regular events, Beachey performed for the spectators. After presenting a series of thrilling feats, he donned a blue silk dress, a blonde wig, an opera cape, and unlimited quantities of "chiffon fleece" and pink ribbon. In this disguise he played the role of Mlle. Lavasseur, a French aviatrix who knew almost nothing about flying. Discarding his usually graceful style, he darted first in one direction and then another. As the crowd became frightened for the safety of the "young lady," he dipped toward the lake, pulling up within a few feet of the water. At one point he put the biplane into a steep dive from which recovery seemed impossible. However, he leveled off in time and flew along Michigan Avenue, sending automobiles and carriages scurrying in all directions. After creating horror among 100,000 spectators, he landed and revealed his true identity.

The 1912 program closed an era of marvelous shows in Chicago. Thereafter, aviation lost much of its artificial luster and assumed the grim realism of a dangerous business for those who performed exhibitions for a livelihood or of a hazardous sport for others who could afford "pleasure" airplanes. The contests of 1911–1912 did not appreciably dispel public distrust but tended to emphasize shortcomings and the need for technical improvements. If the programs had been staged to prove the "air age" a reality, as some enthusiasts hoped, they failed completely.

In the next three years, several long flights were proposed in an effort to demonstrate the reliability of the airplane. In 1913, a group of Chicagoans formed the Great Lakes Cruise to show sportsmen the superiority of flying boats over motorboats. Five contestants started from Chicago on an 885-mile race to Detroit, but only one went the entire distance. In 1914, the Bureau of Aeronautics of the Panama-Pacific Exposition Company of San Francisco proposed a 22,000-mile round-the-world flight, which was canceled at the outbreak of World War I. In 1915, the Aero Club of America planned a mass flight across the United States in 100 days, but this was postponed because of "near war conditions and the fact that orders for aeroplanes and . . . motors . . . are occupying the time of both aviators and constructors." The effect of these schemes, had they been carried out, would have been more damaging than beneficial. The airplane required sound technological study, not promotional "stunts" and "ballyhoo" about reliability and dependability—features it obviously did not have.

6

FLYING POSTMEN: THE AIRMAIL, 1911–1927

In the eight years before the establishment of regular airmail service, so-called "airmail flights" were frequently conducted by exhibition pilots. On numerous occasions the Post Office Department authorized such flights as experiments for testing the possibility of using the airplane for transporting mail, particularly in areas where other forms of rapid transportation were virtually nonexistent. The flights were usually short, often no more than a mile or two from a temporary postal substation at the airfield to the main post office, or from one post office to another in an adjacent community. Upon receipt of the airmail at its destination, letters not addressed for local delivery were forwarded through normal channels. By 1916, some of the flights were performed specifically to show the public and Congress the advantages of transporting mail in speedy airplanes.

The first recorded delivery of mail by airplane in the United States was made in 1911. During an international aviation tournament held at Nassau Boulevard flying field, Garden City, New York, Postmaster General Frank H. Hitchcock authorized a series of airmail flights which Earle R. Ovington made in a Blériot monoplane. Between September 23 and October 1, Ovington carried 43,000 pieces of mail from Nassau Boulevard to Mineola. Each day he dropped a mail pouch onto a field at

Mineola. A courier waiting there then delivered the pouch to the local post office. As a result of these demonstrations, Hitchcock concluded that the "progress made in the science of aviation encourages the hope that ultimately the regular conveyance of mail by this means may be practical."

The airmail service visualized by Hitchcock in 1911 was designed to serve only isolated areas, not large population centers. His idea of utilizing airplane transportation in areas "where the natural conditions precluded other means of rapid transportation" established the policy of the Post Office Department for the next six years. Instead of asking Congress for appropriations to establish airmail service in rural areas and Alaska, the Post Office Department should have asked for funds to open mail delivery by air between large cities. In 1918 the latter type of airmail service was established, but only after more demonstration flights had awakened the government and the public to its advantages.

The first demonstration of airmail service in the Middle West took place in St. Louis less than two weeks after Ovington's historic flights at Nassau Boulevard. On October 4, 1911, during an aviation meet held at Kinloch Park under the auspices of the Aero Club of St. Louis, Walter R. Brookins completed a mail delivery in his Wright biplane. Four days later, Hugh A. Robinson completed another airmail flight, this time in a Curtiss hydroairplane with which he added some daring stunt flying by sailing over or under all the bridges spanning the Mississippi at St. Louis.

The most ambitious of all the early airmail demonstrations, a flight from Minneapolis to New Orleans, was planned in the spring of 1911. Albert Bond Lambert, a St. Louis aviation enthusiast and wealthy industrialist, first proposed the long flight to Glenn H. Curtiss, who did not give the idea serious consideration until advocates of a Mississippi River Deep Waterway adopted it as a means of focusing attention on the river during the Deep Waterways Convention, scheduled to convene in Chicago the latter part of September. Agitation for the flight within the ranks of the Aero Club of St. Louis culminated in mid-September in the formation of the Trans-Mississippi Valley

Flight Association. Funds were solicited in St. Louis, Minneapolis, Memphis, and New Orleans in an attempt to raise a purse of $15,000 for the Curtiss Exhibition Company, which agreed to assign Hugh A. Robinson to make the proposed flight in a hydroairplane. The Association's inability to raise the necessary funds delayed the start of the Minneapolis-to-New Orleans flight until mid-October. After only a portion of the $15,000 purse had been collected, the flight was scheduled to start October 13, but severe rainstorms caused a further delay of four days. Finally, on October 17, Robinson left Lake Calhoun at Minneapolis for New Orleans with 25 pounds of mail.

In three days, Robinson reached Rock Island, where the flight ended. Throughout the 325-mile journey, he had stopped at communities along the river to pick up and deliver mail. On the first day, he damaged a pontoon while attempting to land at Whitman, Minnesota; he was then towed to Winona, where he remained until the following morning. On the second day, he landed briefly at La Crosse and Prairie du Chien, Wisconsin, and reached Dubuque in midafternoon. The next morning, he continued the flight to Rock Island, where he canceled the remainder of the trip after the Trans-Mississippi Association refused to increase the guarantee to compensate for the funds promised but not paid by cities along the route. Robinson's four mail stops between Minneapolis and Rock Island resulted in an estimated loss of $5,000 to the Curtiss Company because several communities reneged on the grounds that the flight occurred four days later than originally scheduled.

In 1912, airmail demonstrations were a popular attraction at exhibitions. Five of the 49 demonstrations given in the United States that year took place in Illinois. The first was on May 25, during which the "flying schoolboy," Farnum Fish, piloted his Wright biplane from Chicago to Milwaukee with letters, four bolts of silk cloth for the local Boston Store, and 7,500 circulars advertising the bargains available at that establishment. The flight (an advertising stunt sponsored by the *Milwaukee Journal*) took Fish two hours and six minutes, a relatively slow trip because he went around over Milwaukee several times in order to scatter the circulars before landing. The cargo of silk cloth overshadowed the little-known fact that the 99-mile nonstop flight was also an unofficial demonstration of airmail service. Fish remained several days in Milwaukee to take part in exhibitions by "The Three Ring Circus" during the Wisconsin State Fair. The "circus" included the flyers Horace F. Kearney, John C. Kaminski, and Lieutenant Kondo. Fish later gave another airmail demonstration, flying from the fairgrounds postal substation to West Allis.

Within a week after Fish's flight, the Aero Club of Illinois conducted a series of airmail demonstration flights. As feature attractions of a four-day aviation program marking the opening of Cicero Field for the 1912 season, the club obtained authorization from the Post Office Department for two daily airmail flights between Cicero, Elmhurst, and Wheaton by George Mestach, a veteran of similar flights in the South. Postmaster Peter McDonald of Cicero administered the oath to Mestach, making him the official aerial postman for the proposed eight flights. Then Mestach refused to serve without pay and the Aero Club, with the approval of the Post Office Department, was forced at the last minute to recruit Max Lillie, Paul Studensky, and Marcel Tournier as aerial postmen. On May 30, though at the time not authorized to carry mail, Lillie saved the day for the demonstration when he accidentally lost his way and landed on the grounds of the Elmhurst Golf Club, where he found a weary mail carrier awaiting the arrival of Mestach. The demonstration had been postponed due to the holiday but someone had neglected to inform the Elmhurst post office. The mail was ready so Lillie loaded it aboard his Wright biplane and delivered it a few minutes later to postal authorities at Cicero. The following day Lillie, with Charles Dickinson as passenger, completed a round trip to Elmhurst with mail. Two days later, Lillie, Studensky, and Tournier engaged in a race with mail; Lillie, because of his slower biplane, was to go to Elmhurst and return, and the other two were to go to Elmhurst and Wheaton and return. Lillie beat Studensky in a close finish; Tournier crashed soon after making a stop at Elmhurst but escaped without serious injury.

Cicero Field was the scene of another airmail demonstration

later the same year. On the first and last days of the International Aviation Meet, September 12-20, contestants competed for prizes in a mail-dropping contest; winners were those whose mail bags, tossed from speeding planes, landed closest to a net on the ground. Anthony Jannus, DeLloyd Thompson, Glenn L. Martin, and Howard W. Gill vied for honors on September 12. Jannus took first place with a toss that landed 19½ feet from the net; Thompson finished second. On the final day of the meet, Martin captured first prize in the mail-dropping contest, followed in order by Lillie, Mestach, and Fish. All the contestants dropped mail bags within 33 feet of the target. Airmail flights from Aurora to Cicero Field were also completed on September 12, 13, and 14 by Thompson, Lillie, and C. Milton Vought.

Illinois' next airmail demonstration occurred during a three-day "aerial exhibition and street circus" in McLeansboro, September 26-28. Horace F. Kearney, known among his fellow aviators as "Sure Shot" Kearney because of his claim that he could take his Curtiss biplane off on a nickel and land on a postage stamp, carried approximately 1,800 pieces of mail, mostly souvenir postcards, a short distance between a substation on the aviation field and the main post office.

Less than two weeks later, Kearney performed a similar demonstration by carrying mail from the State Fairgrounds in Springfield to Williamsville, Illinois. The Illinois State Fair of 1912 featured three top aviators: Farnum Fish, Edward A. Korn, and "Sure Shot" Kearney. All three filled this engagement on short notice after the National Aeroplane Manufacturing Company of Chicago canceled its contract for exhibitions a few days before the fair was to open on October 4. The Johnson Aeroplane Company of Terre Haute, Indiana, had canceled a similar contract with the State Board of Agriculture some weeks earlier. Both Fish and Kearney gave exhibitions in Wisconsin the day the fair opened. Kearney reportedly flew from Watseka to Prairie du Chien, a distance of 25 miles, to catch the Chicago, Burlington & Quincy train for Chicago and then to Springfield, where he arrived on October 6. Korn, a member of the Benoist Airplane Company of St. Louis, easily reached Springfield on the day the fair commenced, but an express company error delayed delivery of his Benoist tractor biplane until too late for it to be assembled and flown on opening day.

An airmail flight from Springfield to Williamsville was announced as the feature attraction of the seven-day aviation program. The Post Office Department co-operated with the fair officials to the extent of authorizing the flight as Route No. 635,002. On the morning of October 7, Korn ascended with the mail, supposedly headed for Williamsville, but, instead, he circled for several minutes and returned to the field after deciding that weather conditions were not right for the cross-country flight. On the following day, Korn went up for a short exhibition flight and once more declined to make the trip. Meanwhile, both Fish and Kearney were grounded by smashed machines. When Kearney's machine reappeared on the aviation field on October 9, fair officials asked him to make the airmail flight because a balky engine prevented Korn's making another trial. Always eager for an outstanding flight, Kearney jumped at the chance. That afternoon he lifted his Curtiss machine off the race track infield and headed for Williamsville with a mail sack full of letters from the Fairgrounds postal substation. Thirty minutes later, he handed the postmaster at Williamsville the first airmail ever dispatched from Springfield. The return flight to the Fairgrounds had to be postponed until the following morning because of a bad leak in the gas tank. After repairs were made, Kearney returned to Springfield to complete his exhibitions for the amusement of fair visitors.

Two airmail demonstrations were held in Illinois in September, 1913, in connection with exhibition flights. On September 4-6, Roy N. Francis, a San Francisco aviator, and James ("Sky High") Irving, a parachutist, appeared in McLeansboro as star features of the second annual three-day aviation program and street circus. A portion of Francis' daily show consisted of an airmail flight from the aviation field to the local post office five miles away. The Post Office Department authorized the flights on an aerial route designated as No. 635,004. Five days after Francis' last airmail flight in McLeansboro, Tony Jannus began the first of two similar flights in Carmi. Over authorized Route No. 635,003, Jannus carried mail on September 10 and 11 from the aviation field to the main post office. As in most flights of this type, he dropped the mail while circling above the post office.

In the three years after 1913, only four airmail demonstrations took place in Illinois. One was a flight which started in Iowa. W. C. Robinson, a familiar exhibition pilot in Illinois before he organized an airplane manufacturing company in Grinnell, Iowa, carried mail on his record-breaking nonstop flight from Des Moines to Kentland, Indiana, on October 17, 1914. The following day, he piloted his parasol monoplane to Chicago, his original destination. Although unauthorized by the Post Office Department, Robinson carried an unknown amount of mail that was turned over to postal authorities in Chicago.

The only airmail demonstration flight in Illinois in 1915 was given in Rock Island on August 15 after being postponed a day because of rain. Over Route No. 635,005 authorized by the Post Office Department, Harry K. Webster, of the Patterson Aviators, Detroit, carried approximately 500 cards and a dozen first-class letters from Exposition Park over the post office and back to the park. They were then forwarded to the post office by carrier. On the same day, O. A. Solbrig joined Webster in exhibition flights with Curtiss pusher-type biplanes. A portion of the program included flights that were co-ordinated with maneuvers conducted by Company A of the Illinois National Guard.

The most ambitious of the early airmail demonstrations took place on November 2, 1916, when the *New York Times* sponsored a "sunrise to sunset" flight between Chicago and New York. A limited amount of mail was carried with authorization from the Post Office Department. Postal officials took advantage of the newspaper's offer to use the flight as an experimental mail route when it became certain that Victor Carlstrom, an instructor in the Curtiss school at Newport News, Virginia, would attempt to break the nonstop flight record in a Curtiss Model R military biplane. Carlstrom's achievement fulfilled the dream of aviation enthusiasts since Eugene Ely made the first attempt to fly from Chicago to New York in 1910. By coincidence, both Ely's and Carlstrom's flights were made through the efforts of the *New York Times.*

The Chicago-New York flight shattered two American records. In approximately 8½ hours, Carlstrom piloted the big 200-horsepower Curtiss-powered biplane, *New York Times,* 967 miles, stopping at Erie, Pennsylvania, and Hammondsport, New York, before alighting on Governors Island in New York Harbor. A nonstop flight of 452 miles from Ashburn Field, Chicago, to Erie set a new American cross-country nonstop record; and the 315-mile flight from Hammondsport to Governors Island at an average speed of 134 miles per hour set a new American speed record for cross-country flight. An emergency landing in Erie, necessitated by a loose connection on the gasoline intake pipe, prevented Carlstrom from compiling a more impressive nonstop record.

Less than three weeks later, Ruth Law broke Carlstrom's mark by flying nonstop from Chicago to Hornell, New York, a distance of 590 miles. Although Miss Law did not reach New York City in a single day, her nonstop record was all the more remarkable because she flew an old-style Curtiss pusher-type biplane powered by a 100-horsepower motor. She not only surpassed Carlstrom's record but outdistanced the latest, most powerful airplane in America with an obsolete machine. Miss Law carried letters from Chicago and Binghamton, New York, to persons in New York City, but the flight was not authorized by the Post Office Department.

Two record-breaking flights between Chicago and New York in the same month stirred up interest in the establishment of airmail and passenger service between the country's two largest cities. Following Carlstrom's flight, and before Miss Law improved upon his record, a group of Chicago businessmen and aviation enthusiasts began investigating the feasibility of organizing airline passenger and mail service between Chicago, New York, and Detroit. Airplane engine manufacturer Glenn Muffly and Walter L. Brock, consulting engineer of the Aero Club of Illinois, proposed to establish a company to open regular airmail service from Chicago to Detroit and New York before the close of 1916. According to a plan announced by Muffly, overnight service was to be operated in each direction for the Chicago-New York route with fueling and maintenance stops in Napoleon and Niles, Ohio, and Williamsport, Pennsylvania. The three maintenance centers would be fully equipped stations complete with lighted landing fields, hangars, spare parts, mechanics, wireless facilities, telephones, and extra motors and airplanes. At Niles, where three planes and pilots were to be stationed, the mail was to be transferred to another airplane with a new pilot, who would complete the trip either to Chicago or New York. The organizers of the route planned to use twin-engine airplanes capable of carrying 500 to 1,000 pounds of mail in addition to fuel for a 400-mile flight. This scheme, though not advanced beyond the planning stage, created a surprising amount of interest in the Post Office Department and among aviation enthusiasts and constituted an important advance in contemporary thought regarding the use of airplanes for transportation of mail. As a result of Muffly's much-publicized plans, the idea of using planes for transporting mail only in isolated rural areas was partially abandoned; for the first time, the airplane seemed to promise speedy, efficient transportation of mail between large centers of population.

For a brief time early in 1917 Second Assistant Postmaster General Otto Praeger had under consideration 37 different temporary airmail routes in addition to a temporary transcontinental service to be conducted under auspices of the Aero Club of America. Because the Post Office Department had requested only $100,000 for experimental airmail service, not more than a few of the proposed routes could be established. Congress appropriated the requested funds, and in May, 1918, one of the suggested routes was opened between Washington, D.C., and New York by way of Philadelphia rather than by the direct route originally proposed. Four of the airmail routes considered by Praeger would have served Illinois communities. One, from St. Louis to Chicago by way of Springfield, anticipated a route inaugurated nine years later by a private contractor. Another, from St. Louis to Memphis via Cairo, Illinois, became a regular route in the late 1920's. The two remaining routes would have served small communities in the southern and central part of the state: one from Harrisburg to Elizabethtown via Rudement, Herod, and Hicks, returning via Golconda, Baum, Eddyville, and Mitchellsville; the other from Perque, Missouri, to Pearl, Illinois, via Golden Eagle, Brussels, Beechville, Meppen, Hardin, Michael, Kampsville, and Beecreek, Illinois. This grand experimental scheme failed to materialize because of the mobilization of America's meager aeronautical facilities and trained personnel that followed the United States' declaration of war on Germany and Austria in April, 1917.

The fact remained, however, that the Post Office had a prewar appropriation of $100,000 with which to set up an experimental service as soon as equipment and personnel were available. During the interim, the Aero Club of America and its 30 affiliated clubs kept up the agitation for regular airmail service. This clamor did not, as might have been expected, appear unpatriotic at the height of the wartime aviation training program. Quite to the contrary, regular airmail service was called a necessary device for providing reserves of skilled aviators for national defense. Airmail advocates shrewdly pointed to the dilemma faced in the spring of 1917 when only a few trained aviators were available and the United States Air Service needed to expand from 1,100 to nearly 170,000 officers and men in less than a year and a half. Lieutenant Colonel George C. Squier, later Brigadier General and Chief of the Aviation Section, Signal Corps, gave support to this argument even before the war began, when he stated that an airmail service operated by the Post Office Department "will be instrumental in creating valuable reserves of trained aviators for national defense." A reiteration of this view by Squier almost a year later helped to make possible the opening of regular airmail service between Washington and New York.

The first regular airmail service in the United States began May 15, 1918, over a 218-mile route between Washington and New York by way of Philadelphia. On that day, two Army Air Service officers in Curtiss Jenny military planes started from opposite ends of the route. Contrary to the schedule, the first mail from Washington ended up in Waldorf, Maryland; the other three flights, two southbound and one northbound, were completed without trouble. Airmail became a reality at last, and with its appearance commercial aviation began to take its rightful place in the complex transportation system of a thriving nation.

Because the United States was at war in May, 1918, the airmail service was inaugurated by the Post Office Department with military equipment and personnel. The original airmail appropriation had been made before the United States declared war on the Central Powers and would revert to the Treasury unless it were used. Post Office officials recognized that if the airmail experiment were delayed beyond that fiscal year, Congress, because of financial burdens arising from the war, might not reappropriate the money for experiment under peacetime conditions. Fortunately, the War Department was willing to co-operate with the Post Office Department. Despite a serious shortage of aircraft, the Air Service needed to improve its public relations, especially with Congress. By participating in the airmail, the War Department hoped to increase public confidence in military aviation. Three months after the Washington-New York route opened, the Post Office Department took over full control of the service, using its own planes and civilian pilots. Captain Benjamin B. Lipsner, the organizer of the first route, resigned his commission in the Signal Corps to become the first superintendent of the airmail service. Once the Post Office Department gained full control of the airmail service, the next logical step was the expansion of operations over a greater area and the improvement of service by utilizing faster, more efficient aircraft capable of carrying heavier loads. Schedules that included both day and night flying were a part of the Department's plans in 1918 but remained untried for nearly four more years.

A coast-to-coast airmail route with feeder lines to St. Louis, Kansas City, St. Paul-Minneapolis, and Pittsburgh formed the first stage of an expansion program planned by Postmaster General Albert S. Burleson and Second Assistant Postmaster General Praeger in 1918. The second stage consisted of a route from Boston to Key West, Florida, with feeder lines linking Pittsburgh, Cincinnati, and New Orleans with the principal cities on the main line. The third and fourth stages envisioned extensions from Key West to Panama via Havana, Cuba, and to South America via the West Indies. Before this plan was publicly announced, Praeger and Lipsner began a survey of a route from New York to Chicago with the hope of opening service in the near future.

A "trail blazing" airmail flight between New York and Chicago on September 5, 1918, pointed to the possible establishment of regular service before the end of the year. Max Miller and Ed Gardner completed the first flights from New York over the terrifying "hellstretch" of the Alleghenies to Lock Haven, Pennsylvania, and on to Cleveland and Chicago. Miller reached Grant Park, Chicago, on the evening of September 5; Gardner arrived 12 hours later after spending the night in Westville, Indiana. On that flight, Miller and Gardner each carried about 400 pounds of mail, and, in addition, Gardner carried a mechanic, Eddie Radel, and spare parts for both machines. The flights were marked by frequent stops for repairs, water for leaky radiators, and directions, since both pilots frequently drifted off course, especially over the rough terrain in Pennsylvania. On the morning of September 9, following a complete overhaul of the planes, Miller set out from Grant Park to establish a speed record, if possible, for the Chicago-New York flight. The New York-Chicago flights had shown the public that airmail service could be operated between the two largest cities in the country: This time, Miller was determined to prove that it could be accomplished with speed. However, a faulty radiator forced him down near Cleveland, interrupting the flight until midafternoon. Because of this delay, Miller had to remain overnight in Lock Haven, Pennsylvania, and fly on to Belmont Park, the New York airmail terminal, the following morning.

Shortly after dawn on September 10, Gardner departed from Grant Park on schedule in spite of a heavy rainstorm. With Radel as a passenger, he pushed his Curtiss R-4 at top speed all the way to New York, but his efforts to complete the long flight in a single day were marred by a crash near Hicksville,

Long Island, just ten miles from Belmont Park. The airplane was completely demolished, but Gardner and Radel escaped with only minor cuts and bruises and delivered the airmail to postal authorities before going to a nearby hospital for first-aid treatment. The near-tragic ending did not detract from the fact that airmail from Chicago had reached New York in one day. The actual flying time, 9 hours 18 minutes, set new records for the Chicago to New York flight and for any flight of equal distance.

Plans for the inauguration of regular airmail service between Chicago and New York were subsequently worked out on the basis of information obtained from the "trail blazing" flights. One change was made in the route, however; to avoid the hazardous approaches to Lock Haven over rugged mountainous country, the first stop on the westward flight was shifted to Bellefonte, Pennsylvania. The new route, therefore, ran from New York to Bellefonte, then to Cleveland and Bryan, Ohio, and on to Chicago. An announcement on October 24 stating that the new route would open between December 1 and 15 precipitated a flurry of action in Chicago. Early in October, Lipsner had selected Ashburn Field as the Chicago terminal and entered into negotiations with the Aero Club of Illinois for the rental of a 42-acre tract at $1,000 per year under a five-year lease with an option to purchase it at $350 per acre. The Aero Committee of the Chicago Chamber of Commerce erected a hangar on the leased portion of the field for the use of the Post Office Department.

Service on the Chicago-New York airmail route opened in mid-December, a time ill suited for launching operation of a 900-mile route with the war-surplus equipment then available. The insistence by Post Office officials that the route be opened at that time was one of many factors which compelled Lipsner to resign as superintendent of the airmail service early in December. Despite Lipsner's warnings of impending disaster, service was opened on December 18. The first flight from Chicago, scheduled to leave Grant Park at 6 A.M., did not depart because of a delay in arrival of airplanes from Dayton. Two planes were to have made the first flight from Chicago to

Cleveland, but only one, piloted by "Mike" Ebersole, reached Chicago; the other was wrecked in Defiance, Ohio.

Airmail service was not actually inaugurated to or from Chicago before December 21, when the Post Office Department ordered a ten-day suspension of operations on the New York-Chicago route. On the afternoon of December 18, Ebersole loaded mail into his DH-4 in Grant Park in preparation for a start from Ashburn Field the following morning. In landing on the Aero Club field, he struck soft wet ground which sent the machine into a somersault, resulting in a smashed propeller, cracked engine, and broken fuselage. The flight to Cleveland was delayed until another machine could be obtained from Bryan, Ohio. Again on December 20, the airmail failed to leave Chicago. On this occasion, an airplane ordered from Cleveland to make the flight spent the night in Bryan, Ohio, with a defective radiator.

Westbound airmail from New York failed to reach Cleveland by air on three consecutive days. On the first day, Leon D. Smith entrained his mail at Bellefonte after missing the relay plane to Cleveland; the next day, R. M. Taylor and Trent C. Fry left Belmont Park on schedule with 250 pounds of mail but did not reach Cleveland; and on the final day, Ira O. Biffle and D. T. Lamb left on schedule with 400 pounds of mail in two machines, but both returned to Belmont Park within two hours because of engine trouble. The main source of difficulty was eventually found to be the Liberty engines used in the modified DH-4 wartime bombers and observation planes. Through inexperience, or oversight, new motors had been installed in Post Office planes and placed in service without first having been sufficiently tested for their capabilities of extended use.

The ten-day suspension of service over the New York-Chicago route ordered on December 21 was later extended to nearly five months. Originally all the Liberty engines were to be overhauled and adjusted in time for resumption of service on January 2, 1919. Before that date, however, the Post Office Department decided to postpone the reopening until May 15 in order to avoid the adverse weather conditions encountered in winter months. During the delay, the Chicago terminal was shifted from Ashburn Field to Grant Park. An attempt to provide a solid landing area by constructing a cinder runway at Ashburn proved futile, and the cost of draining the field, estimated by the Chicago Drainage Canal System at $60,000, finally compelled the Post Office Department to erect a landing field on the lake front.

Airmail service between Chicago and Cleveland began on May 15, 1919. On July 1, service started over the eastern end of the New York-Chicago route. Trent C. Fry carried the first airmail from Chicago on the morning of May 15 as Gardner started from Cleveland on a similar mission. In a DH-4 loaded with six pouches of mail, Gardner landed in Grant Park at 2:25 P.M., 3 hours and 13 minutes after leaving Cleveland. Mail dispatched from Cleveland reached Chicago in the early afternoon in time for delivery the same day, 16 hours ahead of mail transported by railroad. After the opening-day flights, airmail service between Chicago and Cleveland continued without mishap. Continuous service between Chicago and New York began on July 1, when the existing route was extended to Bellefonte and New York. Plans were being formulated for the extension of service westward to the Pacific Coast. The airmail, according to Post Office Department calculations, speeded the delivery of mail between New York and Chicago by 11 hours over the fastest passenger train service linking those cities and expedited actual delivery by 16 hours.

On May 15, 1920, the Post Office Department inaugurated operations over a 440-mile route that extended westward from Chicago to Omaha. Further extensions that year pushed the airmail to San Francisco, creating a coast-to-coast route, and provided feeder-type service from St. Louis and Minneapolis to the main route at Chicago. The Chicago-St. Louis route via Rantoul opened on August 16, 1920. It was the first step in the Post Office Department's long-range plans for linking all important cities in the United States with the transcontinental route. An extension of the Chicago-St. Louis route by seaplane carriers down the Mississippi River to New Orleans, with stops at Cairo, Memphis, and Vicksburg, failed to materialize because of lack of money. On August 10, 1920, service opened over a 344-mile route to Minneapolis from Chicago. After December 1, a daily (except Sunday) schedule became effective between these cities by way of La Crosse, Wisconsin, where a maintenance and service point was established. Service between Omaha and San Francisco, the last link in the transcontinental route, opened on September 10, 1920. On the same day, a coast-to-coast daily service (except Sundays and holidays) replaced the daily (except Mondays and holidays) service that had been in operation between New York and Omaha. Route extensions that had been tentatively planned to link Washington, D.C., and Atlanta, Georgia; and Pittsburgh and Kansas City via Cincinnati, Indianapolis, and St. Louis were abandoned because of insufficient funds.

Government airmail service reached the peak of its development, in terms of route mileage, in 1920–1921. By the close of 1920, it covered 3,461 miles in four separate, interconnected routes and served, in addition to key cities on the transcontinental line, Washington, Philadelphia, St. Louis, and Minneapolis. At this time the government-operated service could have been extended by a system of routes operated by private carriers under contract to the Post Office Department. Although Congress, in 1920, gave the Postmaster General authority to contract for airmail service "between such points as he may deem advisable in case such service is furnished at a cost not greater than the cost of the same service by rail," private contractors refused to bid on routes projected by the Post Office Department. Only one of four proposed routes, Key West to Havana, Cuba, was taken over under contract in 1921. Of the other three, one provided an alternate New York-Chicago route that would have served Harrisburg, Pittsburgh, and Fort Wayne.

Economy measures in the Post Office Department in 1921 reduced airmail operations to the transcontinental route. Because of the need to cut expenditures and because only the New York-San Francisco airmail service had been specifically authorized by Congress, the New York-Washington route was discontinued on May 31, 1921, and the Minneapolis-Chicago and Chicago-St. Louis routes on June 30.

During the 1920's, the manufacturing and repair depots for the airmail service were gradually concentrated in Chicago. Less than a year after the Chicago-New York route opened, the Chicago terminal was shifted from the congested lake front district to Checkerboard Field, a commercial airport operated by David L. Behncke in Maywood. The next year it was moved across First Avenue in Maywood to the grounds of Walter Hines Hospital, where it remained until the Post Office turned over the transcontinental route to private contractors in 1927. A factory in which war-surplus DeHaviland DH-4 planes were adapted for airmail service was built on the Maywood field in 1921. There the famous warplanes, often dubbed "flaming coffins," were subjected to more than 600 structural changes before being released to airmail pilots on the transcontinental route. On June 30, 1921, the repair depot at Bustleton, Pennsylvania, was consolidated with the Chicago facilities, making the latter city the repair, as well as manufacturing, depot for the transcontinental airmail service. Postal authorities moved the airmail warehouse to Chicago a year later in order to obtain a centrally located point for more efficient and economical mail distribution.

From May 1, 1922, until all operations shifted to Chicago Municipal Airport in December, 1927, Maywood Government Field served as the terminal for all airmail flights in and out of Chicago on the transcontinental route. During 1926 and 1927, until accommodations were available at the Municipal Airport, private airmail contractors also used the Maywood field as a Chicago base of operations. Before the installation of lights along the transcontinental route, airmail flights in and out of Maywood were restricted to daylight hours. After night flying was adopted in 1924, working hours of service and maintenance crews were indefinite six days a week. No one worked on Sunday, the one day when planes were grounded. Manufacturing activities at the field ended early in 1926 after the Morrow Committee (President's Aircraft Board) questioned the advisability of the Post Office Department's manufacturing aircraft in competition with the aircraft industry. During the early 1920's, however, the Department had had to manufacture aircraft simply because suitable commercial aircraft were not available.

In spite of the serious handicaps of inadequate equipment and often unsuitable airport facilities, not to mention the absence of navigation aids, pilots of the government airmail service established a phenomenal record for performance of duties. To the men who flew the machines and those who kept them in flying condition, all efforts were directed to a single objective —"The mail must fly." Only the most adverse weather conditions grounded the mail planes; consequently, accidents were not infrequent and numerous pilots died while attempting to keep the mail flying. In March, 1920, one airmail pilot completed a flight from Cleveland to Chicago on a day when a tornado stopped all rail traffic and disrupted other forms of transportation. A report of that flight in the pilot's own words reveals the hazards encountered in the performance of ordinary duties: "The wind was blowing about forty miles an hour. The motor sputtered and missed, and I thought how cold Lake Michigan under me would feel. I ran into the worst rain- and hail-storm I ever flew in near Gary, Ind. For five minutes I could see nothing, not even the instruments on the dash board in front of me. I arrived safely at 1:50 P.M. I think that is pretty good time for mail from New York to reach Chicago—eh, what? I left New York at 7 A.M."

The hero of the first day-night, coast-to-coast airmail flight was an unpretentious pilot from Chicago named Jack Knight, who flew the eastbound mail from North Platte, Nebraska, to Chicago without relief or benefit of guide lights. The flight was undertaken as a desperate effort to arouse public interest in airmail and to save it from possible curtailment at the hands of the incoming Harding administration. The project would have ended in failure but for the efforts of Knight and his determination to keep the mail flying. On February 22, 1921, two flights set out from each end of the transcontinental route. Only one of the eastbound flights reached North Platte, where

Knight continued it to Chicago; the westbound flights ended at Chicago because of a heavy snowstorm.

Starting from North Platte at 10:44 P.M. (M.S.T.), Knight piloted his big DeHaviland through the night until 8:40 A.M. (C.S.T.), when he reached Checkerboard Field. Here a relay waited to continue the flight to New York. As he stepped from his plane in Maywood, the tired, frail-looking pilot commented only briefly about the arduous, record-breaking trip. His words fell far short of indicating the trials encountered on the long flight. He admitted that fog and snow had presented serious obstacles and that twice he had "to go down and mow some trees" in order to determine his position. On approaching Iowa City, Iowa, with fuel for only a few more minutes of flight, he could not locate the airport. The ground crew there had decided that the eastbound flight must have been canceled because of storms between Omaha and North Platte. They knew that the westbound flights, whose pilots were to fly the relay back from Omaha, had been stopped in Chicago; consequently they had gone home, leaving only an aged watchman at the field. Fortunately, the watchman heard Knight and lit a flare to guide him to a landing just before the last drop of gasoline in his tanks was exhausted. From Iowa City to Chicago the flight continued without mishap although the flyer was troubled by the weariness from long hours in the air. His achievement was all the more remarkable because he had never before flown the route between Omaha and Chicago and had only a road map for a guide.

During the next few years, the Post Office Department, under the direction of Colonel Paul Henderson, Second Assistant Postmaster General in charge of airmail, devoted its attention to improving the transcontinental service. Important aspects of this work consisted of lighting the airways for night flights, installing two-way radio communications, and experimenting with radio directional beams. On July 1, 1924, a little more than three years after Jack Knight's historic flight, regular schedules were inaugurated around the clock, day and night. Planes left each end of the route early in the morning and arrived at the opposite end late in the afternoon of the second day. A year later, there arose a demand for airmail service between Chicago and New York that would allow mail of one business day to be delivered early the following morning at the other end of the route. In response, the Post Office Department inaugurated overnight service between these two cities on July 1, 1925.

As efficiency of the service improved, the volume of mail dispatched by air increased proportionately. From May 15, 1918, to June 30, 1927, the government-operated airmail service carried 298,517,670 letters (approximately 7,462,941 pounds of mail) more than 13,500,000 miles. The Post Office had developed the service to the point that private enterprise was able to take over and operate it under contracts. From the start, the Post Office Department had planned to develop airmail service only to the point that the public would recognize its feasibility; once this was achieved, the government-operated routes were to be turned over to private enterprise. By the end of 1924, the first year in which the revenues approached the cost of the service, the time for turning the system over to private contractors appeared near at hand. In February, 1925, a bill known as the Kelly Airmail Law—in honor of its sponsor, Clyde Kelly, of Pennsylvania—authorized the Postmaster General to contract with private operators for the transportation of mails over specified routes devised by the Post Office Department. Under the provisions of the Kelly Law, private airlines commenced airmail service over 14 routes in 1926. The next year, the Department turned over the transcontinental route to private operators. From these contract airmail routes, established in the late 1920's, emerged the large domestic airline systems of the present day.

7

MILITARY AERONAUTICS, 1916–1955

On April 6, 1917, the United States declared war on Germany and Austria, and the stage was set for the greatest period of aviation development to that time. The Allies required munitions and equipment to halt the Central Powers, then engaged in an all-out effort to break through the defense lines of northern and eastern France. Depleted British and French armies asked for reinforcements, and in the air the overtaxed Royal Air Force and French air units, short of machines and men and unable to gain control of the air, looked to America for thousands of airplanes, pilots, mechanics, and other trained personnel. In May, 1917, at the request of the French government, the United States agreed to build an army unit of 4,500 planes, 5,000 pilots, 50,000 mechanics, and other expert technical personnel for combat service within one year. An additional 2,000 planes and 4,000 engines were also to be built and delivered each month to the Allies' air services. This commitment raised serious problems, for in the spring of 1917 the United States owned approximately 100 airplanes, and skilled aviators, military and civilian, totaled probably no more than 1,000. Nor were planes, camps, and instructors immediately available for training more than a small handful of flyers. In spite of these inauspicious circumstances, the United States Army Signal Corps established training facilities: at first only four; then the number jumped to nine and to 31 before the end of the war. Ground schools established at colleges and universities furnished 17,540 cadets, who advanced to preliminary flight instruction.

Between April 6, 1917, and November 11, 1918, the aviation branch of the United States Army expanded from 52 officers, 1,100 men, and about 200 civilian employees to approximately 20,000 officers and 149,000 men at home and overseas. Of this number, 7,726 officers and 70,769 men were in Europe, 6,816 officers and 51,229 men in France, the remainder training in England. Forty-five Aero Squadrons with the American Expeditionary Force included 774 pilots, 457 observers, and 23 aerial gunners.

The part played by Illinois in the wartime aviation program centered around air service training camps near Rantoul and Belleville, a military aviation ground school at the University of Illinois, and the training program for aviation technicians at Great Lakes Naval Training Station near Chicago. However, six months before the United States entered the war, military aviators were trained in a Signal Corps school at Ashburn Field in Chicago.

Early in 1916, aero clubs and aviation enthusiasts in the Middle West urged the federal government to expand training facilities for aviators and drew up plans for a reserve organization of flyers that would augment the small Signal Corps Aviation Section in the event of a national emergency. In January, a group of Chicago businessmen pledged financial support to the Aero Club of Illinois and the Aero Club of America if they would establish training facilities for aviators who, after their flight instruction, would join the state militia or regular armed forces.

Through the efforts of business and civic leaders, the Aero Club of Illinois, and the Signal Corps, the United States Central Aviation Reserve was organized in Chicago on June 29 to train volunteers for flying service in the event of war. Three units were formed: Company A, commanded by Logan A. Vilas, for hydroairplanes, and Companies B and C, commanded by W. C. Woodward and Frank Champion, respectively, for land planes. In order to expedite the program, the Central Aviation Reserve, with Charles G. Dawes as treasurer, launched a campaign to raise $20,000 for the operation of a training school and the purchase of two military airplanes. While the reserve program was in the planning stage, the Aero Club of Illinois offered the use of Ashburn Field to the War Department as a training camp. By mid-July, applications from volunteers for the Central Aviation Reserve had piled up in the headquarters of the Aero Club of Illinois, but before the end of the summer the program was abandoned, since the War Department had decided to establish its own school for reserve aviators in Chicago.

On October 28, Captain Joseph C. Morrow, commander of the 4th Aviation School Squadron of the Signal Corps, officially opened the new school at Ashburn Field. Lieutenants Arthur R. Christie and W. W. Spain and civilian instructors Theodore C. MacCaulay, J. D. Hill, and A. Livingston Allan took charge of the training of volunteers who enlisted as sergeants in the Signal Corps Reserve to qualify for flight instruction. The school remained in Chicago until mid-January, 1917, then moved to Memphis, Tennessee, for the balance of the winter. Before the move, 25 students, selected from nearly 400 applicants, had begun training. Among the military and civilian instructors and twelve civilian-student instructors were many able exhibition pilots who had formerly made their headquarters at Ashburn Field. The civilian-student instructors were not members of the Signal Corps, but they assisted with the training program while at the same time learning military tactics. Those who accompanied the school to winter quarters were: Matty Laird, Elmer Partridge, Lester E. Holt, Charles M. Pond, Fred A. Hoover, Harry Crewdson, Harry Powers, William H. Couch, C. N. Sinclair, Louis Gertson, and Perah Maroney. Joseph Pallissard, another familiar local flyer, accompanied the school as a civilian mechanic, one of four employed to keep the command's nine Curtiss JN-4 training ships in flying condition. Other Chicagoans were included among the students undergoing training. Sergeants Rudolph W. Schroeder and Alexander McLeod were veteran exhibition flyers. Schroeder graduated from the school after it returned to Ashburn in June and later received a commission in the Air Service.

The entry of the United States into war led to a drastic expansion of training facilities. For a time, the War Department sought to acquire land adjacent to Ashburn Field in order to enlarge the camp, but the cost was too high. The necessity of transferring training facilities to a larger camp led to the selection of what later became Chanute Field near Rantoul. While construction at this site continued throughout June, the 4th Aviation School Squadron remained in Chicago. Early in July, all personnel and equipment were transferred to the new camp, and the War Department returned Ashburn Field to the Aero Club of Illinois. The following October, the Air Service again took over the field and used it as a temporary camp for advanced training until winter weather sent the instructors and students south.

In May, 1917, a special representative of the Construction Division of the Office of the Chief Signal Officer selected a mile-square tract of land adjoining the southeast boundary of Rantoul as the most suitable site available in that area for an aviation camp. On May 21, the War Department concurred in the selection and accepted options on the land taken up by local civic and business groups. The following day, the Department concluded a contract with English Brothers Construction Company of Champaign for clearing the site and erecting 53 buildings, including six hangars to house 36 training planes. Two weeks later, a supplemental contract provided for six additional hangars. Construction began immediately, at times utilizing from 1,200 to 1,900 laborers, mechanics, apprentices, and skilled tradesmen, in addition to hundreds of teams and several mechanical shovels. Some buildings were ready for the troops and equipment transferred from Ashburn Field and San Antonio, Texas, early in July, but work continued seven days a week until early August.

Transfer of the 4th Aviation School Squadron from Chicago was the occasion for the largest movement of men and equipment by air ever attempted in the United States. On July 3, Lieutenant W. W. Spain, accompanied by E. A. Johnson, a senior civilian instructor, flew to the new station to chart an air route in preparation for a mass flight of training planes the following week. On July 9, twenty-three planes left Ashburn Field in groups of three or four en route to Chanute Field. Most of the personnel and heavy equipment moved southward on a special train. Only one plane failed to complete the trip on schedule; Fred A. Hoover and a mechanic in No. 132 flew off course and finally landed near St. Joseph, Michigan, 65 miles east of Chicago. Charles Pond, flying No. 141, had to make a forced landing for gasoline at Paxton before continuing to Rantoul. Once at the new station, the personnel from Chicago were either absorbed into the 10th Aero Squadron, which had arrived two days earlier, or transferred to other stations. Nearly all the student instructors either went on to other camps, where they served as civilian instructors, or returned to civilian occupations.

In order to speed the training program for military aviators, the War Department, in May, 1917, established six ground schools to train college students in the basic theoretical and practical courses that were preparatory to flight training. On May 21, military aviation ground schools were established at the University of California, Cornell University, the University of Illinois, Massachusetts Institute of Technology, Ohio State University, and the University of Texas. More than a thousand future flying officers were immediately enrolled. Two weeks later, schools were created at the Georgia School of Technology and Princeton University. Before the last of the ground schools closed, February 1, 1919, a total of 17,540 students had received eight weeks of special instruction preparatory to assignment to training camps throughout the country.

The military aviation ground school at the University of Illinois was under the direction of Signal Corps officers and members of the regular faculty. In eighteen months, 3,453 students were trained here. In all, 2,644 graduates from the University of Illinois ground school went on to flight instruction, many to Chanute and Scott fields. In June, 1917, volunteers from the Officers' Training Corps at Fort Sheridan were allowed to transfer to the Aviation Section of the Signal Corps and were assigned to the ground school in Urbana for preflight instruction. The first officer-candidates to take advantage of this order were Reed G. Landis, F. S. Whiting, Darson Knight, Walter R. Avery, and Keith Jones, all of Chicago, and J. Loy Maloney, of Polo, Illinois. After graduation from the University ground school and Chanute Field, Landis received advanced training in Europe, where he shared with two others the distinction of being America's sixth ranking air ace.

Preliminary flight instruction commenced officially at Chanute Field on July 17, after the arrival of Major James L. Dunsworth, first commanding officer of the camp. Captain Roy S. Brown, commander of the mass flight from Chicago and officer in charge of flying at Chanute, inaugurated the training program. He was assisted by Captains J. C. McDonnell and T. J. Handey, Lieutenants Maurice Laffly and Paul Prevost, veteran French army pilots, and twelve civilian instructors including Harry Crewdson, Eugene Heth, Fred Hoover, Charles Pond, L. G. Smith, C. R. Sinclair, Harry Powers, Bert R. J. Hassell, and Maurice Priest. Each student began with the primary stage and passed, in turn, through dual, first solo, advanced solo, and the reserve military aviator's tests before graduating. He then became eligible for a commission and was transferred to another field for advanced training. The rate of progress was not necessarily uniform, for individual ability, weather conditions, and available equipment determined the length of the course. Some students passed their R.M.A. tests in a month; others required six or, more usually, eight weeks. In addition to flight training, students received instruction in armament, aerial gunnery, signals, and aerial tactics, whenever practical and in varying amounts, depending upon availability of instructors and each student's rate of progress. The first group of 24 graduates departed for advanced training in early September; another group of 24 shipped out six weeks later.

Within three months after the opening of Chanute Field, trained squadrons, of about 150 men each, were transferred to depots in the East for overseas assignments. The 10th and 16th Aero Squadrons were the first to leave, followed closely by the 39th. The first two squadrons were shipped overseas;

the 39th was sent to Waco, Texas. In December, the 152d, 153d, 173d, and 174th Squadrons reported from Kelly Field, Texas, to fill vacancies in shops, hangars, and classrooms; the 210th Squadron was organized at Chanute Field from local recruits. Classes were conducted daily in every branch of aviation related to the maintenance and repair of airplanes, including specialized training for mechanics, carpenters, riggers, and hangar men.

Between December 15 and April 1, flying ceased at Chanute Field, and all instructors and students were transferred to southern camps to continue training during the winter months. Instruction of ground crews and administrative personnel from various aero squadrons continued as before. The training planes, though unused, were serviced and maintained by student mechanics, riggers, and electricians just as they had been during the busy flying season. Early in January, the 153d and 210th Aero Squadrons received orders to prepare for overseas shipment, and two more squadrons left the Kelly Field depot to train at Rantoul. Before the end of that month, all but the 38th, the headquarters squadron, were alerted for shipment. In spite of the steady drain of units and personnel, the number of men at the field did not fall below 500. After the 83d, 268th, and 269th Aero Squadrons were organized in February and were followed to Chanute by the 831st and 832d Squadrons, the field reached its capacity of 1,500 men. In mid-March, the 83d Squadron, composed mostly of local recruits, reported to Langley Field, Virginia, to serve as school squadron; a new unit, the 203d Squadron, was recruited and organized to fill the vacancy. During the wartime program, 19 squadrons received training at the field; of this number, 12 served overseas, 10 in Europe.

Flying commenced at Chanute Field in February, 1918, though student instruction did not begin officially until the following April. A new system of recruiting student flyers inaugurated during the winter gave members of the aero squadrons then training at the field an opportunity to become aviators and commissioned officers. Formerly, all cadets had remained reservists until commissioned; thus, if a student failed to complete flight training, he returned to civilian life. Under the new plan, an enlisted man could apply for flying instruction. If accepted, he was placed on detached service until he was commissioned, but if he failed to complete flight training, he was returned to his former unit.

Preparations for student training began six weeks prior to April 15, the date set for the official opening of the new flying season. In order to accommodate an accelerated training program involving twice the number of planes used the previous year, officers opened negotiations with landowners in the Rantoul area for the lease of a site suitable for an auxiliary airfield. After considering three sites, the War Department secured a lease on 100 acres a mile and a half northeast of Rantoul, and soldiers from the student aero squadrons cleared and leveled the ground in time for use that summer. The Bloomington Association of Commerce constructed another airfield near that city. New hangars were constructed at Chanute Field to house 24 more training planes, and the capacity of the barracks was doubled by enclosing porches that extended the length of each building on the north and south.

Flight instruction for cadets who had recently reached the field from Texas began on April 19. In the next few weeks hundreds of cadets from ground schools, many from the University of Illinois, began the initial stages of flight training. Major Henry Abbey, transferred from Garstner Field, Louisiana, was in charge of flying. He was assisted by Captain Harry M. Smith. Instruction was divided into five stages: dual, solo, aerobatic, formation, and cross-country, each in charge of an expert flyer. Early morning flights were scheduled to acquaint students with the calm air of the dawn; consequently, "first call" was set up to 4:30 A.M., followed by roll call and then breakfast at 4:45. Afterward, ground crews checked the training ships, which had to be ready for the instructors at 5:50. Under this program, six cadets passed the reserve military aviators' test on May 11, twenty-three days after beginning dual instruction.

The accelerated schedule produced the first serious accidents from flying. Cadet Harry Buchannon and an instructor crashed into a moving train on the Illinois Central Railroad near Clinton while distributing circulars advertising a Liberty Loan drive. Buchannon, the pilot, received a broken hip, but the instructor escaped without injury. On July 2, Cadet Harold C. Page, of York, Pennsylvania, crashed near Ludlow as he attempted to dive beneath a storm to make an emergency landing. When about 300 feet from the ground, turbulent winds tossed the plane violently as if it were a piece of paper. Page lost control and the machine spun into the ground. Two weeks later, Cadets John Hooper and Raymond Shirk narrowly escaped fatal injuries when the planes which they were flying for solo instruction collided in midair. Shirk's craft landed upside down, causing extensive damage to the machine only; the other plane crashed in flames, and Hooper suffered lacerations about the face and a broken leg.

Accidents at aviation camps reached an alarming number in July, 1918, and the Chief of the Air Service, Major General Charles T. Menoher, suspended flying at all camps between 11 A.M. and 3 P.M., the hours when a majority of accidents occurred. This curtailment did not reduce the accident rate at Chanute Field, however, for three more fatalities occurred before training ended in early December. On August 7, a student aviator in the act of landing ran into a motorcycle on the field. A cadet passenger in the sidecar was fatally injured by the whirling propeller of the plane. A week later, Lieutenant William C. Gabriel, a recently commissioned graduate of the local flight course, and a cadet crashed on the field because the student misunderstood a signal from his instructor and put the plane into a dive while only 100 feet off the ground. Neither the instructor nor the student was seriously injured. Lieutenants J. W. Johnson, of Trafford, Alabama, and Clifford B. Guthrie, of Robinson, Illinois, were victims of tailspin crashes. Both had recently been transferred from Brooks Field, Texas. Ironically, Johnson was instructing a cadet in the method of recovery from a tailspin when he apparently lost control of his plane.

The Construction Division of the Signal Corps conducted an investigation of available locations for an aviation field on the

Illinois side of the Mississippi River near St. Louis. On June 1, 1917, Captain C. G. Edgar, the officer responsible for selecting training camp sites, accepted an invitation from the Belleville Board of Trade to inspect two areas near that city. One, in Shiloh Valley six miles northwest of Belleville, particularly impressed Edgar, who urged the Board of Trade to secure options on a mile-square tract of flat farm land. After the Airplane Division of the War Department authorized Edgar to proceed with negotiations for the field, Secretary E. A. Daley of the Board of Trade obtained two types of options, one providing for a three-year lease on a monthly rental basis, the other providing for outright purchase at an average price of $200 per acre. On June 15, the Army Aviation Board accepted the option for leasing the land and, a week later, let contracts for the construction of the field. After the war, the second options were taken up by the War Department, and the field became a permanent installation.

The Unit Construction Company of St. Louis, the contractor for Scott Field, commenced work on the new two-squadron camp on June 27, 1917. As many as 3,000 workmen were employed at one time to push the construction of buildings and the clearing and leveling of the landing field. Within two months, 52 buildings, including quarters for students, officers, instructors, mechanics, and enlisted personnel, six large hangars, machine shops, offices, and mess halls were awaiting occupation by troops en route from Texas. Although the work was not completed until September 1, the date on which the War Department officially accepted the field, the 11th and 21st Aero Squadrons moved into the new barracks and quarters on August 12, and training commenced as of that date. Major J. W. Hurd assumed temporary command of Scott Field.

Flying instruction began early in September after the arrival of civilian instructors, cadets, and training planes. On September 10, William Couch, of Stuart, Iowa, a civilian instructor, and Lieutenant Paul Prevost, a French army aviator assigned to the field, completed the first flights in new Curtiss JN4-B training planes. In the next few days, all the cadets began the initial phase of the training program under the supervision of Prevost and either Couch or one of the other civilian instructors, H. T. Lewis, J. D. Hill, and T. C. Jones. The arrival of flying officers, cadets, and planes permitted Major George A. E. Reinburg, commanding officer, to enlarge the training program. By early October, 54 cadets, including 20 recent graduates of the University of Illinois ground school, were engaged in daily instruction flights in 20 planes: 5 Standards and 15 Curtiss Jennies.

In spite of an exceedingly heavy training program involving a score of planes and inexperienced student aviators, Scott Field established a remarkable safety record. During the first season, students learned to fly under a method of instruction commonly known as the "old stage" system, then used in all training camps. Under this system, an instructor in any one stage worked with 12 to 20 students daily from 7:30 A.M. to 4:30 P.M. After 20 or 25 minutes in the air with each student, the instructor returned to the ground for another, repeating this procedure day after day without relief. As a result, mishaps or, sometimes, serious accidents frequently—though only briefly—interrupted field activities. The first accident occurred on September 17 when T. C. Jones stalled a Curtiss ship about 30 feet off the ground. He escaped without injury, although the machine was seriously damaged. On another occasion, Couch had to make a quick landing when the radiator of his machine developed a serious leak in flight. An examination revealed a neat round puncture and slight damage to one propeller blade, which could have resulted from a small-caliber rifle shot. Six weeks later, Couch established an altitude record with one of the training planes by climbing to a height of 9,300 feet.

Shortly before flying activity ended for the year, Lieutenant Colonel James E. Fechet, the new commandant, introduced long cross-country flights as a feature of the training program. Immediately after reporting to Scott Field from San Antonio, Fechet indicated his approval of extra flights by accompanying Major E. A. K. Rheinhardt on a trip to the St. Clair Country Club, where they played a round of golf before returning to the field. Rheinhardt flew some of the longest flights from the field, including trips to Springfield, Decatur, Du Quoin, Pinckneyville, Tamaroa, and St. Louis, where paper "bombs" advertising the Second Liberty Loan drive were dropped. Near the end of October, Fechet and Rheinhardt flew to Salem to arrange for the establishment of a landing field and supply depot for student aviators, who later completed the 50-mile flight as part of the training program. A similar field was established in Springfield the following month, and negotiations were started for establishment of another field in Forest Park, St. Louis.

Other types of instruction developed apace with the flight-training program. Month after month aero squadrons received instruction and practical training in the various jobs related to the actual operations of a combat flying squadron. The 11th and 21st Aero Squadrons left the field before the end of 1917; the 86th departed in mid-February, followed by the 85th, 154th, and 222d, while the 155th, 261st, and 262d, and 263d remained until March. Eight squadrons served overseas, four in France, after advanced training with the Royal Flying Corps in England. Other squadrons were training in England at the close of hostilities. Several squadrons were transferred to camps in the United States.

A new flying season opened officially at Scott Field on April 15, 1918, with the arrival of flying officers, civilian instructors, and cadets from temporary assignments at southern air camps. Instruction ended almost immediately, however, for six days of hail, rain, wind, snow, and generally cold weather grounded every plane on the field. In order to speed up the schedule and also to avoid congestion in the 300-acre landing field, Major John B. Brooks, commandant, leased a 105-acre tract one mile north of Mascoutah as an auxiliary field. With an accelerated program in operation, training continued for seven months, ending shortly after the Armistice. At that time, cadets were released from the service, and the remaining active aero squadrons were transferred to other installations or disbanded, with their personnel returning to civilian life. During this period of Scott Field's activity, 414 cadets received instruction; 244 passed pilots' tests and received commissions.

The officers and civilian instructors at Scott introduced a

new system of flight training that replaced the inefficient stage method used in nearly all Air Service training camps in 1918. The Gosport method originated in Great Britain's Royal Flying Corps training camps during the early part of the war. The British concluded that many potentially good aviators failed to complete the training course because, under the stage method then in use, five to eight instructors worked with each student, and no one knew anything of the student's previous training or any special problems he might have met and left unsolved. As a remedy, the Royal Flying Corps devised a program in which a single instructor worked with a student from the preliminary to the advanced solo stage. In actual practice, it was found that special attention or extra instruction invariably enabled students to overcome serious problems and to complete the training program in record numbers. The United States Air Service borrowed the Gosport method, modified it to conform to conditions in American training camps, and permitted two training camps to experiment with it. Although introduced on a small scale for training instructors at Brooks Field, Texas, the new method was first used throughout a primary training program at Scott Field during the spring and summer of 1918. There it was in general use in October, when the War Department ordered all training camps to use the new system in place of the stage method. Under the Gosport method, approximately three-quarters of all the cadets who entered the training program received commissions as flying officers.

Naval aviation training constituted an important section of the activities at Great Lakes Naval Station. The need for motor mechanics, riggers, and maintenance men in the Navy's growing air fleet led to the establishment of special courses within the training program at Great Lakes early in the war. Before the Great Lakes school could handle students for both pilot and non-pilot (ground school) training, a large share of the Navy's training program outside the Pensacola, Florida, station was handled in the East, particularly by the Massachusetts Institute of Technology. Until Congress appropriated funds for the construction of an aviation school at the Midwestern station in the latter part of 1917, its ground school and flying programs made only a small contribution to naval aviation.

By December, 1917, the school was turning out large numbers of enlisted men with specialized skills, such as quartermasters, armorers, machinist's mates, and some officers from Officers' Material School. During 1918, an accelerated training program and enlarged facilities, particularly after completion of the new aviation school in September, turned out a greater number of aeronautical motor and seaplane construction specialists. The expansion of facilities at Great Lakes resulted in the absorption of a large number of small temporary schools and stations and the reorganization of courses to a standardized curriculum.

Graduates of the Great Lakes Aviation School were specialists trained to keep the Navy's flying boats in flying condition. Men enrolled in the machinists' school were trained to serve as motor overhaul or repair men, trouble shooters, ignition experts, engineer officers, or mechanics on flying boats. Students in the quartermasters' school learned to assemble and align planes and to perform the duties of wire and fabric workers, dopers, and repairmen. A new school in the aviation camp, the armorers' school, appeared late in the war because of development of aircraft weapons. Classes in the armorers' school at Great Lakes were organized early in August, 1918, under the direction of Lieutenant (j.g.) F. B. Christmas and rapidly expanded to a capacity of 360 men in classes of 60 each.

Throughout the war, Great Lakes Naval Training Station remained under the command of Captain William A. Moffet, who, as a rear admiral, later had charge of the Bureau of Aeronautics of the Navy Department. Under Moffet's very capable direction, the base expanded from a small camp to a great station that trained more than 100,000 men during 1917 and 1918. The aviation training program, toward which he was always sympathetic, was under the direction of Lieutenant (j.g.) Lee Hammond during most of the war period. A veteran barnstormer, Hammond had given up flying in 1912 but remained actively interested in aviation. In June, 1917, he entered the Navy as a reserve officer and, on assignment to Great

Lakes, resumed active flying. Associated with Hammond were a number of naval aviators and nonflying officers. Lieutenant (j.g.) Duncan Forbes, a skillful pilot, operated the station's Curtiss flying boats for training exercises and directed a ground school for officers. Another flying officer, Lieutenant (j.g.) E. P. Applegate remained at the station but a short time, as did Ensign Logan A. ("Jack") Vilas, who had made aviation history in 1913 with a flight across Lake Michigan in a Curtiss flying boat.

Flying instruction at Great Lakes was limited to preliminary training during the warm months and experimental work in conjunction with aviation school courses the remainder of the year. Students enrolled in flying classes were sent to other stations for advanced training before they were allowed to qualify for the military aviators' tests and commissions as flying officers. Curtiss NG-type flying boats were maintained at the station and sometimes used for other than training purposes. For a short time in October, 1918, when it appeared that the Post Office Department would soon open regular airmail service between Chicago and New York, Hammond made daily flights between Great Lakes and the airmail service terminal in Grant Park. This service was abandoned when the Chicago-New York airmail route failed to materialize at that time.

A number of instructors in the aviation school received flight instruction from a Chicago flying school. During March, 1918, ten enlisted men of the quartermaster division used their furlough time to study free of charge at the Bud Morriss Airplane School in Chicago. Morriss, a boatswain's mate and head of the quartermaster school, offered the instruction without charge to increase the efficiency of the school. Upon completion of instruction and related courses, the volunteers were assigned as chief instructors in the quartermaster school. Late in June, a second class of 25 men trained at the Morriss School.

The end of the war produced an immediate slowdown in military aviation programs in all camps throughout the nation. By mid-1919, Chanute and Scott fields were all but abandoned and appeared destined for reconversion to farm land. The Navy continued to operate its aviation school at Great Lakes with a skeleton staff of instructors and small classes of enlisted personnel. Despite the efforts of the military services and enlightened leaders in the government, Congress seemed intent upon demobilization to the prewar level, which would have meant the loss of the two Air Service fields and probably the naval aviation training center if not all of Great Lakes. Eventually, however, a program was adopted which permitted the retention of the three training facilities, though all remained virtually inactive for two or three years.

For two years after Air Service demobilization in 1918–1919, Chanute Field remained deserted except for caretakers and guards. But on January 21, 1921, the enlisted mechanics' school was transferred there from Kelly Field, and the field began its role as a technical training center. Over a period of three months, officers and men of the school moved in the personnel and equipment necessary for teaching 24 trades ranging from armorer, blacksmith, and cabinetmaker to parachute rigger, vulcanizer, gas welder, and typewriter repairman. Transfer of the photography school from Langley Field and the communications school from Fort Sill, Oklahoma, in 1922, made Chanute Field a real technical training center with facilities for training personnel in mechanics, photography, communications, and armament. A clerical school was added in 1924.

Since the early 1920's, the technical training program has steadily expanded. In 1955 it included 50 courses in advanced aircraft maintenance, hydraulics, electrical systems, flight engineering, synthetic trainers, and related mechanical phases of military aviation. From the original mechanics' school, in which students learned to operate the 90-horsepower OX-5 and similar engines, technical courses in engines have advanced to specialized instruction in the operation of multi-engined bombers whose R-4360 engines each produce 3,000 or more horsepower. Later, the construction of 32 test cells for jet and reciprocating engines made available larger and more up-to-date facilities for training engine-specialists. During World War II, more than 200,000 men were graduated from the technical schools—62,233 in 1943 alone. In addition to training in mechanics—the largest operation of Chanute's schools—courses have been maintained in other essential categories, particularly in weather observation and forecasting and in synthetic trainers. During the war years, aviation cadets were also offered courses in subjects designed to train them as squadron engineer-officers. At the height of the wartime program, flying instruction was reintroduced for a brief time; a four-engine transitional school qualified single- and twin-engine pilots for four-engine B-24's and B-17's.

The technical schools might have been transferred to Lowry Field, Denver, Colorado, in the mid-1930's had not an aroused community induced government and military officials to retain at least a portion of the technical training program at Chanute. For a time, the future of the Rantoul field appeared uncertain. Finally, in 1938, the photography, armament, and aerial schools were moved to the Denver field; the mechanics' school at Chanute was expanded and housed in permanent buildings. An $8,500,000 construction program in 1938–1939 created modern facilities, centrally located brick buildings, test blocks, and four new hangars.

After the 1918 Armistice, the future of Scott Field remained uncertain until March, 1919, when the War Department bought the mile-square training field. However, the purchase did not settle immediately the question of the field's future use. It served as a storage depot until June 29, 1921, when the Air Service announced the establishment there of the only inland airship port. Balloons, blimps, and semirigid dirigibles (the Navy had been given exclusive responsibility for the development of rigid craft) soon occupied the hangars and fields, originally designed for airplanes. In order to convert from heavier to lighter-than-air craft, the Army spent $5,000,000 on the field and equipment. It constructed a mammoth airship hangar 810 feet long, 150 feet wide, and 150 feet high, larger than any in use at that time at the army airship ports of Langley Field, Virginia; Aberdeen, Maryland; San Antonio or Fort Bliss, Texas; or Ross Field, California.

As the Army Air Corps advanced the development of lighter-than-air craft, Scott Field became the stage for great aeronautical achievements. The RS-1, the Army's first semirigid dirigible, a Goodyear-Zeppelin Company product, was assembled at

Scott Field in 1925 and from there made many record-breaking flights. In July, 1927, this 719,000-cubic-foot ship took on 1,000 gallons of gasoline at Scott Field and then flew nonstop to Bolling Field, Washington, D.C., where Assistant Secretary of War J. Trubee Davidson, staff officers, and a representative of the Navy climbed aboard for a trip to Buffalo, Cleveland, and back to Scott Field in 36 hours. Later the same year, the RS-1 made training flights to Des Moines and Iowa City, Iowa. Also in 1927, the spherical balloon played an important part in Scott Field activities. On March 9 of that year, Captain Hawthorne C. Gray, a 38-year-old veteran of 12-years' service, including six in the balloon section, set a new altitude record for balloons of 77,706- to 105,942-cubic-foot capacity by ascending to an altitude of 28,500 feet (8,690 meters). He set out to surpass the 26-year-old record of 35,424 feet set by two German aeronauts, Suring and Berson, and might easily have done so had he not lost consciousness at approximately 27,000 feet. Although surpassed as a world mark by Joseph Emmer of Germany in 1937, Gray's flight still stands as the American altitude record for balloons of the sixth and seventh categories. Twice more, Gray attempted to set new records. On May 4, he reached 40,000 feet but had to bail out when the balloon fell too rapidly during the final stages of the descent. He landed near Grayville and the balloon near Golden Gate, in east south central Illinois, approximately 300 miles from his starting point. When Gray's instruments and log were sent to the Fédération Aéronautique Internationale for verification, that body refused to recognize the flight as a new world's record on the technicality that Gray had had to abandon the balloon and therefore had not remained in personal possession of his instruments. Six months later, Gray made another attempt to surpass the record and rose to 42,470 feet, but again the flight did not enter the record books, for Gray died from lack of oxygen just before reaching the highest point of the ascension.

Airships, semirigid and nonrigid, were the center of activity at Scott Field during the 1920's. During those years, the 8th, 9th, and 12th Airship Companies, each with as many as six airships; the 21st Balloon Group Headquarters, the 24th Airship

Service Company, and a balloon and airship school carried out extensive training programs, making the field one of the busiest airship ports in the country. During the early 1930's, the Air Corps gave less attention to airships than to airplanes; consequently, the once proud fleet of blimps dwindled in number year by year. In May, 1937, when the War Department ordered the Air Corps to abandon airships, only three TC-type craft remained in operation, and two of those—the TC-11 and T-14—were stationed at Scott Field. The three airships were transferred to the Navy and later became the nucleus around which the antisubmarine patrols were organized in 1941. After the loss of the only airships on the base, activities at Scott Field centered around observation balloons. Only the 21st Balloon Group Headquarters and the 15th Observation Squadron, in addition to base squadrons and special detachments from ordnance, Signal Corps, finance, medical, and quartermaster departments remained on the field.

The next year the Army Air Force began to expand as part of a buildup of national defenses. The War Department decided to move general headquarters from Langley Field to an inland, less vulnerable station, and in July, 1938, Scott Field, an empty airship base, became the new nerve center of the Air Force. A $7,000,000 renovation program converted the base into a modern airfield three times its original area, with a network of eight paved runways and other facilities required by the headquarters units. The program was completed in the spring of 1940, in time to play an important role in the wartime training program.

In the summer of 1939, the Army Air Force transferred its basic training section of the Air Force Technical School to Scott Field. Under an accelerated prewar training program in the late 1930's and the expanded wartime program, this training section turned out thousands of young airmen equipped with the rudiments of mechanics, photography, armaments, and communications. A two-year program involving 2,250 men per month for four-week courses, was expanded to many times that number after December 7, 1941. The demand for communications personnel to operate the hundreds of thousands of radios in aircraft and ground installations compelled the Army Air Force to establish early in the war a "radio university of the Air Corps" at Scott Field for training future radio operators in the use of code, radio telegraph procedure, radio repair, circuit analysis, flight operation, and related subjects. For men designated to receive commissions in the Air Force Reserve there were similar courses.

The Navy reactivated its aviation training program in Illinois in 1938 after establishing facilities on the 300-acre Curtiss-Reynolds airport near Glenview several miles southwest of the Great Lakes Naval Training Station. The following year flying and ground school training programs were greatly accelerated to meet the demands of the naval air fleet for pilots and skilled technicians. To provide training facilities, the Navy in 1940 purchased Curtiss-Reynolds airport outright, plus considerable adjoining acreage, and established the Glenview Naval Air Station.

During World War II, military aviation in Illinois was expanded to include two semimilitary organizations composed of volunteer civilian pilots who operated their own planes but remained subject to the authority of military commands. The Civil Air Patrol, created December 1, 1941, by the Office of Civilian Defense, was transferred to the War Department by order of President Roosevelt less than a year and a half later. After the declaration of war by the United States against Japan, Germany, and Italy, Governor Dwight H. Green ordered the organization of the Illinois Reserve Militia Air Corps under direction of the state's adjutant general, Brigadier General Leo M. Boyle. Both the Civil Air Patrol and the Illinois Reserve Militia Air Corps played important parts in the war effort.

The Civil Air Patrol was created for the purpose of mobilizing civil aviation skills and equipment for the war effort. With a national commander and headquarters staff made up of Air Force personnel, the Civil Air Patrol carried out its duties through wing commands established in each of the 48 states, the District of Columbia, Alaska, and Puerto Rico. Within the command of each state, there were groups composed of separate squadrons through which statewide operations were carried on and co-ordinated with national programs. Each wing commander was appointed by the national commander and was subject to his orders; all Civil Air Patrol personnel were in turn subject to the orders of their respective wing commanders. On the squadron level, membership in the Civil Air Patrol was open to all American citizens, men and women, of good character. Senior members were 18 years of age or older, and cadet members 15 to 17 inclusive.

The Illinois Wing was well organized from the start. Under the able direction of veteran sportsman and military flyer Jack Vilas, the Wing recruited nearly 3,000 men and women who formed nine groups commanded by some of the most experienced pilots in the state. Bill Turgeon commanded Group I with headquarters at Sky Harbor Airport, Northbrook. Group II had its headquarters at Commander Fred Machesney's airport near Rockford. Group III, commanded by Herb Anderson, maintained headquarters at Rubinkam Airport, Harvey. Vern Roberts commanded Group IV with headquarters at the Municipal Airport in Moline. DeWitt Collins, manager of Peoria Municipal Airport, commanded Group V which made its headquarters on that city-owned-and-operated field. Bloomington Municipal Airport served as headquarters for Group VI commanded by airport manager Art Carnahan; Southwest Airport, Springfield, for Group VII commanded by Craig Isbell; Parks Air College Airport near East St. Louis for Group VIII commanded by Oliver Parks; and Salem Airport for Group IX commanded by George F. Lytle. Within each group several squadrons were organized in cities and towns within the jurisdiction of the group command.

The Illinois Wing organized courier service, towed targets, searched for missing aircraft, and performed a variety of services designed to contribute to the buildup of military strength. Under Wing Commander Vilas, Illinois Wing personnel in the Chicago area flew night missions to check the effectiveness of blackout tests and towed targets for antiaircraft training battalions at Fort Sheridan. When Vilas received a commission in the Air Force and an assignment as national executive officer of the Civil Air Patrol, the command of the Illinois Wing went to Herman E. Lacy, who also resigned after a brief tenure to accept an Air Force commission. Under the direction of a succession of commanders—James R. Graham, Robert K. Belt, and Charles W. Schuck—the Illinois Wing flew special missions of various types and in 1943 aided in flood relief work in the southern part of the state. In May and June, 1943, forty planes of the Illinois Wing of the Civil Air Patrol and the Illinois Reserve Militia Air Corps patrolled more than 100,000 miles of levees along the Illinois, Mississippi, Ohio, and Wabash rivers; searched for marooned persons and stock; and summoned aid and ferried emergency supplies to flooded areas.

By the end of World War II, the Civil Air Patrol was a semimilitary organization serving a threefold function: as a training corps, as an Air Force auxiliary, and as a light-plane air force. With the return of peace, the Civil Air Patrol was retained by the Air Force as a civilian adjunct of the military preparedness program. Since 1945, the Civil Air Patrol has served on peacetime military missions such as searches for missing planes, in addition to extending aid, both by flying and ground duties, in civilian emergencies. The cadet training program of the Civil Air Patrol, too, has served as an important source of recruits and officer candidates for the Air Force.

World War II, like World War I, produced remarkable advances in aircraft design and greater appreciation of aircraft as an instrument for commercial travel. Technical improvements in design during the period 1914–1918, coupled with awakening public consciousness of the potential of the airplane, made possible the tremendous expansion of commercial aviation in the 1920's. Similarly, World War II produced advances in aircraft design and performance, which would have taken twenty years or more of peacetime development, and impressed upon the public the value of the airplane for fast, safe travel. Two great wars of the present century perfected the airplane as a weapon of destruction, and from the designs developed under the stress of war came the huge, fast airliners which dominate the nation's airways today. Illinois' contribution to the successful conduct of the two great wars was considerable, just as its contributions to peacetime development have put it in the forefront of commercial aviation.

8

COMMERCIAL AIR TRANSPORT, 1919–1955

Advances in airplane design and performance during World War I led many aviation enthusiasts and promoters to devise schemes for airline passenger and express service after the close of hostilities. A few of the more ambitious promoters announced plans for the organization of airlines between New York, Washington, Philadelphia, and Chicago, and even extensions to the West Coast. But all these prophets failed to make an accurate evaluation of sentiment toward the airplane and air travel. Americans were conscious of the remarkable achievements of aircraft in the war; but no matter how much they marveled, there was almost no popular incentive for air travel, even as late as 1926. The public lacked confidence in the airplane as a means for fast, safe travel, and public apathy precluded air transport operations on a sound commercial basis. A change in attitude came about only after 1926, when the federal government brought order into a hitherto unrestricted industry. Once order was achieved, Charles A. Lindbergh's historic trans-Atlantic solo flight sparked enthusiasm for air travel and provided the initial impulse for almost unlimited expansion of air transport in the lush boom years of the late 1920's.

In the absence of public confidence, former military aviators who wanted to fly for a living turned to barnstorming in war-surplus aircraft. With airplanes available at bargain prices, these young airmen became the "gypsies" or itinerant flyers of the early 1920's. The itinerant flyer set up for business in a convenient field and carried passengers for fees ranging from three to five dollars, sometimes less if business was especially slow. Brief passenger flights and occasional "taxi" service to nearby communities provided a meager existence. When business fell off, or an accident undermined local interest, the flyer moved on to a new community.

Occasionally, a "gypsy" established a permanent airfield from which charter flights became a profitable business. Opportunities were also available, especially in large cities, for aerial advertising, photography, flight instruction, and exhibition work. In the suburbs around Chicago, a number of aviators opened flying fields shortly after the end of the war. David L. Behncke and Bert J. Hassell conducted a delivery service in 1919 from Checkerboard Field, located at First Avenue and Twelfth Street in Maywood. A small open tract of land near Peterson and Lincoln avenues in Chicago was the headquarters for Nimmo Black and other local aviators between 1921 and 1924. During 1923 Black made many long-distance flights carrying photographs of important events for Chicago newspapers. In May, Black and A. Anderson flew in from Louisville, Kentucky, with pictures of the Kentucky Derby in time to make the early morning editions, even though the landing had to be made in the dark with only bonfires in four corners of the field for guides. Three months later, Black made flights from Omaha and from Marion, Ohio, to New York to supply newspapers with pictures of President Harding's funeral procession. At the time of the Jack Dempsey-Luis Firpo fight in New York in mid-September, 1923, he outraced Bert Acosta and Le Roy Thompson, Jim Ray, and Wesley L. Smith to Chicago with photographs for the morning papers.

Similar flights had taken place much earlier. On July 2, 1921, Ross Jacobi, a pilot for the Curtiss Indiana Aircraft Company of Kokomo, flew a Curtiss "Oriole" biplane from Jersey City, New Jersey, to Chicago with pictures of the Dempsey-Georges Carpentier fight. The Sheldon Air Line of Sheldon, Illinois, owned and operated by Harold B. Snow, occasionally engaged in this type of work, in addition to exhibitions, taxi service, and school work. In May, 1923, G. J. McGowan of the Sheldon Air Line flew from Indianapolis to Chicago with pictures of the Memorial Day auto race, and in July, he flew from Shelby, Montana, to Chicago and New York with pictures of the Dempsey-Tom Gibbons match.

The Sheldon Air Line prospered until federal legislation placed firm controls on flying activities. Founded in 1920 by Harold B. Snow, an ex-Army flyer, the company built up a nationwide reputation for daring exhibitions. Snow's troupe of barnstormers, made up of O. B. Freeman and McGowan, pilots, and Forest Reese and Ray W. Meskimen, acrobats, was unrivaled for sheer skill and daring. Performing under the names of "Dick Seals" and "Mark Arnold," Reese and Meskimen devised a repertory of stunts "too daring to watch and too fascinating to turn away from." Reese's super-stunts included wing walking and the "breakaway," a leap from the end of the wing with only a 30-foot rope to prevent an earthward plunge. From the ground, the rope was not visible until the acrobat completed the leap. The "trip of death," a hand-over-hand journey on a wire from the nose of the plane to the tail and back, was another favorite with crowds in all parts of the country.

Aerial acrobatics were the most dangerous of all the many pursuits of barnstormers. On one occasion in Chicago, Reese narrowly escaped death after performing a "breakaway" when the intense cold numbed his hands, making it impossible for him to climb the 30 feet of rope back to the plane. As he started his act from the wing tip, pilot Freeman watched the jump, felt the machine drop slightly as Reese swung below, and waited for him to regain his seat in the plane. Five minutes passed without the appearance of the acrobat. Curious as to why Reese did not climb back, Freeman maneuvered until the acrobat came into view. Reese signaled that he could not climb; his hands were bleeding and numb with cold. If Freeman attempted to land, Reese would probably be crushed under the tail skid of the Curtiss "Canuck" or killed from being dragged along the ground. Only a few weeks earlier, "Tex" McLaughlin, the most famous aerial stunt man of the early 1920's, had been killed in a similar situation. Now Freeman had to find a way to save Reese. In desperation, he decided to make a landing. Carefully he hovered over the field until sure of his plans; then he sent the machine into a gentle glide, swinging into a wide circle as he neared the ground, in order to throw Reese out from under the tail skid as the plane touched down. A perfectly executed landing dragged the unfortunate acrobat only about a hundred feet. Severe cuts and bruises kept Reese out of action less than a month before he and Freeman performed in Dallas, Texas.

Other pilots throughout the state made a living from exhibitions, passenger and charter trips, and flight instruction. In 1921 there were eight fixed-base operators in the state. This number jumped to twelve in 1922 and fourteen the next year, after which fixed-base operations steadily increased in number. In the Chicago area flying activities centered around the Aero Club of Illinois flying field, and smaller fields operated by Behncke and Black, Price Hollingworth's Lincoln Tavern Field at Morton Grove, and Burmeister Field in Evanston; and fields opened by William Westlake, Stanley Wallace, and Edward B. Heath. Passenger and cross-country flights made up the largest share of business. Westlake in 1923 made 200 flights at the rate of $7.50 per passenger for a 15-minute trip, or 60 cents and $1.20 per mile, respectively, for day and night charter flights. From a field leased in Chicago Heights, the same year August Maross completed a hundred or more passenger flights in a Curtiss JN4-D, in addition to aerial advertising flights in 20 states. The Heath Airplane Company, of which Walter M. Meyer served as chief pilot, reported 1,000 flights of an average 25-minutes' duration for passengers at $5 each, plus charter flights to points in Illinois, Wisconsin, and Missouri. Rates for intercity flights were 25 cents per 100 pounds per mile for freight or 35 cents per mile for each passenger. Other flyers at Ashburn Field—Elmer Partridge, Ralph C. Diggins, Henry ("Pop") Keller, Nelson Kelly, and James Curran—offered charter service to any point in the Middle West. Partridge and Diggins also carried on extensive school work. Diggins was particularly active; he headed the Ralph C. Diggins Company at Ashburn Field until it was consolidated in 1923 with the James Levy Aircraft Company.

Outside the Chicago area, fixed-base operators appeared at an early date in Sheldon, Aurora, Moline, Springfield, and Monmouth. Except at Monmouth, all these operators limited their air transport activities to passenger and charter flights, which in some cases provided a substantial business. In 1921, the Sheldon Air Line, using four Curtiss JN4-C Canucks, completed 700 flights and carried a total of 300 passengers. Two years later, using a "Canuck," a Standard J-1, a Thomas-Morse, and a five-passenger Brequet, the same company completed 300 flights and carried a total of 200 passengers. Although the number of flights and passengers carried in 1923 fell far below the number in 1921, total mileage increased from 3,500 to 18,750, mainly because of flights between Sheldon and Louisville, Kentucky, where the Sheldon Air Line maintained a portion of its business activities.

The Aurora Aviation Company conducted passenger flights from a field adjoining Exposition Park in Aurora. Each season between 1921 and 1923, the company made 250 to 400 short passenger flights for which thrill seekers paid $10.00 for a 15-minute flight.

Before the establishment of a permanent airport by the Chamber of Commerce in April, 1926, aviation in Springfield centered around the activities of Leslie H. Smith. In 1925, Smith staged exhibitions, built airplanes, instructed students, and made passenger and intercity charter flights. His students included Earl Smith, Glenn Walling, and Smith Hawkins, all of Springfield; Bill Myers, of Kirksville, Missouri; and Joe Wright, of Altamont, Illinois. Craig Isbell, a graduate of Alex Varney's flying school in Peoria, and Gelder Lockwood opened the L. & I. Aerial Service at the Chamber of Commerce Airport in 1927 and later the same year moved to a new field southwest of the city. In 1926, Les Smith joined the staff of the Robertson Aircraft Corporation, which operated the airmail route between St. Louis and Chicago via Springfield and Peoria. In the summer of 1928 he died in a plane crash in the Ozarks while en route from St. Louis to Denver.

Every attempt to organize airline passenger and express service in the early 1920's ended in failure. Monmouth, Illinois, became one of the leading centers of aviation outside the Chicago area in 1921 when the Curtiss-Iowa Corporation established a branch of its Waterloo, Iowa, operations there. In addition to aircraft sales and service, passenger, sight-seeing, and charter flights, and student instruction, the company devised ambitious plans for the operation of a passenger and freight airline linking Chicago and Kansas City, Missouri, via Monmouth. The rate for passenger service was fixed at 15 cents per mile. Inaugurated on April 17, 1922, the airline failed to win public support, and service ended within a month. Without passenger traffic, which was virtually nonexistent, the airline was doomed to failure from the start. A somewhat similar venture was launched between Chicago and Detroit two days before the Chicago-Kansas City service opened. Eddie Stinson, one of the famous flying Stinson family, opened an express line from Ashburn Field using six-passenger Junkers JL-6 monoplanes. By June 5, Stinson had completed only three round-trip flights and a short time later abandoned the airline. A Chicago-Milwaukee airline, using Nimmo Black's airport for a southern terminal, failed to materialize. Its first flights had been scheduled some time in May, 1922. All these ventures pointed to the need for government aid, for until the American public became air-travel conscious and acquired confidence in the airplane, there was little chance of successfully operating an airline on passenger and express revenues alone.

The Curtiss-Iowa Corporation, after the failure of the Chicago-Kansas City airline, sold its Monmouth field and equipment to a group of local businessmen who took over the field under the name of Midwest Airways Corporation. I. F. Daines, Fred B. Pattee, C. W. Buchanan, and C. G. Jenks were the principal backers of the new enterprise. The new company engaged in the standard business activities of the time. Under the direction of General Manager Jenks and Chief Pilot John H. Livingston, the company prospered. In the first year alone, three planes—a five-passenger Brequet, a Standard J-1, and a Curtiss JN4-D—completed 760 flights carrying 960 passengers at the rate of $5 for a 20-minute pleasure trip or 15 cents per mile for intercity trips. Five years later, pilot Livingston took over the management of the company and expanded its operations to include airport facilities in Aurora and Waterloo, Iowa. By 1928, MidWest's principal activities were aircraft sales and student instruction, though charter flights were still made.

Passenger and charter services were available in a great many Illinois communities by the mid-1920's. Roy Pierce, a former army pilot, operated a Curtiss JN4-D near Macomb during the 1925 season. After a prosperous year, he set up a permanent field, erected a hangar, and purchased a new Swallow biplane for the next season. In 1926, the Sterling Airscape Company, Sterling, purchased a new airplane and hired Howard Coghill, of Rossville, to pilot the craft. William McBoyle conducted passenger and charter flights from Galena as early as 1926 and from Freeport beginning in 1929, remaining in business until 1931. The scope of passenger and charter flight activity in 1926 in downstate communities was revealed by the reported mileage of various companies and individual airmen. The Decatur Aircraft Company reported 25,000 miles; the Hudson Auto Aero Company, Jacksonville, 20,000; Mt. Vernon Flyers, 10,000; E. K. Campbell Airplane Company, Moline, 70,000; Varney Aircraft Company, Peoria, 75,000; and Tony Amrhein, Peoria, 30,000. Alex Varney, owner and operator of the Varney Aircraft Company of Peoria, conducted a large flight-training school and at one time attempted to manufacture airplanes.

Although the American public felt no overwhelming desire to travel by air in 1925, financiers and aviation enthusiasts, with a helping hand from the government, created the first extensive system of private airlines in the United States. The solution to the baffling problem of financing commercial air transport appeared in the form of indirect government aid. Such a policy, nearly as old as the government itself, aroused little opposition. The Post Office Department had for many years paid railroads and steamship companies for transporting the mails. Similar payments to privately operated airlines could not be questioned as outright subsidization, for such payments were for services received. This reasoning prompted Congress, in February, 1925, to enact legislation authorizing the Postmaster General to contract with private aircraft operators for airmail service.

The Kelly bill, so named in honor of its sponsor, Representative Clyde Kelly of Pennsylvania, laid the foundation upon which commercial air transport was organized and expanded in the 1920's. With the possibility of receiving up to four-fifths of the revenue from mail carried, private operators visualized the creation of successful airlines. By 1926, thousands of inquiries from tentative airline operators had poured into the Post Office, and intercity airlines were being hastily projected wherever there appeared to be a chance for profitable operation.

Although airlines were projected with the approval of the Post Office Department soon after the passage of the Kelly bill, the growth of commercial air transport had to await the enactment of regulatory legislation the following year. Unregulated commercial aviation appealed to few investors, and only on a very limited scale. The nature of air transport, particularly its inherent risks and expensive equipment, demanded the creation of commercial air travel as a big business with strong financial backing. Such investments were unlikely, however, until aviation came under effective and constructive federal control. Many government officials and businessmen, whether or not directly associated with aviation, recognized the need for federal controls, but Congress refused to act until 1926. In part, the transfer of airmail to private contractors awakened Congress to the need for legislation. Too, a number of investigations aroused the public, as well as the legislators, to the chaotic condition of military and civil aviation and to the need for federal action. More than any other single influence, General William Mitchell's one-man fight to bring about a reorganization of the military air services stimulated the agitation for regulation of civil aviation. As a result of congressional investigations, the way was cleared for the enactment of the Air Commerce Act of 1926, creating the Aeronautics Branch of the Department of Commerce.

The Kelly bill, signed by President Calvin Coolidge, February 2, 1925, defined the manner in which the Post Office Department could participate in the organization of air transport routes. This bill authorized the Postmaster General to contract with any individual, firm, or corporation for the transportation of mail by aircraft between such points as he chose to designate at a rate not to exceed four-fifths of the revenues derived from airmail; and to formulate rules, regulations, and orders necessary for the conduct of airmail routes. Under the provisions of the bill, Postmaster General Harry S. New and Second Assistant Postmaster General W. Irving Glover contracted for the private operation of twelve airmail routes totaling 5,500 miles, all of which served as feeder routes connecting with the New York-San Francisco route operated by the Post Office Department. Four of the new routes served Chicago, linking that city with St. Louis, via Peoria and Springfield; with Dallas, Texas, via Moline, Illinois, St. Joseph and Kansas City, Missouri, Wichita, Kansas, Oklahoma City, and Fort Worth; with Detroit and with St. Paul and Minneapolis, via Milwaukee and La Crosse, Wisconsin.

The Robertson Aircraft Corporation began service between St. Louis and Chicago on April 15, 1926. The company, formed in April, 1919, by William B. Robertson and located on what later became Lambert-St. Louis Airport, had won an enviable reputation for its flying service before it received an airmail contract. At the time the airmail route opened, William B. and Frank H. Robertson and Harry C. Willson were the principal officers of the firm. An angular, shy young man named Charles A. Lindbergh, a former barnstormer, served as chief pilot on the route. He was aided at first by Philip L. Love and Thomas Nelson. The Robertson company continued in business until 1931. In November, 1928, it had become a division of the Universal Aviation Corporation, and, in 1931, this company merged with several others to form American Airways, Inc.

Throughout the five years, the operations of the Robertson company had remained remarkably efficient. During 1926, when all flights were completed in the old but reliable DH-4's used so effectively by the government airmail service, Lindbergh, Love, Nelson, Leslie H. Smith, and Clyde Clevenger completed

Early exhibition pilots. Left: Art Smith; right: Mickey Mc-Guire. (*Charles A. Arens*)

Above: Aviatrix Blanche Stuart Scott in a Curtiss biplane similar to the machine which she displayed in Chicago in July, 1910. (*Walter C. Scholl*) Below: Ruth Bancroft Law seated at the controls of her Curtiss pusher-type biplane. (*Charles A. Arens*)

International Aviation Meet, Grant Park, Chicago, August, 1911. (*Paul B. Zaring*)

Above: James J. Ward's Curtiss biplane and (below) James V. Martin's biplane at the International Aviation Meet, Grant Park, Chicago, August, 1911. (*Joseph M. Pallissard*)

Above: Harry N. Atwood leaving Chicago's Grant Park enroute to Elkhart, Indiana, August 15, 1911, during his St. Louis–New York flight. (*Walter C. Scholl*) Below: Frank Kastory standing in front of C. Hartman's Curtiss-type biplane, which he piloted on exhibitions in 1911. (*Frank Kastory*)

Nineteen Hundred Twelve
Aviation Events
Chicago, U. S. A.

Under the auspices of The Aero Club of Illinois

Gordon Bennett World's Championship Aeroplane Race

September 9, Clearing, Ill.

Four Day International Aviation Meet

September 12, 13, 14, 15, Cicero Flying Field

Cross Country and Hydroaeroplane Races

(Passenger and Mail Carrying)

September 16 to 21, Grant Park, Chicago

Weekly Matinees

Every Saturday and Sunday during flying season, Cicero Flying Field

HOW TO GET THERE

To Clearing, by Automobile:—Michigan Boulevard to 55th Boulevard, west to Western Avenue, south to 63rd Street, west to 56th Avenue, south to field.

By Train:—From Polk and Dearborn Streets Railway Station.

By Street Cars:—Transfer from north and south surface lines to 63rd street car line, west.

To Cicero Flying Field, by Automobile:—Washington Boulevard to 48th Avenue, south to 22nd Street Field Entrance.

By Metropolitan Elevated Railway:—Douglas Park Branch to 52nd Avenue Station.

By Street Cars:—Transfer south onto 48th or 52nd avenue surface lines from west bound car lines.

Aerial Age, Vol. I (July, 1912)

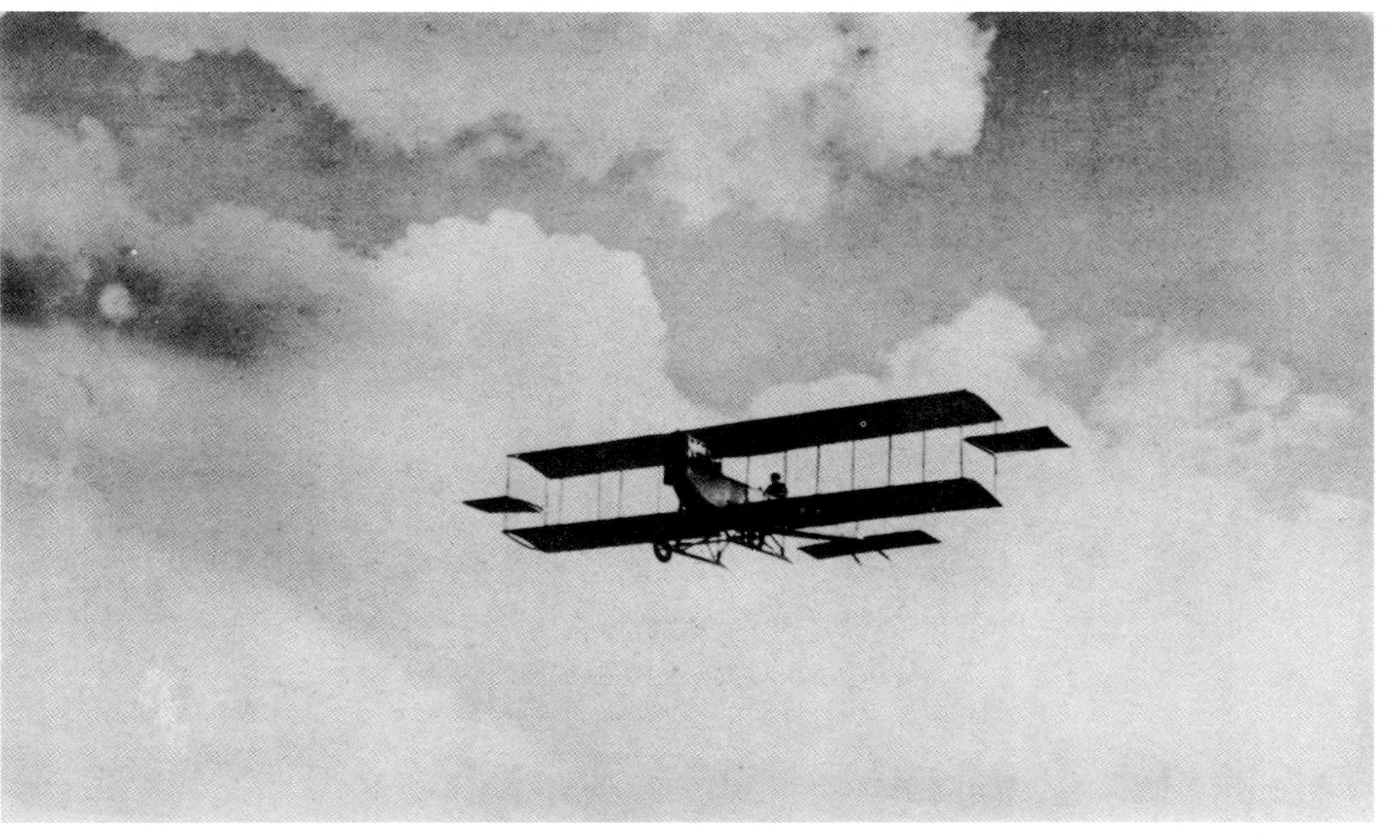

Edward A. Korn in a Benoist biplane over Anna, Illinois, July 4, 1912. (*Edward A. Korn*)

Left: Horace Kearney (left) and Edward A. Korn standing beside a Benoist biplane at the Illinois State Fair, Springfield, 1912. (*Edward A. Korn*) Right: Horace Kearney with his Curtiss biplane, picture taken from a post card carried by Kearney at the McLeansboro Aviation Meet and Street Circus, September 26-28, 1912. (*Earl H. Wellman*)

Above top: Biplane used by Roy N. Francis, San Francisco, for exhibitions in Illinois in 1914. Picture taken at Cicero Flying Field. (*Charles A. Arens*). Above center: Frank Kastory in a biplane built by Elmer Partridge and Henry "Pop" Keller, Cicero Flying Field, 1913. Below: William E. Somerville, Coal City, Illinois, seated in the cockpit of his monoplane with upturned wing-tips, 1912. (*Richard Hill*)

Above: Mills Aviators hydroaeroplane in the water, Clarendon Beach, Chicago, 1912. (*James R. Mills*) Below: Lincoln Beachey seated in a Curtiss biplane similar to the machines he used for exhibitions throughout the United States, 1911–1915. (*Earl H. Wellman*)

Above: Max Lillie, operator of the Lillie Flying School and Station, Cicero Field, Chicago, 1912–1913. (*Joseph M. Pallissard*) Below: DeLloyd Thompson (right), chief instructor of the Lillie Flying School and Station, and Harry Wells, a student, in a Wright school machine equipped with dual controls. Picture was taken at Cicero Field, 1913.

Exterior (above) and interior (below) views of the Mills Aviators factory, Chicago, owned and operated by George P. and James R. Mills, and A. P. McArthur. (*James R. Mills*)

Aerial Age, Vol. I (July, 1912)

Walter L. Brock, Chicago, winner of the world's three most important airplane races in 1914. (*Charles A. Arens*)

Above: The parasol monoplane with which W. C. Robinson established a new American record for non-stop flight, October 17, 1914. Robinson's flight from Des Moines, Iowa, to Kentland, Indiana, covered approximately 332 miles in 4 hours and 44 minutes. Below: A Curtiss flying boat similar to aircraft flown by Harold F. McCormick (C. C. Witmer, pilot) and Logan A. "Jack" Vilas, Chicago, 1913–1914. (*Charles A. Arens*)

Above: Katherine Stinson standing in front of her Partridge-Keller biplane, Cicero Field, 1915. Below left: Marjorie Stinson, in front of Charles A. Arens' biplane, Ashburn Field, Chicago, 1916. Below right: Charles Kirkham, Art Smith and Victor Carlstrom standing beside the Curtiss Model R biplane which Carlstrom piloted to New York City, November 2, 1916. On this flight, sponsored by the *New York Times*, Carlstrom set two new American speed records for distance and speed. (*Charles A. Arens*)

97.89 per cent of all scheduled flights. At that time, the Robertson company operated an early morning flight from the government field at Maywood to St. Louis and a return trip the same evening. Aside from the opening-day flights, only one plane made each trip and even then a single bag was more than enough to hold all the mail. At first, the morning flight started and the evening flight ended in darkness. The hazards of night flying, though initially of little consequence except during winter months, increased appreciably before the end of the first year because the start of the evening flight was set a quarter of an hour later to allow additional time for business mail to reach the field for the Chicago flight. On two northbound flights, Lindbergh had to ditch his plane and make an emergency landing by parachute when he was unable to find the Maywood field in heavy fogs.

In May, 1925, a group of Detroit and Chicago financiers organized National Air Transport, Inc., the first large air transport company formed in the United States. Capitalized at $10,000,000, of which $2,000,000 was paid in on the day of organization, National Air Transport planned to establish mail and express, and later passenger, service between Chicago and the Southwest. Officers of the company were Howard E. Coffin, president; Clement M. Keyes, chairman of the executive committee; Charles Lawrence, Wayne Chatfield-Taylor, and Eugene W. Lewis, vice-presidents; Carl B. Fritsche, secretary; and John M. Mitchell, Jr., treasurer. Colonel Paul Henderson, former Assistant Postmaster General, became general manager. A year after National Air Transport, Inc., came into existence, service along its 995-mile route from Chicago to Dallas opened with ten Liberty-powered Curtiss carrier pigeon biplanes.

Even before the Robertson Aircraft Corporation and National Air Transport, Inc., planes became familiar sights on the airmail field at Maywood, the Ford Motor Company had opened mail service over its Chicago-Detroit route. On April 13, 1925, a big Ford all-metal transport, the product of William B. Stout's genius, opened a private airline service between Dearborn and Chicago. When Postmaster General New contracted with private operators for the transport of airmail, the Ford company was operating an airline complete with experienced personnel and the safest planes known. In October, 1925, the Ford Motor Company received contracts for routes from Detroit to Cleveland and Chicago and, on February 15, the first contract airmail service in the United States went into operation.

The contract for a 377-mile route between Chicago and St. Paul-Minneapolis, by way of Milwaukee and La Crosse, went to a Chicago millionaire aviation enthusiast, Charles Dickinson, whose bid of 48 per cent of the revenue from mail transported doomed the venture to failure from the start. Aided by Elmer Partridge, "Pop" Keller, "Billy" Brock, Charles A. Arens, "Matty" Laird, and William A. Kidder, the last-named as manager, Dickinson equipped three Laird biplanes with Wright Whirlwind engines in preparation for inaugurating service over the route on June 7. A fourth craft, a cabin plane designed and built by Partridge, completed the equipment of the "C. D. Air Line." On the appointed day, Partridge opened the service in the cabin plane. The next day he suffered fatal injuries in a crash during a snowstorm in Wisconsin. After Partridge's death, bad luck plagued the airline, and its personnel, particularly Dickinson, soon lost interest. After two months, during which the airline piled up huge operating deficits, Dickinson asked to be relieved of his contract. The Post Office subsequently readvertised the route and awarded the contract to Northwest Airways, effective October 1, 1926.

The cancellation of Dickinson's contract for the Chicago-Twin Cities airmail route in August, 1926, induced Colonel L. H. Brittin to organize a new company to take over the route rather than allow Minneapolis and St. Paul to go without airmail service. First he interested Minneapolis, St. Paul, and Detroit financiers in the venture, and, with their financial backing, he organized Northwest Airways. Airmail service over the route commenced with three Stinson "Detroiter" cabin planes and a single Laird "Commercial" under the supervision of Brittin as general manager and Charles W. Holman as operations manager. On July 4, 1927, regular passenger service began over the line. The inaugural flight took 18 hours and included a forced landing, a terrific storm, and a great deal of skillful piloting by Holman. In the next two years, a fleet of two Ford tri-motors and two six-passenger Hamilton monoplanes shuttled passengers as well as mail over the route. By September 30, 1928, Northwest Airways had flown 459,452 miles without injury to any of 6,360 paying customers.

Although in later years passenger traffic became a prime source of revenue, the four airlines that served Chicago in 1926 began with little intention of carrying more than airmail. Almost without exception, the equipment initially installed on the routes was unsuited to passenger travel. Some companies, like the Robertson corporation, used modified DH-4's, similar to the rebuilt war-surplus craft used by the Post Office. Although more modern and speedier, the Curtiss "Carrier Pigeon" and Laird "Commercial" planes used respectively by National Air Transport and Dickinson were nevertheless unadaptable to passenger business. These and other early planes were two-place, open-cockpit ships in which the front cockpit was enclosed to form a compartment for mail bags. If an occasional passenger desired to make an intercity flight, the only available accommodation was the small, unlighted mail compartment with a mail bag for a seat. In spite of the inconvenience, some passengers were carried. Almost without exception, however, they resorted to the airmail flights only because of emergencies. Most people would have been reluctant to fly even in a luxury liner at that time. More commodious aircraft were available to airline operators; the all-metal Ford tri-motor, a favorite for many years with operators and passengers alike because of its safety record, had appeared in 1925, and Anthony Fokker had introduced a plywood tri-motor transport the same year. Eddie Stinson was producing a single-engine biplane with an enclosed cabin suitable for passenger service, as were many other manufacturers. These aircraft were not used to any large extent in 1926 simply because the public was not willing to travel by air.

In the spring and summer of 1927, the attitude of the American public toward air travel suddenly changed from outright skepticism to unbounded enthusiasm. The turning point came with Charles A. Lindbergh's solo flight across the Atlantic Ocean on May 20-21. Almost overnight, people who previously thought airplanes unsafe became aviation-conscious and looked upon air travel as both safe and efficient. This transformation was by no means universal but a sizable portion of the population was willing to travel by air; consequently, the airlines found a new source of income, though nearly all continued to carry mail.

Fortunately for the future of air transport, the Post Office Department decided to turn over the transcontinental airmail route to private operators at the very time public interest in aviation reached its peak. The Boeing Air Transport Company, a subsidiary of the Boeing Airplane Company of Seattle, took over the operation of airmail service between Chicago and San Francisco on July 1, 1927. Two months later National Air Transport added to its Chicago-Dallas route the eastern section, from Chicago to New York. The Boeing company inaugurated passenger service along with the airmail, making available for the first time airline service from Chicago to the Pacific Coast. National Air Transport, however, hesitated to establish passenger service on the New York-Chicago route, even though regular passenger service was opened between Chicago and Kansas City in 1927, with Travel Air cabin planes that could carry three passengers in addition to baggage and mail. The Boeing Airplane Company developed for its transport subsidiary the famed Boeing 40-A, a biplane with an open cockpit for the pilot and an enclosed cabin for two passengers and mail. A subsequent modification of the B40-A, the B40-B, provided two cabins, each for two passengers. In 1929, Boeing inaugurated night service with tri-motor transports between Oakland and Salt Lake City and the following year placed the big transports in service along the entire route, providing 30-hour service between Chicago and Los Angeles by way of San Francisco and the Boeing-owned Pacific Air Transport.

The Post Office Department awarded contracts for nine new airmail routes in 1927. Only one of these, between Cincinnati and Chicago, entered Illinois. T. Higbee Embry and John Paul Riddle had organized the Embry-Riddle Company as a flying school, with headquarters at Lunken Airport, Cincinnati, but during the summer of 1927 the company decided to enter a bid for a recently projected airmail route to Chicago. Its bid was accepted, and on December 7, 1927, Riddle, general manager, opened the airmail service with six Waco biplanes and a Ryan monoplane, all with enclosed cabins.

Also in 1927, the older air transport companies expanded operations to accommodate passenger traffic. The oldest of the mail carriers, the Ford Motor Company, hesitated to enter the passenger business. Although scheduled passenger service opened in August, 1926 between Chicago, Detroit, and Cleveland, Ford relied mainly upon revenue from mail to meet operating expenses. Until Ford suspended service in 1929, at which time Stout Air Services took over the routes, the Chicago-Detroit-Cleveland airline lost money, but it did not suffer a single fatality. After four years in air transport, Henry Ford closed out the route because of its burdensome expenses. During the existence of the airline, Ford's reputation and influence did much to stimulate public confidence in air travel.

Under the terms of the Airmail Act of 1925, the infant air transport industry struggled under burdensome restrictions that hindered progress and expansion. An amendment to the original act in 1926 changed the rate of compensation from a percentage of revenue to a weight system. Despite the change, routes were generally unprofitable. A ten-cent per ounce airmail postage rate did not encourage the use of available services. On August 1, 1928, after the air transport industry clamored for relief, additional legislation lowered the airmail postage rate to five cents per ounce and awarded route certificates to operators on a ten-year franchise basis. The resulting increase in the volume of airmail and the security of long-term franchises permitted the operators to build up their respective routes and engage in long-range planning. These changes did not bring about complete relief from financial distresses, however, for the various airlines continued to pile up expenses in excess of revenue. The McNary-Watres Act of April, 1930, finally provided needed relief and gave the Postmaster General authority to forge the heterogeneous airlines into an efficient system of financially stable trunk lines dedicated to the service of the air traveler as well as of the Post Office Department. By authority derived from the act, Postmaster General Walter F.

Brown located airmail routes to best serve public interest, prescribed and enforced route extensions and consolidations, dictated types of equipment to be used, and determined the compensation for carrying mail on a space-weight basis. Brown held the whip hand and the airlines had no choice but to conform to his dictates. In less than two years, he brought into existence a stabilized airline network that has served as the foundation for air transport growth and expansion to the present day.

In the five years that followed the establishment of contract airmail routes, commercial air transport in Illinois expanded at a phenomenal rate. In 1926, four companies with routes totaling 1,938 miles served Chicago and other communities in Illinois. By 1931, as the result of mergers and consolidations, virtually every route in the country was accessible through the facilities of the eight companies serving Chicago with routes totaling 5,072 miles. Four large holding companies maintained control of most of the principal airlines, and, because of their strong financial backing, provided the air transport industry with the basis for sound growth.

The strongest of the holding companies, the United Aircraft and Transport Corporation, controlled operating units in the air transport field and airplane- and engine-manufacturing companies. Formed in 1928, the United Aircraft and Transport Corporation represented one of the largest consolidations in the aviation industry to that date. Subsequent mergers and consolidations built up the company's air transport system. The acquisition of Stout Air Lines extended the Boeing system eastward to Detroit in April, 1929. Efforts were then turned toward the acquisition of National Air Transport, Inc., holder of routes from New York to Chicago and thence to Dallas. In 1930, National Air Transport came under control of the company through an exchange of stock; thus, by the close of that year, a single company controlled and operated the vital transcontinental route linking New York, Chicago, and San Francisco. Additional lines extended United's operations from Chicago to Dallas and from San Francisco to Los Angeles. On July 1, 1931, United Air Lines was created as the operating company, placing under a single management and name the airlines formerly operated by Boeing Air Transport, Pacific Air Transport, National Air Transport, and Varney Air Lines.

The Aviation Corporation of Delaware, another giant holding company, formed in 1928, vested in a single company control over a vast system of transport and manufacturing firms. Air transport lines taken over by American Airways, the operating unit of the holding company, eventually included a network 6,293 miles in length, extending from New England through the Middle West and the West to California.

The Universal Aviation Corporation, which became a subsidiary of Aviation Corporation of Delaware in 1930, was itself the product of consolidations and mergers two years earlier. More than 4,000 miles of airlines merged with Universal Airlines, Inc., operating between Cleveland, Chicago, and St. Paul-Minneapolis. The Robertson Aircraft Corporation, Northern Air Lines and Universal Air Lines were the only transport companies involved in the merger. Other companies taken over by the holding company were the Universal Air Line System Terminal Company, Midplane Sales and Transit Company, Northern Airplane Company, Air Transportation, Inc., Robertson Flying School, Inc., and Egyptian Airways, Inc. The last-named operated a flying school in Marion, Illinois. The new organization projected airlines that augmented existing routes in the Middle West and Southwest and doubled its airline mileage before merging into American Airways.

The genesis of American Airways as a leader in air transport took place in 1928, but the company did not acquire its predominance until two years later. Under the direction of Frederick G. Coburn, the loosely organized routes that made up American Airways' network gained a semblance of efficiency and order. After four years of tireless effort, Coburn, president of Aviation Corporation of Delaware, resigned to make way for the elevation of Lamotte T. Cohû, president of Air Investors, Inc., underwriters of Aviation Corporation stock. Cohû succeeded in effecting many necessary financial reforms before being ousted when E. L. Cord, president of the Auburn Automobile Company, gained control of the holding company.

In March, 1931, the Cord Corporation, then in the aeronautical field through its ownership of Stinson Aircraft Corporation and Lycoming Manufacturing Company, entered the air transport field with the organization of Century Air Lines and a subsidiary, Century Pacific Lines, Ltd. Without benefit of airmail contracts, Century Air Lines operated a system of passenger and express routes radiating from Chicago and serving Detroit, Cleveland, St. Louis, and intermediate points; Century Pacific Lines, Ltd., operated passenger lines on the Pacific Coast. By maintaining the strictest possible economy, Cord sought to underbid established operators for routes which paralleled those of his own company. He might have succeeded had not a strike by the Air Line Pilots' Association in February, 1932, focused attention on his high-handed methods, with the result that the Commerce and Post Office departments (who wanted more than cheap transportation) refused to award airmail contracts to Century Air Lines. After failing to secure a mail contract, Cord sold his unprofitable lines to Aviation Corporation for sufficient shares of American Airways stock to gain a directorship in the holding company.

The sale of Century Air Lines to Aviation Corporation paved the way for Cord's eventual control of American Airways. In the fall of 1932, when Aviation Corporation proposed to purchase certain assets of North American Aviation, the holding company for Eastern Air Transport, Cord stopped the transaction with an injunction and deliberately set out to buy control of Aviation Corporation, of which he was by then the largest single stockholder. Finally, as the result of a compromise, Cord gained control of American Airways. He placed Lester D. Seymour, former vice president of United Air Lines, in charge of American, and, under the latter's direction, the company obtained complete independence from Aviation Corporation. Its general offices were moved to Chicago, and the line prospered.

Other mergers and consolidations reshaped air transport facilities that served Illinois. Trans-World Airlines, known until 1950 as Transcontinental and Western Air, Inc., appeared in 1930 as the operating company for a consolidated group made up of Transcontinental Air Transport, Maddux Air Lines, and Western Air Express. Transcontinental Air Transport was formed in 1928 and opened the following year to provide coast-to-coast combined air and railroad service. On October 25, 1930, under a new name, Transcontinental and Western Air, this line opened mail and passenger service between New York and Los Angeles on a 36-hour schedule by way of Columbus, Indianapolis, St. Louis, Kansas City, Oklahoma City, and Albuquerque. After the completion of a lighted airway from coast to coast, planes were flown day and night. Transcontinental and Western Air inaugurated passenger service to and from Chicago on May 1, 1931.

Mail and passenger service between Chicago and a number of the larger cities in Michigan opened in July, 1928, over routes of the Thompson Aeronautical Corporation of Cleveland. In 1927 Edwin G. Thompson, president of Thompson Products Corporation of Cleveland, purchased a Laird biplane and hired veteran airmail pilot R. C. ("Tex") Marshall to pilot the ship on company business. Within less than a year, the Thompson fleet grew to six planes, which were used for sightseeing and taxi service when not engaged in business flights. The following year, in response to advertisements for bids on a proposed airmail route between Chicago and Bay City, Michigan, the Thompson Aeronautical Corporation entered the low bid. The company provided passenger, mail, and express service between Chicago, Kalamazoo, Grand Rapids, and Muskegon; Kalamazoo and Flint; Kalamazoo, Battle Creek, Jackson, Ann Arbor, and Detroit; Cleveland, Toledo, Detroit, Pontiac, Flint, Saginaw, and Bay City; and amphibian service between Cleveland and Detroit. Night airmail service began on April 1, 1929, between Cleveland and Bay City, and on May 27 between Chicago and Kalamazoo. In 1931, Thompson Aeronautical Corporation established a new operating division, Trans-American Airlines Corporation, with Marshall as president, to co-ordinate mail, passenger, and express activities serving eighteen cities in Ohio, Michigan, and Illinois. At the time of the struggle for control of American Airways, Cord bought out Trans-American Airlines Corporation and, in turn, sold a controlling interest to Aviation Corporation. Beginning January 1, 1933, the Trans-American Airlines Corporation became a part of the American Airways system. The Chicago-to-New York route, opened in 1933 by way of Detroit and Buffalo over lines pioneered by Trans-American Airlines and its predecessor, became one of the most important links in the American system. By the end of 1933 passenger service to the East Coast was augmented by a new route between Chicago and Atlanta and another between Chicago and Washington.

Eight years of development and growth were temporarily set aside on February 9, 1934, when the Post Office Department canceled all contracts with operators flying mail on routes within the United States. Postmaster General James A. Farley justified the wholesale cancellations on the ground that the contracts had been obtained through collusion and fraud during the previous administration. The operators denied the charge, and, although subsequent investigation failed to produce evidence to support the charges, the Post Office Department maintained its position. To fill the void, an executive order by President Franklin D. Roosevelt directed the United States Army Air Corps to take over the airmail.

Air Corps operations commenced February 19, 1934, and ended June 1. During that time, except for ten days (March 10-19) when mail flights were suspended to allow a reorganization of the service, Army pilots carried 768,215 pounds of mail, spent 14,745 hours in the air, and flew 1,707,555 miles. It turned out to be a disastrous experiment, costing the government 12 lives, 66 accidents, and expenses out of proportion to the cost of similar services by private operators. The average cost per mile for mail service under Army supervision soared to $2.21 compared to an average of 54 cents per mile paid to private operators during 1933. Immediately prior to the wholesale cancellation of contracts, the average rate had fallen to a record low of 42.6 cents per mile. It should be kept in mind that the Army's mail transportation was an emergency service; a more efficient organization might have reduced costs, and proper equipment and experienced personnel might have reduced loss of life. The Army did not have an opportunity to establish a more effective organization, however, for, as a result of public criticism of its service, the Post Office Department awarded new contracts to private operators in April and May, 1934.

Because Farley insisted that no airline that had been represented in the so-called "collusion" contracts of the previous administration could receive a new contract, the major air transport companies effected transparent reorganizations that gave birth to the leading airlines of the present time. No one could fail to recognize American Airlines as the former American Airways, or Eastern Air Lines as the former Eastern Air Transport. Transcontinental and Western Air, Inc., was the new name of Transcontinental and Western Air. United Air Lines, formed by a recent merger of older lines, remained untainted by the actions of its subsidiaries. The new contracts were awarded for three months, but the passage of the Black-McKellar Airmail Act nullified them within a month after they went into effect.

Mail contracts awarded between April and July, 1934, were taken up principally by the larger air transport companies. American Airlines won eight of the 33 routes turned over to private operators, including No. 7, Newark, New Jersey, to Chicago; No. 25, Washington, D.C., to Chicago; and No. 30, Chicago to Fort Worth, Texas. Its other awards included routes linking Newark, Nashville, and Fort Worth; Fort Worth and Los Angeles; Boston and Newark; Newark and Cleveland; and Cleveland and Nashville. Though operating with reduced mileage under the new system, American controlled not only the profitable southern transcontinental route but also important connecting lines serving population centers of the Middle West and East. Although Cord remained the largest single stockholder in American Airlines, he resigned in 1934, and the company came under the capable direction of C. R. Smith. Employing huge Curtiss Condor transports, and later the famous Douglas airliners, American rapidly climbed to the top rank among passenger carriers, a position it has retained for the past twenty years.

United Air Lines emerged from the cancellation period in

possession of the northern transcontinental route it had pioneered and all of its smaller lines except the Chicago-Dallas route, which went to Braniff Airways. United continued to dominate transcontinental traffic after 1934, but eventually lost ground to American Airlines and Transcontinental and Western Air, Inc., operators, respectively, of the southern and central coast-to-coast air routes. United gained a temporary edge over its competitors in 1933 by introducing twin-engine, all-metal, ten-passenger Boeing 247 airliners, offset by the appearance of Douglas DC-2's on both rival lines the following year. The leading executives of Transcontinental and Western Air, Jack Frye, Howard Hughes, and Paul Richter, all veteran pilots, seriously threatened United's grip on transcontinental traffic by pioneering high altitude or "over-weather" flying, for which they obtained the first deliveries of Boeing's excellent four-engined Stratoliners.

Northwest Airlines, reorganized from the former Northwest Airways, emerged from the contract controversy in control of the valuable Chicago-Twin Cities-Seattle route. When operation of the line resumed on June 1, 1934, Northwest began a daily flying schedule of about 5,200 miles, using Lockheed Orions and Ford tri-motors. Early the following year, a fleet of speedy Lockheed Electra transports began three round-trip flights daily between Chicago and Minneapolis-St. Paul, and one round trip daily between the Twin Cities and Seattle. Northwest also resumed operations in 1934 on its former international route between Chicago, the Twin Cities, Fargo and Pembina, North Dakota, and Winnipeg, Canada, after purchasing the line from Hanford Tri-State Air Lines.

As a result of the new airmail contracts awarded in 1934, three new companies commenced operations to and from Chicago. Although a newcomer in airmail transportation, Braniff Airways, operators of the Chicago-Dallas route, had operated a passenger line between Oklahoma City and Tulsa since 1927. For several years Paul Braniff carried on the airline business while his brother, Thomas E. Braniff, paid the expenses from the profits of a successful insurance agency in Oklahoma City. The cancellation of all mail contracts in 1934 offered them an opportunity to expand, and they were successful bidders for the Chicago-Dallas route. Thereafter, Braniff Airways expanded throughout the Southwest and eventually into Mexico and Latin America.

The second newcomer to air transport in Illinois, Pacific Air Transport, Inc., commenced operations over the Chicago-New Orleans route on June 3, 1934. On July 15 of the same year, that company, under the new name Chicago and Southern Airlines, opened passenger service over the 900-mile route with single-engine Lockheed Bellanca aircraft. Service points included Peoria, Springfield, St. Louis, Memphis, and Greenwood and Jackson, Mississippi.

Chicago and Southern Airlines enjoyed a large volume of airmail and passenger traffic in the midst of the depression because of its fortunate location. Much of its traffic constituted feeder service to the three transcontinental routes it intersected at Chicago, St. Louis, and Memphis. During Pacific Air Transport's brief venture as a non-mail-carrying passenger line between Los Angeles and San Francisco in 1933 and 1934, Carleton Putnam, dynamic founder and president of the airline, learned the futility of attempting to operate an air transport company on passenger revenues alone. Because of Postmaster General Brown's determination to build a nation-wide network of large airlines, small companies like Pacific Air Transport were denied government subsidization in the form of airmail contracts. Putnam's fledgling airline might have gone out of business in the spring of 1934 had not the cancellation of airmail contracts offered an opportunity to stave off bankruptcy. Putnam decided to go after the Chicago-New Orleans route formerly operated by American Airways. By computing operation costs with single-engine aircraft at a bare minimum, Putnam won the chance to combine airmail and passenger service the length of the potentially profitable Mississippi Valley from the Gulf to the Great Lakes.

The route from Chicago to Pembina, North Dakota, went to Hanford Tri-State Air Lines, which opened service June 1, 1934. Reorganized in 1934 with A. S. Hanford the controlling stockholder, this firm had operated air passenger service between Minneapolis and Omaha since 1928. The company sold the Chicago-Pembina route to Northwest Airlines within less than a year but retained one from St. Paul-Minneapolis to Omaha, which it had placed in operation July 3, 1934. The Omaha-Kansas City portion of the line was leased in 1934 to Rapid Air Lines. In 1936 Hanford sold his majority stock to Thomas Fortune Ryan III, and two years later a new name, Mid-Continent Airlines, removed the last evidence of Hanford's once dominant role in the company's administration. Though its routes were extended to St. Louis and Tulsa, Mid-Continent did not venture out of its original territory until 1945 when the Civil Aeronautics Board approved an extension to New Orleans. The following year the federal agency approved two new routes between Chicago and the Twin Cities, one by way of Duluth and the other by way of Milwaukee.

The termination of airmail contracts in February, 1934, prompted Congress to enact a series of acts regulating various aspects of civil aviation, particularly the activities of mail carriers. For a time Senator Hugo Black's investigating committee scrutinized the operations of all former airmail contractors. Charges of fraud and collusion against the airline operators and the previous Republican administration were proved groundless. However, because of the publicity given to the investigation, the public demanded some form of remedial legislation. Subsequently, Congress enacted the Airmail Act of 1934, which repealed all antecedent legislation affecting the transport of mail by air and made the operations of airmail contractors subject to three separate governmental agencies. The new act gave the Post Office Department authority to award contracts and to determine routes and schedules; the Interstate Commerce Commission, already overtaxed by the burden of regulating railroads, received powers to fix rates and payments for the transport of airmail; and the Department of Commerce regained ample powers for continued regulation of civil airways and licensing of airmen and aircraft—functions performed by its Aeronautics Branch since the enactment of the Air Commerce Act of 1926. On July 1, 1934, the Air Commerce Bureau of the Department of Commerce assumed the responsibilities and powers previously held by the Aeronautics Branch.

The Airmail Act of 1934 also provided for the creation of a commission to investigate all phases of aviation and to recommend legislation for more effective, constructive control of civil aviation, particularly the air transport industry. Under the very able direction of Chairman Clark Howell, assisted by Jerome C. Hunsaker, Franklin K. Law, Edward P. Warner, Albert J. Berres, and J. Carroll Cone, the Federal Aviation Commission compiled more than 100 recommendations, many of which were included in bills drafted by Senator Pat McCarran and Representative Clarence F. Lea and introduced in Congress in January, 1935. Further, the Commission recommended that Congress create a separate administrative body to regulate commercial aviation in much the same way the Interstate Commerce Commission regulated the railroads. The provision for an independent regulatory agency had been included in a bill sponsored by McCarran the previous year. During the next two years, administration and congressional leaders argued the merits of an independent agency; some, including the President, considered that the Interstate Commerce Commission was best suited to control civil air transport; others supported a separate agency. Meanwhile air transportation struggled along under inadequate legislation. Not until President Roosevelt finally consented to support the original McCarran bill did the air transport industry obtain legislation suited to its constructive growth. The Civil Aeronautics Act of 1938 placed the regulation of air transportation in the hands of an independent Civil Aeronautics Authority. In 1940, this agency was replaced by the Civil Aeronautics Administration, in the Department of Commerce, and the Civil Aeronautics Board, an independent agency.

World War II temporarily halted the expansion that, despite the depression, had characterized the air transport industry throughout the 1930's. In spite of the loss of many veteran pilots and aircraft to the military forces, the airlines carried on a near capacity business. Air travel suddenly came of age during the war years as the public turned to the sky for fast, efficient travel. The exigencies of war demanded speedy communications and the quickest possible movement of priority materials and personnel over vast distances, often halfway around the world or farther.

Important postwar developments have been the establishment of feeder-line service to supplement trunk-line routes and the extension of domestic carriers into international operations. By 1946, approximately 400 applicants for feeder-type airlines had filed requests with the Civil Aeronautics Board for certificates of public convenience and necessity required for the operation of airlines. Local and feeder-type air service was inaugurated by 14 separate airlines with Civil Aeronautics Board approval on an experimental basis between 1945 and 1950. The benefits of scheduled air transportation were thus extended to smaller cities. Such feeder-line and local service has been so effective that it is now recognized as an important and profitable part of the transport industry.

The projection of domestic airlines into the international field, where Pan-American Airways System once held a tight monopoly, came about largely as a result of the world-wide operations of Transcontinental and Western Air, American Airlines, Eastern Air Lines, and others under wartime contracts with the Air Transport Command and the Naval Air Transport Service. Juan Trippe, Pan-American's resourceful president, fought stubbornly to exclude them from his exclusive domain, but he eventually lost the fight. On July 5, 1945, the Civil Aeronautics Board awarded certificates for North Atlantic routes to Transcontinental and Western Air and American Export Airlines (American Overseas Airlines). Once Pan-American's monopoly was broken, other domestic carriers quickly entered the competition for international air business.

Local service airlines that affected air transport in Illinois were established between 1948 and 1950. Lake Central Airlines, North Central Airlines, and Ozark Air Lines established service points throughout the Middle West. For the first time hundreds of communities were directly connected with trunk-line routes at Chicago and other points. Of the three, Ozark has served the greatest number of communities in Illinois.

Lake Central, established in 1949, has served communities in Illinois, Indiana, Michigan, Ohio, and Pennsylvania. Its only service point in Illinois outside of Chicago, in 1955, was Danville. North Central Airlines serves intermediate points in Indiana and Michigan on its Chicago-Detroit route, and many Wisconsin communities on routes from Chicago to Duluth and to Minneapolis-St. Paul.

The feeder-type service throughout Illinois and four adjacent states that was originally awarded to Parks Air Lines eventually came under the control of Ozark. Certificates for routes between Chicago and Sioux City, Chicago and St. Louis, St. Louis and Paducah, and St. Louis and Indianapolis were awarded on March 31, 1948, by the Civil Aeronautics Board to Parks Air Lines, of which Oliver L. Parks, prominent aviation pioneer and founder of the internationally known Parks Air College, was president. The opening of the airline was delayed for two years while Parks sought financial support and suitable facilities along the proposed routes. Not until June, 1950, was service inaugurated between East St. Louis and Chicago, and that was put into effect solely to prevent possible license revocation. The move was unsuccessful, however, and a few months later the routes were awarded to other lines. Parks's determination to fight the revocation order in the courts led to a settlement with Ozark Air Lines, the new operator of a portion of the disputed routes. Under terms of the agreement, Ozark purchased most of Parks's equipment and gave Oliver Parks a sizable share of stock as well as three of the eight places on its eight-man board of directors.

Ozark Air Lines commenced operations on September 26, 1950. Initially, service was limited to the St. Louis-Chicago route, serving Springfield, Decatur, and Champaign. In November, the St. Louis-Quincy-Keokuk-Burlington-Moline-Peoria-Bloomington-Champaign-Danville-Indianapolis route opened, followed eleven days later by service over the St. Louis-Cape Girardeau-Paducah-Dyersburg-Jackson-Memphis route. The Chicago-Sioux City route was opened in January, 1951. Over these various routes residents of Illinois enjoyed connections with all parts of the country and were quick to take advantage of Ozark's fast, safe DC-3 service. In three years, from September, 1950, to September, 1953, nearly a quarter of a million passengers flew more than 36,000,000 passenger miles over Ozark's routes without a single accident to passenger or crew. In 1954, Ozark's transports carried 156,391 passengers, a considerable increase over the average for the three previous years.

The end of World War II and the removal of restrictions on air transport operations opened a boom period of expansion unknown since the late 1920's. Since 1945, all the major airlines have doubled and redoubled passenger traffic, and routes have been expanded through local service extensions, consolidations, and mergers. Even more significant advances in passenger traffic and route extensions have resulted from the penetration of domestic airlines into the international field. As a result of international expansion by domestic and foreign air transport companies, Chicago has become a great center of international as well as domestic air travel.

The greatest strides in the field of international air transportation in the 1945–1955 decade have been achieved by Trans-World Airlines, a new name for Transcontinental and Western Air. In July, 1946, Transcontinental and Western Air expanded from 7,700 miles to some 25,000 miles as a result of awards of routes stretching from New York to Europe, the Middle East, Africa, India, and Ceylon. In keeping with the greater scope of its operations, the company in 1950 adopted its new name, which permitted retention of the familiar initials "T.W.A." For both domestic and international service, Trans-World Airlines set the pace for the industry by adopting 51-passenger super-transports, the famous Lockheed Constellations. This ship was conceived in 1939 but was produced exclusively for the military services until 1945. In 1949, the late Ralph S. Damon resigned from American Airlines to take over Trans-World Airlines' operations. Since that time, the company's routes have increased to 33,000 miles, extending as far east as Shanghai, and its passenger traffic has grown to 4,000,000 annually. Trans-World Airlines now serves 60 American cities from coast to coast and 21 cities in Europe and other parts of the world.

American Airlines entered the international air transport field by purchasing control of American Export Airlines. This company, organized in 1937 by the American Export Line of steamships, began North Atlantic air service in 1940 under a temporary certificate. Pan-American protested against this invasion of its monopoly in international service but succeeded only in forcing the American Export Line to give up control of the airline. The latter continued operations on a temporary basis until awarded a permanent certificate in 1945. Legal action ended when American Airlines purchased a controlling interest in the firm and incorporated American Export Airlines into its own system under the name American Overseas Airlines. By this purchase, American added to its vast domestic routes an overseas route that served most of the principal cities of Europe.

Beginning in 1946, the major airlines gave Chicago direct connections with cities on four continents. In 1946, Braniff, Chicago and Southern, and Eastern obtained permission to extend their routes into Latin-American countries. In the same year, Northwest Airlines received a certificate for service to the Orient by the Great Circle route through Anchorage, Alaska, and Shemya in the Aleutians, to Tokyo, Shanghai, Seoul, and Manila. Northwest's service to Anchorage from Seattle began September 1, 1946, and from Minneapolis-St. Paul on January 2, 1947; on the latter date, flights were also inaugurated to the Orient. United Air Lines entered the international field in 1947 with the opening of service between San Francisco and Honolulu. By 1955, international operations from Chicago had been greatly expanded by the addition of direct service to other countries over foreign airlines, particularly Royal Dutch Airlines (KLM), Air France, and Scandinavian Air Lines.

Among the thirteen scheduled air carriers in the United States, the four serving Illinois, Trans-World Airlines, American Airlines, Eastern Air Lines, and United Airlines, control the greatest unduplicated route mileage and carry the largest number of passengers. Each of these companies carried more than three million passengers in 1953 over routes aggregating more than 65,000 miles. Four other companies—Braniff, Capitol, Delta-C. & S., and Northwest—each carried a million or more passengers during the same year. American Airlines has retained its leadership in passenger service for nearly 25 years; its total scheduled passengers flown in 1953 fell just short of six million. Eastern Airlines, second-ranking passenger carrier in 1953, reported approximately four and three-quarter million scheduled passengers.

Local service airlines, since their organization after World War II, have enjoyed an era of prosperity similar to that of the larger companies. Lake Central, North Central, and Ozark, the only three of the fifteen companies in operation in the United States that serve Illinois, flew a total of 6,802 miles of unduplicated routes and carried a total of 398,419 passengers in 1953. Since that time, local service flights have increased appreciably in response to a growing volume of passenger traffic.

The airlines have served an ever-increasing proportion of the traveling public in the past thirty years. The rapid growth of the industry is reflected in the expansion of passenger and air freight business, especially in the 1945–1955 decade. An indication of the airlines' growth can be seen in the operations of American Airlines, which in the early years of air transport carried a million passengers in approximately ten years. The second million passenger mark was passed in less than three more years, and the third in slightly more than a year. Other lines have experienced similar increases in passenger traffic. Trans-World Airlines, for example, has carried approximately 25,000,000 passengers since Western Air Express, its predecessor, commenced passenger and mail service 30 years ago.

The large volume of business conducted annually by both trunk-line and local service airlines is an outgrowth of increasing public confidence in air travel and recognition of its advantages. Public opinion, in turn, has been shaped and molded by developments within and without the air transport industry. Constructive regulation and supervision of the airlines by federal and state agencies, coupled with the industry's deliberate policy of fostering safe, efficient service at reasonable rates, has enabled air travel to gain over rival modes of transportation. Trunk-line air passenger miles, which in 1948 equaled approximately one-half of first-class railroad passenger miles, were about 70 per cent greater than Pullman-type traffic in 1953 and equaled about one-half of total railroad passenger traffic (excluding commuter service). A big factor in this increase has been reduced-fare operations in the form of family, coach, and tourist fares at savings of as much as 50 per cent when compared with first-class air fares. Superior equipment and unexcelled personnel have also contributed to the shaping of public opinion. In recent years, a variety of air transports ranging from the 40-passenger Convair 340 to the larger Lockheed 1049-C Super Constellations and Douglas DC-6B's and DC-7's have offered speed, safety, luxury, and economy to the air traveler. A decrease in the accident rate to 0.48 fatalities per 100,000,000 passenger miles in 1953 reflects in part the use of such improved ground facilities as instrument and radar-controlled landing devices. The big increase in local service business in Illinois since 1948 has come about largely because of local, state, and federal co-operation in the construction and improvement of airports which can accommodate transport planes of the DC-3 class.

Further gains may be achieved in the future if, as expected, small twin-engine craft and helicopters are utilized for passenger and mail service from communities having excellent but small commercial airports. Initial successes in this direction have been achieved by Illini Airlines of Sterling with scheduled passenger service daily between Sterling-Rock Falls and Meigs Field, Chicago, in twin-engine Piper Apache aircraft. Another possibility lies in the adoption of a passenger schedule by Helicopter Air Service, operator of a 1,200-mile route daily through 40 Chicago-area communities. At the present time, Helicopter Air Service's Bell 47-D helicopters are used exclusively for transporting mail.

If the past and present are a reliable indication of the future, residents of Illinois can anticipate a wide extension of airline service in the 1955–1965 decade. The most significant advances will be made by existing lines. Such recent developments as the Piasecki YH-16 helicopter, capable of carrying 35 to 40 passengers, and convertiplanes, now undergoing tests, may bring mail service to more hundreds of communities in the next few years. The passenger-carrying helicopter seems especially suited to commuter traffic in the Chicago and East St. Louis areas. But whatever the future trend of air transport, the long-range outlook for the industry is a bright one. The potential for unlimited expansion exists; the air transport industry and interested local communities need only to exploit it.

9

EXPANSION OF AVIATION: AIRPORTS, 1919–1955

When United States military forces were demobilized in 1918, thousands of young men in new civilian clothes chose not to abandon the flying for which they had been trained in the Air Service. Many former military aviators who had experienced the thrill of flying found nothing in the ordinary business and industrial enterprises of 1918 that would permit them to utilize the skills acquired in the service; consequently, they turned to aviation, purchased war-surplus aircraft, and began making a living by flying. Many former military aviators joined the ranks of itinerant flyers or "gypsies" so familiar throughout the United States during the early 1920's. It was a hard, lean, nomadic type of existence, one that lured the itinerant flyer from city to city and from state to state in search of business. Stops were frequent and brief. If the demand for short passenger flights or stunts was good, the "gypsy" often remained in one place until business dropped off, then loaded his meager possessions into the front cockpit and set out in search of business elsewhere.

The "gypsy" performed both a service and a disservice to aviation in general, but in the final analysis the former far outweighed the latter. On the credit side, it must be said that the "gypsy" spread the gospel of aviation throughout the country.

He was usually a fanatic in his faith in the airplane and the future of air travel; consequently, wherever he conducted business, he passed on his views to others. But critics loudly decried the inadequate equipment of the itinerant and charged that he undermined public confidence in air travel. While the charges were justified in some cases, they should not have been hurled indiscriminately at all itinerants, some of whom worked earnestly to avoid accidents. In three years (1921–1923), 419 accidents involving 196 fatalities were attributed to the itinerants, whose ranks numbered approximately 500 to 600. In the same period, 125 fixed-base operators throughout the country reported 51 accidents with only 25 fatalities. A detailed analysis of the reports revealed that the majority of accidents among itinerants resulted from deficient flying skill; faulty aircraft, engines, or accessories; or inadequate landing facilities. Such problems did not usually face the fixed-base operator, whose business depended largely upon establishing and maintaining public confidence. Thus, the case against the itinerant flyer was stated; but the figures ignore the fact that the "gypsy" was a pioneer and that, good or bad, he was all that was known of aviation in many sections of the country for several years.

In time, the itinerant flyer virtually passed from the scene; commercial aviation assumed respectability based on permanent fields, shops, hangars, and repair facilities. Itinerant pilots in Illinois after 1924 or 1925 generally located at semi-permanent airfields, often remaining in a single community throughout the spring, summer, and fall flying season but turning to other occupations or moving southward with the advent of winter. For several years before the regulations of the Aeronautics Branch of the Department of Commerce ended the abuses of the "gypsy" flyers, the establishment of fixed-base operations in Illinois tended to stabilize and direct aviation along constructive lines. Numerous landing fields appeared in Illinois as early as 1919, but only four were established as permanent facilities with adequate hangars, regular attendants, and maintenance and repair facilities. These four fields—two military, one airmail, and one commercial—deserved the name "airport"; 129 unimproved landing fields were at best only emergency facilities. By 1926, the number of landing sites in the state had grown to 246, an increasing proportion of which were permanent, improved airports and landing fields. Ten were operated and maintained, at least in part, by municipalities or civic agencies; 15 were privately owned commercial airports which offered maintenance and repair services of varying extent. Nine so-called "emergency" fields were operated and maintained by the Post Office Department along the transcontinental airmail route, and 197 were privately maintained as temporary landing fields. By 1926, Illinois ranked third in the nation in number of airports and landing fields. It held the same rank in 1955.

In the post-World War I period, the landing field, as distinguished from the airport, was generally a temporary facility with no more than makeshift hangars and buildings, if any. Almost all of the landing fields opened in Illinois between 1919 and 1926 remained in operation no longer than a year or two. In many instances, the so-called landing fields were simply public or private golf courses, or vacant lots on the edge of communities. Sometimes local civic associations erected signs and markings for the fields—others could not be distinguished from the air. In Joliet, Pontiac, and Sterling, vacant lots adjacent to the city limits were designated as landing fields in 1920. The Sterling Association of Commerce marked the local field with the word "Sterling" in 40-foot letters on a broad roof near the field. During the same year, the Carbondale Rotary Club considered a proposal to install air-markings on a field at the north edge of the city. Elsewhere, golf courses—like the public links at Champaign and Colonel Frank L. Smith's private course at Dwight—served as local landing fields.

Aside from two nearly inactive military fields, there were in Illinois in 1919 only two recognized airports—Ashburn Field and Grant Park Air Mail Field, both in Chicago. The older and busier of the two was Ashburn Field on South Cicero Avenue between 79th and 87th streets. Elmer Partridge and Henry "Pop" Keller operated an aircraft manufacturing plant and flight training school at the field from the time it was first opened by the Aero Club of Illinois in 1916 until Partridge died in an airplane crash in Wisconsin ten years later. In 1920, Ralph C. Diggins opened the Diggins School of Aviation at Ashburn and continued to train pilots at the rate of 15 or 20 a month until the school merged with the James Levy Aircraft Company in 1923. Levy continued the operation of the flight training school in conjunction with a plant for modifying war-surplus aircraft for civilian pilots. Diggins, after selling out, became a vice-president of the Chicago Air Park Company, which operated an 80-acre flying field at 63d Street and 48th Avenue. The company had five ships that were engaged in general aviation business—flight instruction, passenger and charter flights, aerial photography, and mapping.

In 1925, Matty Laird left the E. M. Laird Company of Wichita, manufacturers of the famed Laird Swallow. He returned to Chicago and opened the E. M. Laird Airplane Company at Ashburn Field. In the next five years he built Commercial biplanes, renowned for reliability, and speedy racers, which Charles W. ("Speed") Holman and Ed Ballough piloted to many honors in racing events throughout the United States between 1925 and 1930.

Many other Chicago aviators made Ashburn Field their flying headquarters during the 1920's. In addition to student flyers, many sportsmen and professional pilots flew regularly from the field. Field manager Gordon R. Thomas and veteran hangar chief Johnnie Metzger frequently served such outstanding pilots as Joe and Mike Cafferallo, O. R. Younge, Art Phillips, William P. Burns, Dallas M. Speer, La Pierre Cavender, James Curran, William Westlake, Stanley Wallace, William Worden, Bert D. Burley, and many others. Ashburn Field remained in operation as a privately owned commercial airport until 1949 and continued as a private airport (restricted landing area) until 1951, at which time the remaining members of the Aero Club of Illinois sold the land to make way for a residential and business area.

In 1920, after remaining in Grant Park for two years, the airmail terminal of the Post Office Department was moved to Checkerboard Field at the edge of Maywood. David L. Behncke and Bert R. J. Hassell had opened this field in 1919 and used it as a shipping center from which they delivered clothes to retail merchants for Alfred Decker & Cohn, Chicago clothing manufacturers. When the clothing company discontinued airplane delivery service in 1920, Behncke bought its two Curtiss Jennies and equipment and, together with Bert J. Blair and Lutz Myers, operated the field as a commercial airport. Three years later, Behncke sold the field to Wilfred Alonzo Yackey, a former military and airmail pilot. From 1923 until Yackey's death in an airplane crash five years later, the Yackey Aircraft Company and Checkerboard Field were the center of aircraft manufacturing activities in the Chicago area. The company specialized in rebuilding war-surplus airplanes for civilian use, particularly large French-made Brequet bombers, which Yackey converted into five-place transports for the growing charter-flight business among fixed-base operators in the Middle West. The Brequet, marketed under the name Yackey Transport, was a popular craft with airmen engaged in passenger flights because of its high load capacity, top speed of 125 miles per hour, and remarkably slow landing speed. The Yackey Sport, a small two-place biplane, was popular with sportsmen-aviators in the Chicago area and the Midwest. A number of Chicago pilots, including O. R. Younge, Art Phillips, and Mike Cafferallo, piloted Yackey ships. Shortly after Yackey's death, operations at Checkerboard Field ceased, and the once active airport became a part of the Cook County forest preserve.

In 1921, a year after moving its terminal to Checkerboard Field in Maywood, the Post Office Department opened a new airmail field across First Avenue on the grounds of Walter Hines Hospital. At that time, the repair depot formerly located at Bustleton, Pennsylvania, was moved to the Maywood airmail field, and the following year the airmail warehouse was transferred to Maywood from Newark, New Jersey. Until December, 1927, at which time all airmail operations were transferred to Chicago Municipal Airport, the Maywood field served as the Chicago terminal for the government-operated transcontinental route. Beginning in April, 1926, the field also served as terminal for the many airmail routes conducted between Chicago and distant cities by private contractors.

More than a dozen commercial airports, municipal and private, were established in or near Chicago by 1926. Chicago Municipal Airport, now known as Midway Airport, was officially opened May 8, 1926, although it was not completed until two years later. Along the northern and western limits of the city, mostly in adjoining communities, numerous small, privately owned commercial facilities appeared as early as 1921. In that year, Nimmo Black leased a 50-acre airport on which he built a large hangar to house seven machines. Three years later, Black closed the airport when the land was sold and portions of it subdivided for residential buildings. However, Edward B. Heath, president of the Heath Airplane Company, used a part of the field for student training and passenger flights during the spring and summer of 1924 before moving to another location east of Park Ridge on River Road near Touhy Avenue. The Park Ridge site remained in operation until shortly after Heath's death in a plane crash in 1931, at which time the company was dissolved and the airfield abandoned. To the south, on Irving Park Road east of the Des Plaines River, the Western Airplane Corporation of Chicago opened the Chicago Flying Club Field in 1925. Farther north, Lincoln Tavern Aviation Field, near Morton Grove, and Guthier Flying Field, near Mt. Prospect, were centers of aviation activity, the former dating from 1921 when opened by Price Hollingworth, and the latter from 1925 when opened by Roy Guthier. Guthier's field later became the site of Palwaukee Airport. Burmeister Field, located east of Niles, opened in 1923 for a single season. On the south side of Chicago, Ogden Park Field, operated and maintained by the Ogden Park Flying Club, opened about 1925. Three years later, Russell C. Mossman established a flying field at 95th Street and Western Avenue in Chicago Heights. Both the Ogden Park and Chicago Heights fields were used for several years.

Wilson Airport in Schiller Park remained in continuous operation from 1922 until 1945. Max Schusin, a former German military aviator, and Stanley Wallace, a Chicago flyer, opened the field in 1922 with surplus military planes. Wallace was in charge of the field until 1926, at which time Ralph Wilson, another

Chicagoan, took over and changed the name to Wilson Airport. In 1927, Wilson sold the field to Greer Airways, a subsidiary of the Greer School of Aviation, operators of two other fields in the Chicago area at that time. The firm operated the field as Greer Airways Field No. 2 during that flying season. Its name reverted to Wilson Airport the following year, when it was purchased by Roy C. Wilson. Wilson died in 1933 as the result of an accident while instructing a student, but Mabel K. Wilson kept the field going until 1945. Although she had taken up flying in 1927, Mabel Wilson did not solo until July 14, 1934. She won her private and limited commercial license in 1935 and a transport license in March, 1937. From Wilson Airport she gave flying instruction and made passenger flights. She also engaged in the aeronautical activities of the Illinois Chapter of the "Ninety-Nines" and the Chicago Girls Flying Club. When Wilson Airport closed in 1945 to make room for a residential building project, Mabel Wilson moved to Elmhurst Airport, where she instructed "G.I." students under the veterans' education program for a time before retiring from aviation.

By 1925, when the use of private airmail carriers seemed imminent, Chicago faced the problem of securing adequate airport facilities. The government airmail field was too small and in a poor location. Ashburn Field, the only other airport large enough to warrant development, was in a fine location but was too wet for year-round service. The best solution appeared to be a municipally operated airport. At the urging of the Chicago Air Board, an advisory group created several years earlier by the Association of Commerce, the city of Chicago created a municipal airport, owned, operated, and maintained by the Bureau of Parks, Playgrounds, and Bathing Beaches. Although the new airport was officially opened in 1926, the formal dedication was delayed until December 13, 1928, following the completion of all field and administrative facilities. All airmail services into and out of Chicago (with the exception of Ford Air Transport, which had its own field near Lansing) were transferred to the Municipal Airport in December, 1927, and the Government Air Mail Field in Maywood was then restricted to limited commercial use.

Chicago Municipal Airport consisted originally of a 300-acre tract, oblong in shape, of which only the east half was developed. When completed in 1928, the field had nearly two miles of "modern" cinder runways, the longest 3,600 feet in length and 186 feet wide. Buildings on the field included an office for John A. Casey, superintendent of operations, a small passenger station, and offices and hangars for the various companies which operated from the field. On the southeast portion of the field, National Air Transport, Boeing Air Transport, Robertson Aircraft, Aviation Service and Transport Company, and the 33d Division of the Illinois National Guard maintained hangars and offices. On the south side, Universal Air Lines and Northwest Airways shared one hangar, and Grey Goose Air Lines, Embry-Riddle, and Standard Oil Company, another. Thompson Aeronautical Corporation and Interstate Air Lines, the only other companies that handled airmail from the field, did not have separate hangars at that time.

An ever increasing flow of air traffic into and out of Chicago soon emphasized the need for enlargement of the new field. Also, large, heavy airliners, Boeing 247's and 147-D's and Douglas DC-2's and DC-3's, which appeared in the mid-1930's, required long, surfaced runways. The Chicago Belt Line Railroad track, which marked the northern boundary of the field, blocked possible expansion to an unused tract of land. Relocation of the railroad in 1934 cleared the way for the extension of runways and construction of additional facilities to accommodate the largest airliners, making possible the development of the field as the world's busiest airport.

Outside the Chicago area, airports appeared in numerous communities during the mid-1920's. In 1919, two former army flyers from Iowa, E. K. ("Rusty") Campbell and Roy McElvain, set up barnstorming operations near Prospect Park in Moline in a farm pasture—the city's first landing field. Soon thereafter, Gustaf DeSchepper, a flying instructor at Wallace Field, Bettendorf, Iowa, formed a partnership with Wesley L. Smith of Geneseo, Illinois, for the operation of an airport on the Weaver farm on Colona Avenue. With a Jenny purchased by DeSchepper, Smith began training students at Moline's first airport in

1922. Floyd Ketner, Dr. C. C. Sloan, and Al Hedlund were the first residents of Moline to learn to fly at the local airport.

In November, 1922, DeSchepper, Ketner, and Sloan formed a partnership and leased 30 acres of Franing Field, now a portion of Quad-City Airport, which Smith managed until he decided to go East the next year. Before the new flying season opened, the partners invited Campbell to return to Moline to operate Franing Field. Campbell and Roy T. Quimby put the field in order during the inactive winter months and returned to Moline the following spring to manage operations. More hangars and planes were added that year, and the partners obtained a lifetime lease for the small field.

The creation of the Chicago-Dallas airmail route in 1926 gave Moline and Franing Field the opportunity to acquire airline connections. Campbell and the Rev. J. B. Coleman persuaded the Moline Chamber of Commerce to offer National Air Transport the use of the airport and a new $6,000 hangar in return for daily airmail connections with Chicago, Dallas, and intermediate points. Daily flights each way over the route, with stops in Moline, began on May 12, 1926. The airline's services multiplied rapidly, leading to passenger service between New York, Chicago, and Kansas City in 1928. That same year, the Curtiss-Wright Flying Service purchased the field, placing it under the management of Campbell. Later, when Campbell became division chief of the Curtiss-Wright Flying Service, the management of the Moline base went to Frank Le Mann.

In 1935, the city of Moline purchased the airport from Curtiss-Wright. With the aid of the Works Progress Administration, the city expanded the airport by clearing 205 acres of ground and constructing eight runways, each 3,000 to 4,000 feet in length. A combination restaurant, service station, and office was also added. By the time this work was completed in 1937, construction costs had soared to $629,000, of which local funds amounted to $165,000; at the end of 1938, airport expenditures over a four-year period totaled approximately $800,000. The following year, Moline residents approved a $175,000 bond issue to provide for completion of the airport and the construction of a large building designed to provide hangar space for small planes, offices for federal and city agencies, a weather bureau station, and offices for United Air Lines officials. No further improvements were made until the end of World War II, at which time a local planning group sponsored by the Moline Chamber of Commerce rallied support for expansion of the airport to a metropolitan-type Class IV port.

In less than three years after Lindbergh's 1927 flight across the Atlantic, at least 39 airports were opened in as many communities; approximately one-fourth of this number were still in operation in 1940; and three remain active at the present time. The Moline Quad-City Airport has been in continuous operation on the same location since 1922. The first section of Chicago Municipal Airport opened in 1926 is still in use as a part of Chicago Midway Airport. Airports opened in 1927 and still in operation at the same location are Aurora Airport; Machesney Airport, Rockford; Ford Airport, now Lansing-Hammond Airport, Lansing; and Springfield Airport (Southwest).

Aurora Airport, though opened in 1927, did not begin operation as a commercial airport until 1928, when it was taken over by the Midwest Airways Corporation of Monmouth under the direction of John H. Livingston. On the 93-acre field located next to Exposition Park, Livingston built a hangar from which he operated Aurora Airways, a subsidiary of the Monmouth concern. In 1932, Livingston sold out to Paul Thornberg, who managed the field for a year before turning it over to Ralph Swaby, who also remained only a year. In 1935, Ernest H. Spiller and W. E. Thatcher, operators of the Fox Valley Flying Service, set up their equipment on the Aurora field; Thatcher continued running the airport as manager of the Fox Valley Flying Service until 1942. At that time James F. Bird took over the management of the company. In March, 1945, Spiller and Peter L. Julius assumed control of the company and since then have continued operating the field.

Southwest Airport in Springfield has been in continuous operation since 1927. Craig Isbell managed the airport from that time until February, 1955. Isbell and J. Gelder Lockwood opened the L. & I. Aerial Service in 1927 on the Chamber of

Commerce airport near Bradfordton. The latter airport had opened in April of the previous year as the Springfield terminal for airmail service over the St. Louis-Chicago route. In the autumn of 1927, the L. & I. Aerial Service moved from the Bradfordton field and, with L. B. Van Meter, established a new airport 4½ miles south of Springfield. Originally confined to 37 acres, the airport was enlarged to 107 acres the following spring. The expansion was financed with the help of the Springfield Chamber of Commerce in anticipation of transferring the airmail service to the new field, and, in the fall of 1928, Universal Airlines opened daily mail and passenger service from Southwest Airport. Until 1933, the Springfield Aviation Company (formed by Lockwood and Isbell in 1929 to succeed the L. & I. Aerial Service, and Van Meter) operated the airport, the only one in Springfield. The city of Springfield leased the field in December, 1933, but the actual operation remained in the hands of the Springfield Aviation Company. City and federal funds, the latter provided by the Civil Works Administration, produced needed improvements, including two shale runways, a system of taxi strips, fences, walks, and parking areas, which make the field one of the best small airports in central Illinois.

During the late 1930's, commercial airlines serving Springfield began to find it difficult to utilize Southwest Airport with their larger, heavier aircraft. American Airlines used huge Curtiss Condor twin-engine craft, Stinson tri-motors, and single-engine Vultees until 1938, then DC-2's and eventually DC-3's. As a result, in November, 1938, the stop at Springfield had to be taken off the Chicago-St. Louis-Memphis flight. Similarly, Chicago and Southern Airlines eliminated Springfield from its schedule the next spring after changing from Stinson tri-motors to Lockheed "Electras" and Douglas DC-3's. Springfield remained on the route structure of both airlines, but the service was not reinstated because the runways were not extended. Two paved highways and a railroad surrounded the field on three sides, making expansion impractical if not impossible. As early as 1938, the city of Springfield had sought federal and state aid for the construction of an airport that could handle large airliners. Nothing came of this effort, however, until 1945.

At that time a municipal airport authority, approved by referendum, began the construction of Capital Airport north of the city on the plateau where the first airmail field had been located nearly twenty years earlier.

A former Kewanee barnstormer, Fred L. Machesney, well-known operator of Machesney Airport in Rockford, has the distinction of being the oldest airport operator on a single location in Illinois. He established his present airport in June, 1927, after operating airports in Kewanee and Rockford during the three previous years. A one-time motorcycle racer, he started flying in 1919 in Sikeston, Missouri, after ten hours' instruction, of which more than half were solo cross-country flights. After returning to Kewanee, he worked for nearly five years before saving $1,000 with which to buy a second-hand Curtiss Jenny. As soon as he had a plane, he established an "airport" in a convenient pasture. Like other pilots of that time, Machesney barnstormed, carried passengers, and distributed handbills over cities to make a meager living and to keep flying. While dropping handbills over Rockford for a local business house in 1925 —one of the 97 similar tasks he performed that season—Machesney first saw from the air the community he was to make aviation-conscious. In June, 1926, he moved to Rockford and opened an airport on the Miller farm on North Second Street about half a mile south of the present site of Machesney Airport.

In June, 1927, Machesney opened a new airport, which has remained in operation in the same location since that time. A five-year lease on a 130-acre tract of land lying between North Second Street and Rock River provided ample room for what was then Rockford's largest commercial airport. At that time, Thomas Van Stone and Elmer Etes operated Blackhawk Airport near Loves Park, south of Machesney's field. The operation of an airport, Machesney learned, was an uphill struggle, especially during the lean years of the 1930's. To meet expenses he regularly barnstormed at fairs and picnics in the summer, and even then fell behind in his rent. During the period 1930–1933, the Chamber of Commerce extended limited financial aid so that the airport could be used by Northwest Airways after

Rockford voters turned down a proposal to convert the field into a municipal airport. About half the funds promised by the Chamber of Commerce remained unpaid, but Northwest Airways used the airport as its Rockford terminal for 38 months. After barely hanging on during the depression years, Machesney enjoyed more prosperous times when the wartime training program for pilots went into effect. Between 1939 and 1944, he trained 1,139 military and 2,000 civilian students. The Veterans' Administration flight training program brought about an enlargement of the instruction program in the postwar years. In 25 years, the airport played host to 23,800 visiting aircraft; and the airport's own planes—more than 100 in all—flew 81,213 hours or 8,121,300 air miles and carried 76,000 passengers. During the same 25 years, Fred Machesney flew 77,330 hours or 7,633,000 miles as a part of his teaching or on other airport business.

In the central and southern part of the state, airports were less numerous and generally less prosperous than in the north—particularly in the Chicago area. There were, of course, notable exceptions, such as St. Elmo, Marion, and East St. Louis. The development of aviation in the state reflects the distribution of trained aviators. Although reliable statistics were not recorded until after the creation of the Aeronautics Branch of the Department of Commerce in 1926, available sources for the early 1920's indicate that the majority of aviators in Illinois resided in the Chicago area; the northern portion of the state contained far more than half—perhaps as many as three-fourths—of all aviators in Illinois. Only in the 1945–1955 decade did the distribution become more nearly equalized, with northern Illinois still ahead because of the aeronautical activity in the Chicago area.

By 1927, airports had begun to appear in greater numbers in downstate counties. At St. Elmo, Smith Aviation Field, opened that year by Dr. W. E. Smith, became a center of aviation activity because of its strategic location on the Indianapolis-St. Louis airway. This field remained in continuous operation until 1952. The Egyptian Transportation System opened an airport at Marion in May, 1926, and gave student instruction, charter-flight service, and aircraft sales and services for nearly four years. Universal Aviation Corporation added the Marion airport to its nation-wide chain of flight schools in 1928. Two years later, however, when Fred C. Valentine took over the field, it was all but abandoned. Valentine Air Service operated the field until the city of Marion leased it in the early 1930's in order to participate in federal relief airport programs. With federal funds, the city laid permanent tile to drain the field and constructed runways of mine refuse and cinders. Valentine continued to manage the airport and to operate the Valentine Flying Service until 1954, at which time he moved to the newly constructed Marion-Herrin Airport. The old airport, better known by the name "Macarin Airport," was then closed.

One of the oldest and most active airports in the state opened in East St. Louis in April, 1928, as a training field for Parks Air College, the forerunner of Parks College of Aeronautical Technology of St. Louis University. Oliver L. Parks, founder and for many years president of Parks Air College, moved the small school to the East St. Louis field from Lambert-St. Louis Airport. Since its move to Illinois, the Parks school has developed into one of the leading aviation technical training centers in the United States. Its more than 3,000 graduates now serve in key positions throughout the aviation industry.

In addition to the school airport, Oliver L. Parks has owned or operated Parks Metropolitan Airport at East St. Louis since 1940. The Curtiss-Wright Flying Service constructed and operated the field as Curtiss-Steinberg Airport in 1929, as one of a chain of airfields that company built in all parts of the United States. In the mid-1930's, the Curtiss-Wright Flying Service leased the field to C. R. Wassel, who maintained a flying service there until 1940, at which time Parks acquired temporary use of the field for training Air Corps personnel. When Parks released the field in July, 1944, it reverted to Wassel's control for a brief time but was soon taken over by the Missouri Institute of Aeronautics of East St. Louis, under the operation of its subsidiary, Parks Aircraft Sales and Service. Subsequently, Parks Aircraft Sales and Service obtained outright ownership of the field, which was renamed Parks Metropolitan Airport. Although still owned by Parks, the airport has been operated by Mel Walston and Walston Sales and Service, Inc., Alton, since 1948.

In the middle of the depression decade of the 1930's, the federal government, in conjunction with various relief agencies, launched a nation-wide airport construction program designed to expand existing facilities to a point adequate for serving the nation's licensed pilots and registered aircraft. In Illinois, the Civil Works Administration and Works Progress Administration financed eleven airport improvement projects, of which only six were completed. The airport improvement projects of the federal relief agencies marked the beginning of municipal airport development. The expansion and improvement of Chicago Municipal (Midway) Airport, a ten-million-dollar project, produced one of the finest airports in the world from the standpoint of handling traffic. Improvement projects were also carried out with federal funds at Joliet, Moline, Galesburg, and Rockford (Camp Grant). The federal airport program led many communities to acquire land for airports in anticipation of obtaining funds from the government for improvements. Because of the federal program, there was a large amount of construction in the midst of the depression, especially in 1933–1935, when local finances were generally chaotic. At least nine cities acquired sites for airports at that time. In a single week in October, 1934, Governor Henry Horner participated in dedication ceremonies at municipal airports in Bloomington, Danville, Dixon, Harrisburg, Joliet, Marion, Peoria, Quincy, and Springfield.

Between 1930 and 1934, the total number of airports in Illinois fell from 69 to 59, but because of the development of municipal airports during the depression years, the number of the latter jumped from 9 to 14 between 1934 and 1939 while the total number of airports—municipal, commercial, intermediate and military—fell from 59 to 56. Small privately owned commercial airports, many of which were partially supported by local chambers of commerce or other civic groups, were the hardest hit in the early 1930's. Many other commercial airports all but ceased to exist for a time and survived only because operators turned, temporarily, to other occupations.

In the closing years of the 1930's, aviation enjoyed a brief revival of prosperity before the entry of the United States into World War II severely restricted all nonscheduled flying activities. Nonmilitary flying was prohibited over certain areas; airports, except those used by aircraft operating on regular schedules, were temporarily closed; and private pilots and nonscheduled aircraft were grounded until a system of controls could be worked out by the Civil Aeronautics Administration and the military services. Although controls over civil aviation were somewhat relaxed as the war progressed, nonscheduled aircraft continued to operate under some restrictions until the end of 1945. Military guards were placed at such strategic airports as Springfield, Peoria, Chicago, and East St. Louis, and civilian guards were required elsewhere. All airports were required to maintain clearance officers to record flights of nonscheduled aircraft. As a result, many small commercial airports that could not afford to hire guards and clearance officers were forced to close.

In spite of wartime restrictions, the number of airports in Illinois rose appreciably during World War II. Municipal airports increased from 44 to 74, and the total number of all types, from 56 to 71. Much of the credit for the increase belongs to the Illinois Aviation Conference, a group composed of representatives from the aviation industry, the Illinois Chamber of Commerce, and the Illinois Aeronautics Commission. These groups conducted a thorough study of aviation facilities in Illinois as a basis for recommendations submitted to the Illinois General Assembly. On the strength of these recommendations, the General Assembly approved a research and training airport for the University of Illinois and passed enabling legislation designed to accelerate the development of airports.

By the end of World War II, Illinois had fallen behind other states in the development of airports. This condition resulted partly from the depression and partly from the fact that municipalities, counties, and public corporations did not have sufficient authority to raise tax revenue for the acquisition and

AIRPORTS IN ILLINOIS 1928–1955

Year	*Commercial*	*Private*	*Total*	*Total in U.S.*
1928			58	1,036
1929			60	1,364
1930			69	1,550
1931				1,782
1932			53	2,093
1933			54	2,117
1934			54	2,188
1935	48		59	2,297
1936				2,368
1937	47		58	2,342
1938	44		56	2,299
1939	44		56	2,374
1940	44		56	2,280
1941	44		56	2,331
1942	48		54	2,484
1943	76		85	2,809
1944	74		80	2,769
1945	60	11	71	3,427
1946	88	12	103	4,026
1947	113	10	126	4,490
1948	179	168	350	5,759
1949	166	240	409	6,414
1950	163	335	501	6,484
1951	186	382	571	6,403
1952	159	408	570	6,237
1953	145	417	565	6,042
1954	137	442	582	6,760
1955	129	486	618	

maintenance of a public-use airport. In general, enabling legislation had been of a haphazard nature for nearly twenty years. Illinois statutes contained four separate and distinct acts, dating back to 1929, granting cities and villages various powers for acquiring and developing airports. These laws had been principally enacted to meet special problems of particular communities and were therefore not broad enough to meet general requirements. Other acts pertained only to counties and park districts. Almost without exception, enabling acts required bond issues to be paid off from the future income of airports, but because airports were not producers of profits, revenue bonds for their construction were not an attractive form of investment. Even though the enabling acts were generally ineffective, many communities did make use of them during the 1930's to acquire airport sites in order to qualify for relief funds through the federal airport act. Under provisions of the several acts for cities and villages, Moline, Galesburg, Salem, Mt. Vernon, Bloomington, Quincy, Dixon, and Centralia created public-use airports prior to 1943. Similarly, Joliet, Peoria, and Decatur built airports under the park district acts.

Agitation for new enabling legislation influenced the 63d General Assembly to consider the problem in May, 1943. After a thorough investigation of airport development and operation, the General Assembly passed the Municipal Airport Authority Act, which empowered cities to create, with referendum approval, separate corporations known as airport authorities. The airport authorities, in turn, had power to acquire, maintain, and operate public-use airports. Although it was a step in the right direction, the act fell short of providing a sound basis for a state-wide airport system. Also, before it could be used effectively by communities, the Illinois Supreme Court ruled the act unconstitutional, and Springfield, Freeport, and Rockford had to abandon projects after authorities had been approved by referendum vote.

In addition to the Municipal Airport Authority Act, the 63d General Assembly approved a special act authorizing the University of Illinois to construct and operate a model research and training airport. The University Airport was largely an outgrowth of local agitation which began more than a year before the state government agreed to finance the project with the help of federal funds. In January, 1942, a committee of private citizens appeared before the University Board of Trustees with a petition asking that the Board request funds in the next biennium to purchase land for an airport. On the same day, President Arthur C. Willard of the University recommended that the Board ask for an appropriation of approximately $200,000 to purchase 640 acres of land for an airport. President Willard also requested permission to make a thorough study of the question and submit a report to the Board.

During the regular session of the 63d General Assembly, supporters of the University airport won approval for the plan and an appropriation for the purchase of a site. As soon as the title was assured, University officials opened negotiations with the Civil Aeronautics Administration for funds under terms of the National Military Airport Program. Within a week, the federal agency approved the project and later allocated $1,500,000 for its construction. Less than two months later, on July 1, 1943, Governor Dwight H. Green signed a bill which appropriated $500,000 of state funds for construction. The new airport was to be located four miles south of Champaign-Urbana.

Construction took slightly more than two years. The Civil Aeronautics Administration accepted the airport in December, 1944, though shops, hangars, and administrative buildings were not completed. On October 26, 1945, dedication ceremonies officially opened the airport as a center of aviation education, research, and service. Since that time the University of Illinois Airport has been a model for many others constructed by educational institutions throughout the United States. The airport is operated by the University's Institute of Aviation, under the direction of Dr. Leslie A. Bryan. It is not only the state's largest center but also one of its busiest commercial airports. With a total area of 772 acres and three miles of paved runways, it is one of the largest in Illinois. In addition to its major functions, the airport is also the base for the University's fleet of 39 airplanes, utilized for education and business.

Since 1943, Illinois has made great strides toward the creation of a state-wide airport system of publicly owned public-use airports. In December, 1943, municipalities and public corporations owned only 13 airports outside the city of Chicago. On November 7, 1955, there were, in addition to three municipal airports in Chicago and the University of Illinois Airport, 45 airports owned and maintained by municipalities or public corporate agencies—15 by municipal airport authorities, 21 by municipalities, 7 by counties, and 2 by park districts. This increase has resulted largely from state and federal airport plans designed to create integrated airport systems.

In 1945, the 64th General Assembly appropriated $2,875,000 for airport construction and improvement in anticipation of the passage of the Federal Airport Act. Under terms of this act, approved May 13, 1946, the United States Government, through the Civil Aeronautics Administration, proposed to participate with state and local governments in a nation-wide airport construction and improvement program. Illinois' share of the federal funds was expected to total approximately $40,000,000 over a seven-year period. In order to match federal funds, the state appropriated $2,500,000 for airport construction and improvement and $375,000 for research, survey, and planning of a state-wide airport program. The latter program was delegated to the Illinois Department of Aeronautics, a newly created code department of the state government.

The state appropriation for construction and improvement of airports in the 1945–1947 biennium made possible for the first time full utilization of the enabling legislation dating back to 1929. Counties, municipalities, and park districts began to consider the possibility of establishing publicly owned public-use airports. One section of the Illinois Aeronautics Act of 1945 paved the way for a co-ordinated local-state-federal airport program. It authorized the Aeronautics Department to act as agent for the local government in all negotiations with the Civil Aeronautics Administration. Because the responsibility for negotiating for federal funds was placed entirely in a single agency, state and national airport plans were easily co-ordinated, and federal participation in airport construction and improvement commenced almost immediately. In the 1945–1947 biennium, state and local political subdivisions, or corporate agencies, jointly carried out construction and improvement projects in 13 localities, six of which were financed in part by the Civil Aeronautics Administration. Federal funds totaling $1,715,740 were expended on projects at Chicago's Northerly Island (Meigs Field), Danville, Mt. Vernon, Salem, Marion-Herrin, and Alton. During the same period, federal funds were tentatively allocated for projects at Bloomington, Chicago (O'Hare International Field), Freeport, Jacksonville, Quincy, and Rockford (Greater Rockford). In the absence of federal aid, state and local authorities conducted surveys for construction or improvement projects at Cairo, Harrisburg, Carbondale-Murphysboro, Lacon, Lincoln, Moline-Rock Island, Sullivan, and Mattoon-Charleston.

By the close of 1948, federal, state, and local funds already expended or contracted for the coming year, totaled more than $21,000,000. In the previous two and a half years, state funds had been allocated for 20 projects, consisting of work on airports at Alton, Bloomington, Chicago (Meigs Field), Chicago (O'Hare International Field), Vermilion County (Danville), Decatur, Freeport, Jacksonville, Logan County (Lincoln), Metropolis, Williamson County (Marion-Herrin), Quad-City (Moline-Rock Island), Mt. Vernon, Peoria, Quincy, Rockford (Greater Rockford), Shelby County (Shelbyville), Springfield, and the University of Illinois (Champaign). Early in 1949, contracts were awarded for the construction of new airports at Murphysboro-Carbondale (Murdale), Alexander County (Cairo), and Harrisburg-Raleigh, and for the development and expansion of Douglas Airport near Park Ridge, known today as Chicago O'Hare International Airport. Over a period of three and a half years, federal participation in Illinois airport projects totaled nearly $9,000,000. State expenditures during the same period, representing the costs of planning and supervising all airport construction and improvements under both the state and federal airport plans as well as direct aid to localities, totaled more than $6,900,000.

The state-wide airport program reached its peak during the 1949–1951 biennium when the 66th General Assembly appropriated $3,190,000 for "financial assistance to municipalities and other subdivisions in planning, construction, extension, development, and improvement of air navigation facilities owned, controlled or operated or to be owned, controlled or operated by municipalities or political subdivisions of the state." Of this amount, $1,300,000 was earmarked for the modernization and expansion of O'Hare International Airport. The funds were not used during the 1949–1951 biennium, but were reappropriated by the 67th General Assembly and used to complete the first phase of construction work on the huge airport prior to its official opening, October 30, 1955. By that time, more than $24,-000,000 in city, state, and federal funds had been expended on the big northside Chicago air terminal, and more than twice that amount was expected to be spent before the development period ended. O'Hare's 5,700 acres, to which 675 were to be added, make it the largest in the world and more than 1,000 acres larger than New York's busy Idlewild Airport. Within two or three years, it was planned that O'Hare International Airport would serve as the terminal for all international flights into and out of Chicago and for a large percentage of the domestic flights then using Chicago's overcrowded Midway Airport.

State funds in the 1949–1951 biennium supplemented local and some federal funds for the construction of two new airports and the improvement of 21 others. First-stage construction began on airports at Litchfield and in Coles County (Mattoon-Charleston), and contracts were awarded for improvements at Rockford, Vermilion County (Danville), Williamson County (Marion-Herrin), Alton, Quad-City (Moline-Rock Island), Peoria, Lacon, Springfield, Shelby County (Shelbyville), St. Charles, Salem, Harrisburg-Raleigh, Bloomington, Freeport, Jacksonville, Logan County (Lincoln), Murdale (Murphysboro-Carbondale), Alexander County (Cairo), Quincy, and Decatur. The expansion of Peoria Municipal Airport into Greater Peoria Airport was made possible in 1950 by the creation of the Greater Peoria Airport Authority. This agency took over operation of the airport from the Pleasure Driveway and Park District, which had controlled it since its creation in 1939.

Since federal and state airport plans were placed in effect in 1946, the major portion of expenses for airport construction and improvement has been provided by the federal and state governments, but in every case initiative for construction or development of an airport has come from the local community. Land for an airport site had to be in the possession of the municipality or its agency before state funds could be allocated for actual construction costs. If a community's proposed airport project fell outside the scope of the federal plan, the cost of land acquisition had to be absorbed entirely by the community before state funds could be allocated. Many airports were built in the post-World War II period with only local and state funds. When a local project fell within the scope of the federal airport plan, funds equal to as much as 25 per cent of the cost of the land and 50 per cent of the cost of construction could be allocated by the Civil Aeronautics Administration.

Since 1951, state aid for airport construction and improvements has kept pace with that of the previous six years, while federal participation in local airport projects has lessened appreciably. For the 1951–1953 biennium, the 67th General Assembly appropriated funds for 29 downstate projects—all improvements of existing facilities—and for the expansion of O'Hare International Airport, the recipient of the largest share of the funds. Commencing in 1953, nearly all airport improvements were carried out by state and local governments with little aid from the federal government. The virtual withdrawal of the federal government from the Illinois airport program necessitated drastic modifications and reductions in the scope of the state plan. An appropriation of $20,000,000 by Congress for improvements at Chicago's O'Hare International Airport and facilities in Peoria, Rockford, Cairo, and Quincy indicates the possibility of further federal aid under the Monroney Act. On the state level, an appropriation of $3,107,500 for the 1955–1957 biennium reflects the need for expanding publicly owned public-use airports even at a time when the post-World War II boom in civil aviation seems to have slackened appreciably.

To a large extent, the expansion of airport facilities in the 1945–1955 decade was achieved through the development of privately owned commercial fields that catered almost exclusively to the operators of small personal aircraft. Postwar enthusiasm for flying and the Veterans' Administration G.I. flight training program combined to produce a tremendous increase in the activity of privately owned aircraft between 1945 and 1948. During the height of the boom, the number of commercial airports in Illinois rose to 166. After 1948, because of the gradual curtailment of the Veterans' Administration training program, the number of commercial airports declined steadily to 129 as of January 1, 1955. The total decrease in privately owned commercial airports was partially offset by the construction of publicly owned public-use airports under federal and state airport plans. A further indication of the decrease in civil aviation since 1948 can be seen in the number of aircraft licenses registered with the state. The number of civil aircraft in Illinois fell from 3,530 in 1949 to 2,928 in 1953, with a jump to 3,406 the following year. However, during the same period, the number of federal airmen's licenses registered with the state agency increased steadily. The number of approved G.I. flight training schools in Illinois fell from a high of 162 in 1948 to 106 in 1951 and to 84 as of June 30, 1953.

Since 1945, the growth of personal or private airports (restricted landing areas) has continued at a steady pace. In spite of the relative decrease in private flying activity in recent years, these small fields, which also serve as emergency fields, have increased out of proportion to the number of aircraft in use in Illinois. After a slow start, the number of private airports reached 148 in 1948 and thereafter jumped rapidly to 486 by the close of 1954. To some extent, the apparent sudden increase in private facilities after 1948 represents the conversion of small privately owned commercial airports to restricted landing areas when the decline in the G.I. flight training program removed the principal source of income for many fields. Even more significant has been the influence of organized groups of private aircraft owners such as local flying clubs, the Ninety-Nines, the Civil Air Patrol, and the Illinois Chapter of the Flying Farmers. The last named group, since its founding in 1945, has been especially influential in encouraging owners and operators of private aircraft to establish their own airports.

The future development of airports will determine the expansion of civil aviation in Illinois. Without a farsighted program of airport construction and expansion and improvement of existing facilities to handle a greater volume of traffic, civil aviation will soon reach the point where inadequate facilities will retard its natural growth and development. Only in the

1945–1955 decade did airport development keep pace with the growth of aviation. The fine publicly owned public-use airports that have been developed in Illinois through the co-operation of local, state, and federal governments in the decade indicate an awareness that aviation is as dependent upon improved airport facilities as the automobile is upon an improved highway system. At the present writing Illinois ranks among the leaders in aviation. If this position is to be maintained, both state and local governments must co-operate to improve and expand airport facilities in the same manner that airport construction has been accomplished during the ten years prior to 1956. The key to the future of aviation lies in the maintenance of proper terminal facilities, whether for private or commercial aircraft. Air travel in Illinois was largely restricted to the Chicago area for many years because of the absence of adequate airports in downstate communities. In the future, air travel in the United States may be largely restricted to other states if Illinois neglects to provide facilities that keep pace with technological improvements in aircraft.

10

FLYERS AND FLYING ACHIEVEMENTS, 1919–1955

The ranks of private, commercial, and transport pilots in Illinois have grown steadily since the close of World War I. Throughout the 1920's, the number of qualified aviators was probably no more than a few hundred at any time, and the number fluctuated greatly, with a noticeable increase taking place after 1927. By 1931, soon after the Illinois Aeronautics Commission began its operations, there were approximately 800 pilots who maintained their residences in Illinois. After that date, the number increased more rapidly until by 1956 there were approximately 17,000, of whom about 9,000 were active. Perhaps as many as half of this number have obtained pilot's licenses since the end of World War II.

Thirty years ago, the qualified pilot enjoyed an entirely different status in society from what he had in the 1945–1955 decade. In 1920, at a time when there were probably not more than 100 pilots in the state, and many of them transients, the pilot was set off from others who were gainfully employed in the usual types of businesses and industries. Flying was a peculiar profession that made the pilot the constant object of curiosity and wonder. On seeing an aviator, little boys would boast that they too would someday pilot an airplane, but parents almost universally looked upon flying as an undignified way of making a living. In part, the prejudice against both the pilot and the airplane was justified, for at that early date, aside from recent wartime activity, aviation had accomplished little for which it deserved public acclaim, respect, or confidence. In the next two decades, outstanding achievements elevated the aviator to a more respectable status and created almost universal confidence in the airplane as a method of convenient, efficient travel. Aviation's struggle to win respect and confidence is a story of flyers and flying achievements. It is the narrative of a few people who sought to promote air travel by performing remarkable flights as evidence of the potential of the airplane.

Over a period of nearly four decades, most aviators have had relatively few opportunities to gain more than occasional local publicity. For the most part, the pilot who engaged in flying for business or pleasure, or a combination of the two, had little inclination to seek publicity and often shunned public attention, even when he deserved special notice. However, these little-known and unknown men have been the real boosters of aviation and the main strength of flying activities in the state. It would be unfair to judge the relative importance of any pilot, or group of them, simply according to the number of times their names appeared in print. But in the final analysis, there is no other way to single out pilots for special mention in a work such as this. It is well, indeed it is necessary, to point out that the main strength of flying activities in Illinois has always rested with the nameless flyers.

In many instances, pilots who lived in Illinois, or conducted a large part of their activities in this state, have performed outstanding achievements that set them apart from their fellow flyers. Generally, the outstanding pilots have gained distinction by participating in one or more especially difficult or dangerous activities, such as transoceanic flights, establishment of new records for speed, altitude, or endurance, and other events that were the focus of public attention. As a result of outstanding achievements, some pilots have gained lasting fame; but others won acclaim for only a brief moment and were then soon forgotten. In the 1920's and early 1930's, transoceanic flyers—those who survived—were the darlings of the press, though participants in national racing events also received considerable public acclaim. For a time, when commercial air travel was new, pilots of airliners were often given special attention. And, from time to time, private flyers have made outstanding rescue and emergency relief flights that won special notice, though usually of a local nature.

Although several Illinois men won military honors in combat against German aircraft during World War I, the greatest figure to emerge from the United States Army Air Service after the war spent all his time either training flying officers or experimenting with airplanes. Major Rudolph W. ("Shorty") Schroeder, a Chicago resident, served his aviation apprenticeship as a mechanic for early exhibition flyers such as Otto W. Brodie, Lincoln Beachey, and Mickey McGuire before becoming a barnstormer in his own right with McGuire and Katherine Stinson. When Shorty—so called because of his lanky six-foot four-inch stature—first entered the United States Army Signal Corps Aero Reserve training program at Ashburn Field, Chicago, in the fall of 1916, he had already spent nearly seven years as an aviation mechanic and pilot.

The entry of the United States into World War I resulted in a promotion for Sergeant Schroeder to the rank of lieutenant in the Aviation Section. In July, 1917, he was assigned to a new training camp, Chanute Field near Rantoul. In the next five years, promotions and assignments to more responsible duties followed in quick succession. From Chanute Field, Schroeder went to Wright Field at Dayton, to Kelly Field at San Antonio, Texas, and finally to McCook Field at Dayton. Here he remained in charge of experimental work as chief pilot for the Engineering Section of the Air Service until he resigned his commission as major in 1921. While at McCook Field, he earned lasting fame as a pioneer of stratospheric flight and paved the way for subsequent advances in high altitude flying.

In the short space of five years, Schroeder established three official records for altitude and, on unofficial flights, shattered existing records a dozen or more times. Two of his official records were for an airplane carrying a pilot and passenger; the other was for an airplane and pilot alone. All three records were achieved under hazardous conditions, and, on the last, Schroeder narrowly escaped with his life when his oxygen supply ran out at a height of 33,000 feet.

The outstanding altitude flight of Schroeder's career occurred on February 27, 1920. Lessons learned from countless previous trips into the stratosphere were put to the test on this occasion in an effort to shatter the existing record of 32,450 feet, for the Air Service wanted to regain the honor it had held until Roland Rouff of the Curtiss Aeroplane & Motor Company had set a new record several months earlier. In order to allow complete attention to handling the airplane, a La Pere biplane powered by a supercharged Liberty engine, Schroeder decided to use two types of apparatus for controlling the flow of life-sustaining oxygen to his face mask: one, an automatic type that he hoped to use until he reached a height of approximately 29,000 feet; and the other, a manual-type control that would be needed for higher altitudes, where extreme cold might cause the other control to freeze. Had he been able to utilize his oxygen supply as anticipated, he might have climbed 12,000 feet higher that day.

Dressed in the warmest flying clothing obtainable, Schroeder lifted his big La Pere biplane from McCook Field. The plane was equipped to spend several hours in the stratosphere and had enough oxygen for three hours in the rarefied upper air. Schroeder hoped to do much more than just set a new altitude record. His official orders directed him to explore the upper air, particularly the trade winds which blew from west to east with terrific force above 25,000 feet. At 18,000 feet, Schroeder noticed that his instruments registered 67 degrees below zero as he turned on the oxygen flask fitted with automatic controls that regulated the flow according to altitude. Had this control worked properly, he would have been able to climb at least 10,000 feet more before turning on the second and only other flask. However, before climbing half that distance, the automatic control failed. He knew then that there was time enough to surpass the existing record but little to spare.

The faulty oxygen-feed control nearly cost Schroeder his life. On reaching 33,000 feet, he gasped the last of the second flask. Without oxygen at that height, life would not last long. Frantically he whipped frost-covered goggles from his eyes in order to switch the controls on his mask from the exhausted flask to the partly full one he had discarded earlier. Still the oxygen failed to flow through the faulty control mechanism. Finally, in desperation, he pushed the nose of the ship down into a steep dive and switched off the engine. Without oxygen he had only a few minutes in which to act. As the plane started its long plunge to earth, Schroeder slumped forward, unconscious of the speed at which he was falling.

From the ground, anxious observers caught sight of the plunging plane after more than an hour during which it had completely vanished into the limitless heights of the stratosphere. Spinning and out of control, with its pilot unconscious, the plane neared the ground. A crash appeared unavoidable. At a height of only 3,000 feet, the careening plane slowly leveled off; Schroeder had regained consciousness. With apparent difficulty, he circled above the field, approached for a landing, touched down with a jolt, and rolled to a stop. When aid reached the plane Schroeder was in a coma, slumped forward on the controls, with his eyes frozen wide open. Twice within the space of a few minutes, he had barely escaped almost certain death; he had survived both a lack of oxygen at extreme height and a nose dive in an uncontrollable plane. And, in spite of these mishaps, he had set a new altitude record of 33,000 feet.

After leaving the Air Service in 1921, Schroeder served in many key positions in the aviation industry. For four years he was aviation engineer with Underwriters Laboratories in Chicago, computing the safety factors of aircraft and the risks connected with their operation as a basis for insuring both airmen and airplanes. Because of the work of the Underwriters Laboratories, and particularly the research directed by Schroeder, many insurance companies extended coverage to aircraft and operators of aircraft for the first time. Though insignificant at the time because of the limited number of airplanes in the country, this extension of insurance to aviation had a tremendous bearing on the expansion of flying activity before the close of the decade.

From the Underwriters Laboratories, Schroeder went to Ford Air Transport in 1925. As superintendent of the airline operated by the Ford Motor Company between Detroit, Chicago, and Cleveland, he had charge of one of the oldest, though financially not the most successful, carriers of airmail and passengers in the United States. At the time, Ford Air Transport had the best safety record among all airlines in the United States. In spite of Schroeder's efforts, the airline failed to prosper, largely because Henry Ford refused to encourage traffic over the company's potentially important routes. Under such conditions there was little that Schroeder could do for Ford Air Transport; consequently, he left the firm to specialize in aircraft design and research.

His new position, as a senior member of Schroeder-Wentworth and Associates, in Chicago, gave him time to contribute to the advancement of aviation by aiding in the promotion of air shows and meets, the organization of flying and glider clubs, particularly for youngsters, and in the promotion of air safety. The safe operation of planes, he believed, depended upon coordinated regulation by active pilots and local, state, and federal governmental agencies. With Reed G. Landis, a fellow-aviator and aviation booster, Schroeder campaigned actively throughout 1928 and 1929 for more effective local and state controls over the operation of airplanes in an effort to reduce the especially high accident rate among airplanes in the Chicago area.

The construction of Curtiss-Reynolds Airport near Glenview by the Curtiss Flying Service in 1929 opened a new career for Schroeder, who became superintendent of the new base. Under his management, the company's services were extended to technical as well as flight training. In August, 1929, the Curtiss Flying Service opened a downtown aeronautical university as a center for academic and laboratory training in conjunction with flight instruction carried on at the Glenview field. With the merger of the Curtiss Flying Service and the Wright Aeronautical Corporation late in 1929, all units of both organizations adopted the Curtiss-Wright name. Thereafter, the Glenview activities continued under the name Curtiss-Wright Flying Service, and the downtown school became the Curtiss-Wright Aeronautical University. In 1933, the school was taken over by L. M. Churbuck, Kenneth L. Borroughs, and other members of the staff, who operated it under the name Aeronautical University.

Schroeder remained with the Chicago branch of the Curtiss-Wright Flying Service until 1931. He then became a part owner of Sky Harbor Airport (Northbrook) but served only a brief time before joining the Aeronautics Branch of the Department of Commerce as Chief of Airline Inspection in 1933. Soon after Fred D. Fagg, Jr., was appointed to the directorship of the Bureau of Air Commerce (successor to the Aeronautics Branch) in 1937, Schroeder was elevated to the post of assistant director.

A member of the faculty of the law school of Northwestern University and former member of the Illinois Aeronautics Commission, Fagg gave the federal agency the type of leadership it had long needed. By appointing Schroeder as assistant director of the bureau, Fagg made certain that the enforcement of federal aeronautical regulations would be effective and constructive. The aviation industry applauded the appointment enthusiastically. But the hope for more enlightened regulation quickly faded when, after only a month and a half in the new post, Schroeder resigned to take a position with United Air Lines as vice-president in charge of safety, and a few months later Fagg returned to Northwestern. Schroeder remained with United Air Lines until failing health forced him to resign in 1941.

During the next eleven years "Shorty" Schroeder was almost completely incapacitated due to a paralytic stroke, but his indomitable enthusiasm for aviation continued to inspire those who knew and admired him. On July 14, 1945, at a special dinner held in his honor in Chicago, Shorty's many friends paid tribute to him as one of aviation's greatest pioneers. On that occasion, Lieutenant General Harold L. George, commanding general of the United States Army Air Force Air

Transport Command, presented Schroeder with the Distinguished Flying Cross, belated recognition of the extraordinary achievements of the first explorer of the stratosphere. At the conclusion of the presentation, General George acknowledged America's debt to such pioneers as Schroeder whose work had made possible the tremendous advancements in aviation. The public has all but forgotten Shorty, but in aviation circles his fabulous achievements are a legend which will live on as long as men continue to fly.

Many of the heroes of the first war in the air gained lasting acclaim, probably more as a result of their untiring efforts in behalf of aviation after World War I than because of military honors won in combat with the A.E.F. in France. Among the seven Illinois men who won in battle the distinguished title of flying ace, two gained national reputations for their efforts to promote civil aviation during the two decades following the Armistice. They were Reed G. Landis, of Chicago, and Howard C. Knotts, of Springfield, who were largely responsible for the enactment and implementation of effective state legislation for the control of civil aviation in Illinois.

Illinois' top-ranking ace in World War I, Reed Landis, was the son of Kenesaw Mountain Landis, famous jurist and later commissioner of baseball. Reed Landis joined the United States Signal Corps Aviation Section in June, 1917. After attending primary flight school at Chanute Field, he went on to advanced training and assignment with the 40th Squadron of the British Royal Air Force in France. Landis remained with the English pursuit squadron until September, 1918, at which time he was transferred to the American Air Service and became commander of the 25th Aero Squadron which had recently arrived in France. In action against the Germans, Landis was officially credited with the destruction of nine airplanes and one observation balloon, placing him among America's top aces.

After leaving the Air Service in March, 1919, Landis worked in the aviation industry for a short time, then turned to advertising and publicity when it became apparent that the public was not ready to accept air travel. Even though aviation suffered from a lack of public support, Landis remained firm in his faith and continued to advocate the wider use of airplanes for pleasure, business, and commercial travel. In 1928 and 1929, when a high accident rate among airplane operators in the Chicago area further threatened public confidence in aviation, Landis became an outspoken advocate of local and state regulation to supplement the limited powers of the Aeronautics Branch of the Department of Commerce. Even though local and state authorities were slow to act, and many aviators bitterly opposed additional controls of any type, Landis and others who joined the fight eventually gained their objective, first locally, then throughout the state.

In August, 1929, the Cook County Board, headed by Anton J. Cermak, took action to curb the high accident rate among flyers in the Chicago area. First the board appointed Landis special supervisor with authority to prevent pilots from operating unsafe aircraft in the county. Landis was to serve only three months. Unfortunately, he had neither the time nor the authority to prevent the operation of unsafe airplanes, for he could only enforce existing laws, which were totally unsatisfactory. Ralph Royce was appointed Cook County's first air policeman under Landis' supervision. In spite of determined effort on the part of both men, little could be accomplished until the state legislature enacted needed legislation to supplement federal regulations; flyers who operated airplanes entirely within the state and outside the federal airways were in no way subject to federal laws at that time, nor could they be regulated under existing state laws and local ordinances.

The recognized need for state aircraft regulation induced the Illinois General Assembly to take action in 1929. In May, the legislature, by joint resolution, created an Aerial Navigation Commission to study aeronautical laws then applicable to the regulation of civil aviation and to compile recommendations for new legislation, which were to be submitted for consideration to the 57th General Assembly convening in January, 1931. Landis served as chairman and Howard C. Knotts as secretary; legislators appointed to the commission were Senators Lowell B. Mason and Richard R. Meents and Representatives Charles H. Weber and Elmer C. Wilson. The recommendations contained in the report of the commission were embodied in the Aeronautics Act of 1931 creating the Illinois Aeronautics Commission. Landis served as the first chairman of that body.

During the tense months preceding the Japanese attack on Pearl Harbor, Landis, because of his knowledge of civil and military aviation, served as special consultant to Fiorello H. LaGuardia, Director of the Office of Civilian Defense. Recognizing the impending national emergency, Landis had resigned as a regional vice-president of American Airlines to accept the post. In the following year, United States' entry into the war prompted him to seek a commission in the Army Air Corps, and, in May, 1942, Major Landis was again in uniform, more than twenty years after he had fought with German pursuit planes over the battlegrounds of France. During most of the war, he was assigned to the Office of the Chief of the Air Forces in Washington.

Another prominent booster of civil aviation, and a colleague of Landis in the campaign for state regulation of aeronautics, was Howard C. Knotts, of Springfield, an outstanding legal authority on civil aviation. Like his friend, Knotts had earned his wings as a military aviator and the title of ace as a member of the British and American air squadrons in France. Following graduation from Knox College in 1916, he enrolled in the Harvard Law School but gave up his studies to enter the Aviation Section in 1917. After completing flight training, Knotts was assigned to the 17th Aero Squadron, an American unit within the 13th Wing of the British Royal Air Force in Belgium and France. First in Flanders and later at Cambrai, France, Knotts officially destroyed six enemy aircraft. While winning distinction in combat, he was twice wounded—the second time, on October 14, 1918, his Clerget Camel pursuit plane fell behind German lines, and for nearly a month he was held prisoner with other captured airmen until the retreating Germans abandoned the group shortly before the Armistice.

Knotts returned to Harvard after the war and received his law degree in 1921. He then went back to Springfield where he soon became interested in aeronautical law. Until his death in 1942, he devoted nearly all his professional and private efforts to the study of that subject and soon gained nationwide recognition. As an expert in a little-known legal area, he was called upon time and time again for advice in making new laws for more effective regulation of civil aviation. He was a member both of state and federal agencies for the regulation of civil aviation and thus played an important role in the enforcement of aviation law. He was also secretary of the Illinois Aerial Navigation Commission and was largely responsible for the wording of the Illinois Aeronautics Act of 1931. For more than twelve years, beginning in 1930, Knotts served as aviation adviser for the Illinois Commerce Commission, and, from 1937 to 1939, he was on the staff of the Bureau of Air Commerce and its successor in 1938, the Civil Aeronautics Authority. During that time, he completed the codification of aeronautical regulations and laws, a colossal task which produced the first complete aeronautical code in the United States. In this work, he was closely associated with two friends, Fred D. Fagg, Jr., who carried on the work until he was appointed director of the Bureau of Air Commerce in 1937, and John H. Wigmore, dean emeritus of the Northwestern University School of Law. In addition to state and federal government posts, Knotts held numerous important positions in aviation organizations such as the National Aeronautical Association, the American Association of Airport Executives, and the National Association of State Airport Officials. He was also a member of the American section of the *Comité Internationale Technique d'Experts Juridiques Aériens.*

In addition to Landis and Knotts, five other Illinoisans earned the title of ace in World War I: William P. Erwin, Frank K. Hayes, Charles G. Gray, and John J. Seerley, all of Chicago, and Victor H. Strahen, of Evanston. It is unfortunate that these men who gave so much to the people of America should have been forgotten within so short a time.

Most of the early flyers in Illinois were veterans of the Air Service. At least ten, possibly more, pioneer airport operators were former military pilots. Nimmo Black, David L. Behncke, Bert J. Blair, William Westlake, Stanley Wallace, and William W. Meyers opened and operated airports in the Chicago area shortly after the war. Downstate, E. K. ("Rusty") Campbell, of Moline, David L. Bondurant, of Cairo, and Harold B. Snow, of Sheldon, conducted commercial flying service from privately maintained fields. All these men had refused to give up flying after returning from the Army; all of them devoted much of their lives to aviation from that time on. Other former military pilots played important parts in the expansion of civil aviation between 1919 and 1940. Walter J. Addams, a native of Loda, was general manager of the Yackey Aircraft Company, operators of Checkerboard Field, Maywood, before becoming an air transport pilot in 1929. Leslie B. Coombs, who had worked as an engineer for the Heath Airplane Company before serving with the Air Service during the war, returned to Chicago as chief designer for the Western Airplane Company. Here, he designed the Kingbird, a popular biplane of the mid-1920's. In 1925, Coombs organized the Chicago Flying Club and served as president until 1927. Similar experiences could be traced for dozens of other aviators who were prominent in Illinois after the war.

Many former military pilots became the flying mail carriers of the Post Office Department's airmail service. Intrepid airmail pilots flew the mail from coast to coast along the transcontinental route in all types of weather and, after 1924, by day and night. These men prepared the way for the emergence of the air transport industry in 1925 when the Post Office first contracted for the transportation of mail by private airlines. Few airmail pilots survived the hazardous flights over the primitive mail routes of the early 1920's. Twisted wreckage of DeHaviland mail planes in the Allegheny Mountains, the sparsely settled plains, or the Rockies was the price of progress. The lives sacrificed for the airmail were not lost without results, for out of the early government-operated service came the forerunners of the great domestic and international air carriers.

Prominent among pilots in the Post Office Department's airmail service were several Illinois residents: Shirley J. Short, E. Hamilton Lee, Daniel Kiser, Jack Knight, and Art Smith, to name only a few. Short learned to fly in the Air Service and was a barnstormer with Omar Locklear and Tex McLaughlin before joining the airmail service in March, 1923. He remained with the Post Office Department for more than four years, joining National Air Transport as an airline pilot in September, 1927, when that company took over the New York-Chicago segment of the old transcontinental airmail line. Dan A. Kiser, a Chicago pilot, learned to fly in 1916 and served as a civilian instructor in the Air Service throughout the war. After the Armistice, he engaged in exhibition and passenger work for nearly two years before joining the airmail service in 1921. Two years as an airmail pilot were enough for Kiser, who resigned in 1923 to take up commercial flying and airplane construction in New Butler, Wisconsin.

One of the greatest of the airmail pilots, Jack Knight became a legendary figure of the government service before entering the air transport industry. Knight's heroic flight from North Platte, Nebraska, to Chicago in February, 1921, saved the airmail and pointed to the possibility of regular night service. He also compiled a record of outstanding performances, including many intercity speed records. When Boeing Air Transport took over the western segment of the transcontinental route, Knight stayed on as a pilot. Later, following the formation of United Air Lines, he became its Director of Public Education, a post he retained until 1942.

E. Hamilton Lee was the "grand-daddy" of all airline pilots in length of service when he retired from United Air Lines in 1949. He became a government airmail pilot in 1919, soon after leaving the Air Service, and in 31 years of flying compiled a record of more than 4,400,000 air miles.

Countless other Illinois pilots flew for the old government airmail service and for the private airlines that appeared after 1925. Some, like Knight, Lee, and Kiser, began flying before the war; others received their flight training in military camps; but the largest number learned to fly after the Armistice, entering air transport after first engaging in various types of commercial flying. The outstanding figure of this group was Charles A. Lindbergh, who flew airmail over the St. Louis-Chicago route in 1926 and 1927. Among the others was David L. Behncke, founder and, for many years, president of the Air

Line Pilots' Association, who served as a pilot with Boeing Air Transport after selling Checkerboard Field, Maywood, to the Yackey Aircraft Company. William S. ("Billy") Brock, who, with Edward F. Schlee, flew from Detroit to Tokyo on a projected round-the-world flight in 1927, was a pilot on Charles Dickinson's short-lived Chicago-Twin Cities airmail route in 1926. Elmer L. Partridge lost his life flying mail over the same route that year.

The St. Louis-Chicago airmail route was the training ground for Lindbergh, whose solo flight from New York to Paris in 1927 was one of the most important achievements in aviation. "Slim" Lindbergh was virtually an unknown airmail pilot, one of several hundred in the country, before his epic flight caught the public imagination. Lindbergh had learned to fly in 1922 and barnstormed throughout the West for two years before joining the Air Service Reserve. In 1925, he was graduated from the Army Air Service flight training program at Brooks and Kelly fields, and later that year he joined the Robertson Aircraft Corporation of Anglum, Missouri. He quickly rose to the position of chief pilot in charge of flight instruction and passenger flights, and, when the company began operation of the St. Louis-Chicago airmail route, April 15, 1926, he flew the first mail from Chicago to St. Louis, via Peoria and Springfield.

After the opening-day ceremonies, airmail flights between St. Louis and Chicago became almost a matter of routine. Five days a week, Lindbergh and his two flying partners, Philip Love and Thomas Nelson, made flights in each direction. Shortly after dawn and the arrival of the night mail from New York, one of the three pilots flew from Chicago to St. Louis, stopping at Peoria and Springfield en route. Later the same afternoon, after the delivery of late mail from St. Louis businesses, another flight went north in time to reach the Government Air Mail Field at Maywood before the night plane left for New York. Month after month, Lindbergh continued to fly the mail, seldom carrying more than enough to meet the expenses of the flight. Twice during that time, he had to abandon his DeHaviland plane after running out of gasoline when heavy fog forced him to turn back from the Maywood field.

One day while flying the airmail, Lindbergh's mind turned to thoughts of long-distance flights in modern ships capable of carrying more weight over a greater distance at less cost than his war-surplus mail ship. The obvious shortcomings of the modified DeHavilands used by the Robertson corporation stirred up dreams of nonstop airmail service from St. Louis to New York in the new Wright-Bellanca monoplane or the speedy Laird biplanes he had seen with Northwest Airways markings at the Maywood field. Vast distances could be easily traversed in modern airplanes, Lindbergh knew, but in his sluggish DeHaviland the St. Louis-Chicago flight was no easy task. These thoughts led quite naturally to the idea of transoceanic flights. In fact, Raymond Orteig, of New York, had offered a prize of $25,000 for the first nonstop flight between New York and Paris as early as 1919—and the offer was still good. Other flyers were making preparations for the flight; why couldn't he? In the Wright-Bellanca, it would be easy. All he needed was sound financial backing and a good airplane; the rest would be simply a matter of human endurance. With the aid of a group of St. Louis businessmen and ardent aviation enthusiasts, Lindbergh purchased a Whirlwind-powered monoplane from the Ryan Aircraft Company of San Diego in April, 1927, and a few weeks later flew to New York to complete preparations for a flight to Paris.

Trans-Atlantic flights had long been considered practical; in fact, the first flight between the United States and Europe occurred before Lindbergh learned to fly. In the nineteenth century, John Wise, Samuel Archer King, and other aeronauts, proposed trans-Atlantic flights in balloons; in 1910, Walter Wellman and Melvin Vaniman actually attempted such a flight in a dirigible. After World War I, many aviators believed that an airplane could make the flight, and several set out to prove that it was possible. The first to succeed were Captain John Alcock and Lieutenant A. Whitten Brown, who, in 1919, flew a Vickers-Vimy bomber from Newfoundland to Ireland. Later the same year, the United States Navy accomplished a similar feat by way of the Azores. Other outstanding achievements of the early 1920's indicated that a nonstop flight between New York and Paris was within the capabilities of modern airplanes. A series of marvelous flights during those years began gradually to create public confidence in aviation. Lindbergh's remarkable solo flight to Paris completed the change in public opinion, removing forever the apathy that for two decades had delayed the advancement of commercial air travel. The great flights of 1927, of which Lindbergh's was the most significant, produced an era of unprecedented progress for aviation.

Shortly before dawn on the morning of May 20, 1927, Lindbergh lifted his heavily loaded *The Spirit of St. Louis* from Roosevelt Field, New York, on the start of his nonstop flight to Paris. Slightly more than 33 hours later, he circled above Le Bourget Airport outside the French capital and landed amid thousands of excited spectators who heralded his achievement as the greatest flight in history. With modesty and humility, the former airmail pilot from the Midwest accepted the accolades extended by people of every nation. Rather than exploit his popularity to his own selfish advantage, Lindbergh chose to use his good fortune for the advancement of the one thing closest to his heart, the progress of civil aviation, particularly commercial air travel. Wherever he went during the next decade, he was a salesman for civil aviation and air travel. After returning to the United States in June, 1927, he made a tour of all the states in *The Spirit of St. Louis,* followed by a goodwill tour of Latin America. At each stopping place, he called attention to the progress of aviation and the need for even greater advances. The public listened to "Slim" Lindbergh and believed him. Aviation experienced a period of expansion beyond anything known up to that time.

The late 1920's witnessed a mania for long-distance flights, particularly transoceanic flights, first across the Atlantic and then the Pacific. Several transoceanic flights of lasting significance were made by Illinois residents or by flyers who were especially active in the state. Nearly all successful transoceanic flights had a direct effect on the progress of civil aviation, for the ability of airplanes to cross vast bodies of water on flights of 25 hours or more was a particularly impressive example of dependability of both airplane and engine that was not unnoticed by the public.

Seven months before Lindbergh completed his New York-Paris flight, another Illinois flyer had attempted the same trip. On September 21, 1926, Lieutenant Lawrence Wynn Curtin of Beardstown, a naval pilot, attempted to fly to Paris in a tri-motor Sikorsky S-35 biplane piloted by Rene Fonck, with Jacob Isliamoff and Charles Clavier, the other members of the crew. During the takeoff, the heavily loaded craft crashed and exploded; Fonck and Curtin escaped, but the others perished when flames, fed by hundreds of gallons of gasoline, prevented their rescue.

Soon after Lindbergh's flight, a number of pilots attempted to cross the Atlantic. Within little more than a month, two other airplanes flew from the United States to Europe. Clarence D. Chamberlin, with Charles A. Levine as passenger, flew the Bellanca monoplane *Miss Columbia* from Floyd Bennett Field, Brooklyn, to Eisleben, Germany, setting a new nonstop distance flight record of 3,911 miles. The other flight, that of Commander (later Rear Admiral) Richard E. Byrd and a crew of four in the *America,* a Fokker tri-motor monoplane, actually reached Paris, but ended in the Atlantic off Ver-sur-Mer when the pilot was unable to find Le Bourget Airport in a dense fog. Byrd ordered Bernt Balchen to turn back and ditch the plane in shallow water off the French coast rather than risk the lives of the crew in an emergency landing on unknown terrain in the fog. In September, 1927, Lloyd Bertaud and James D. Hill vanished on a flight from Old Orchard, Maine, to Rome. The first successful flight from the United States to Rome was completed almost two years later by a Chicagoan, Lewis A. Yancey, and Roger Q. Williams. Like Bertaud and Hill, Yancey and Williams started from Old Orchard, Maine. However, they did not complete the flight nonstop. A decade later, transoceanic flights became routine when Pan-American Airways opened mail and passenger service to England and the Continent in addition to flights to the Orient across the Pacific and to nearly all Latin American countries to the south.

While flights across the Atlantic were increasingly frequent

Above: Envelope of a letter carried on the first airmail flight from Springfield, October 8, 1912. Although Edward A. Korn was originally scheduled to make the airmail flight from Springfield to Williamsville, the flight was actually completed by Horace Kearney after Korn's Benoist biplane developed engine trouble. Below: Post card carried by aviator Horace Kearney on an early airmail flight at McLeansboro, Illinois, September 26-28, 1912. (*Earl H. Wellman*)

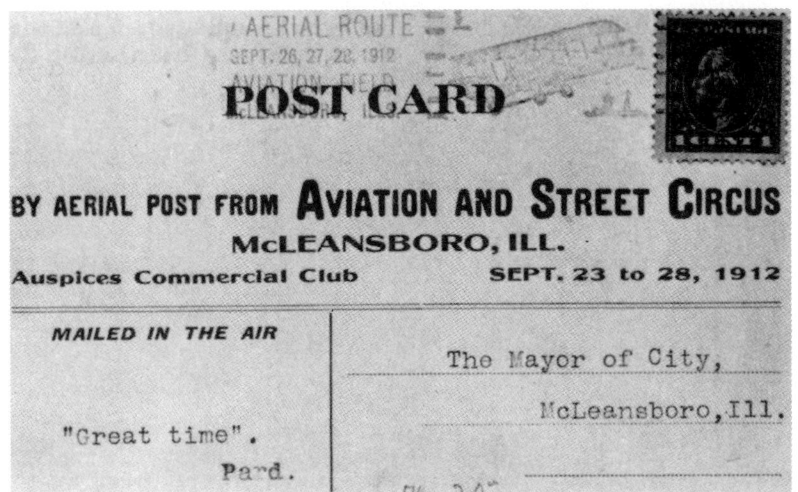

First City-to-City Aerial U. S. Mail Service
New Orleans to
Baton Rouge
April 10, 1912.
Baton Rouge to
New Orleans
April 11.
GEORGE MESTACH and his Somerville Monoplane

George Mestach, a French aviator, performed exhibitions in the United States, 1911–1913. On April 10-11, 1912, Mestach piloted his Morane-Borel monoplane on a flight from New Orleans to Baton Rouge, Louisiana, and back, carrying U.S. mail. During the 1913 flying season, Mestach piloted the same Morane-Borel monoplane, then owned by William E. Somerville, Coal City, Illinois. (*Mrs. Constance B. Smith*)

Above: Junkers all-metal monoplane, one of eight used by the United States Post Office over its airmail routes in 1920. These aircraft were later abandoned after several crashed because of structurally weak landing gears. Below: An L.W.F. biplane, with front cockpit enclosed to form a mail compartment, modified for the United States Post Office Department in October, 1920. (*Charles A. Arens*)

Above: Charles A. Lindbergh (in cockpit) loading the first "official" airmail sent from Springfield, Illinois, April 15, 1926. (*Illinois State Historical Library*) Below: "Cranking up" a DeHaviland mail plane at Government Air Mail Field, Maywood, Illinois. (*Clarence K. Stewart*)

The first pilots on C.A.M. No. 2, St. Louis to Chicago, operated by the Robertson Aircraft Corporation, Anglum, Missouri. Left to right: Thomas Nelson, Charles A. Lindbergh, and Philip R. Love. (*Illinois State Historical Library*)

Harry Crewdson (above left) and Al Johnson (above right) early exhibition flyers and wartime instructors for the United States Army Air Service. (*Charles A. Arens*) Below: Student instructor C. R. Sinclair (in cockpit) and mechanic, Sergeant Rubner, prior to start of mass flight of twenty-one airplanes from the Signal Corps training camp, Ashburn Field, to newly opened Chanute Field, Rantoul, Illinois, July 7, 1917. (*Joseph M. Pallissard*)

Classrooms in aircraft rigging and controls, Military Aviation Ground School, University of Illinois, Urbana, 1917–1918. (*Illinois State Historical Library*)

Above: L.W.F. military biplane powered with a 12-cylinder Liberty motor, used by the United States Air Service, 1918. Below: Thomas-Morse Scout (LeRhone motor) used by the Air Service, 1918. (*Charles A. Arens*)

Above: Captain Hawthorne C. Gray (right) and Colonel Paegelow, prior to start of stratospheric flight from Scott Field, March 9, 1927. (*National Archives*) Below: Six-engined Barling bomber of the early 1920's. (*Clarence K. Stewart*)

Above top: A single-motor, all-metal, transport aircraft designed by William B. Stout and built by the Ford Motor Company, Detroit. This craft is the forerunner of the famous Ford tri-motor transport of the late 1920's. (*Charles A. Arens*) Above center: A twenty-passenger luxury air transport, built by Alfred W. Lawson to transport passengers between Chicago and New York City. Although scheduled to begin operations in 1920, the Lawson Airline did not open the intercity service as planned. (*Gordon H. Snow*) Below: One of the Curtiss "Jennies" used by David L. Behncke and Bert R. J. Hassell to deliver clothing to retail merchants within a radius of 200 miles of Chicago for Alfred Decker & Cohn Company, 1919. (*Lutz Myers*)

Above: Miss Florence Klingensmith of Minneapolis, Minn., a member of the Chicago Girls' Flying Club and prominent woman flyer in Illinois in the early 1930's. Miss Klingensmith was killed while participating in the International Air Races, Glenview, Illinois, September 4, 1934. (*Charles A. Arens*) Below: Aerial exhibitionists who made their headquarters at Checkerboard Field, Maywood, during the early 1920's. Left to right: Walter C. Scholl (parachutist); Dick Kruickschank (parachutist); Ethel Dare (aerial acrobat and parachutist); David L. Behncke (operator of the field and aerial troupe); Chick Wheeler (aerial acrobat); and Jack Cope (parachutist). (*Walter C. Scholl*)

Above: Aerial acrobat Lillian Boyer performing on the wing of a Curtiss "Jenny." (*Charles A. Arens*) Below: An aerial acrobat for the Sheldon Air Line, Sheldon, Illinois, performing beneath a Curtiss "Jenny." (*Gordon B. Snow*)

Right: Major Rudolph W. "Shorty" Schroeder, Chicago. (*Emaline Hunter*) Below: Art Chester, Downers Grove, Illinois, with his 1948 version "Swee' Pea," entry in the Goodyear Trophy Race, Cleveland Air Races, 1948. (*Wilbur Bohl*)

Above: View of the inside of airship hangar, Scott Field, 1930. (*National Archives*) Below: Aerial crop dusting. (*Illinois Department of Aeronautics*)

Aerial view of Chicago Municipal Airport (Midway) in 1928. (*Clarence K. Stewart*)

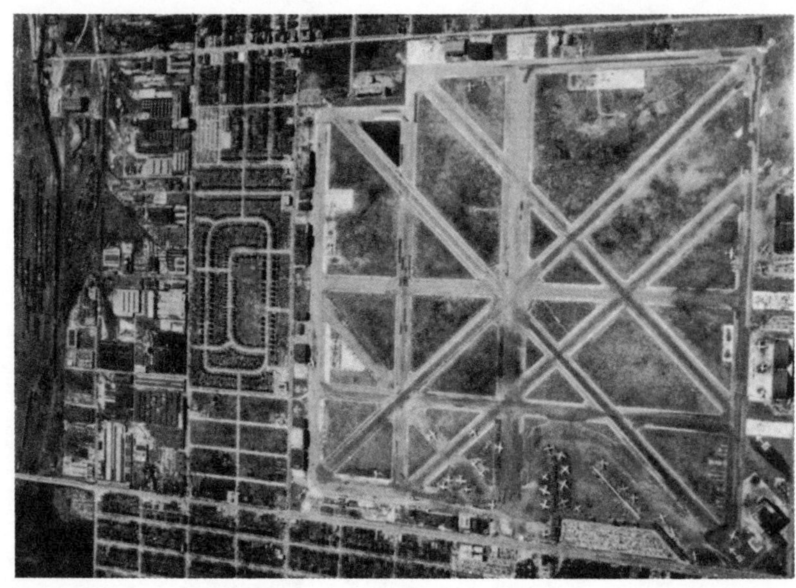

Above: Midway Airport, Chicago. (*Illinois Department of Aeronautics*) Below: Aerial view of the University of Illinois Airport, Champaign, Illinois. (*Institute of Aviation)*

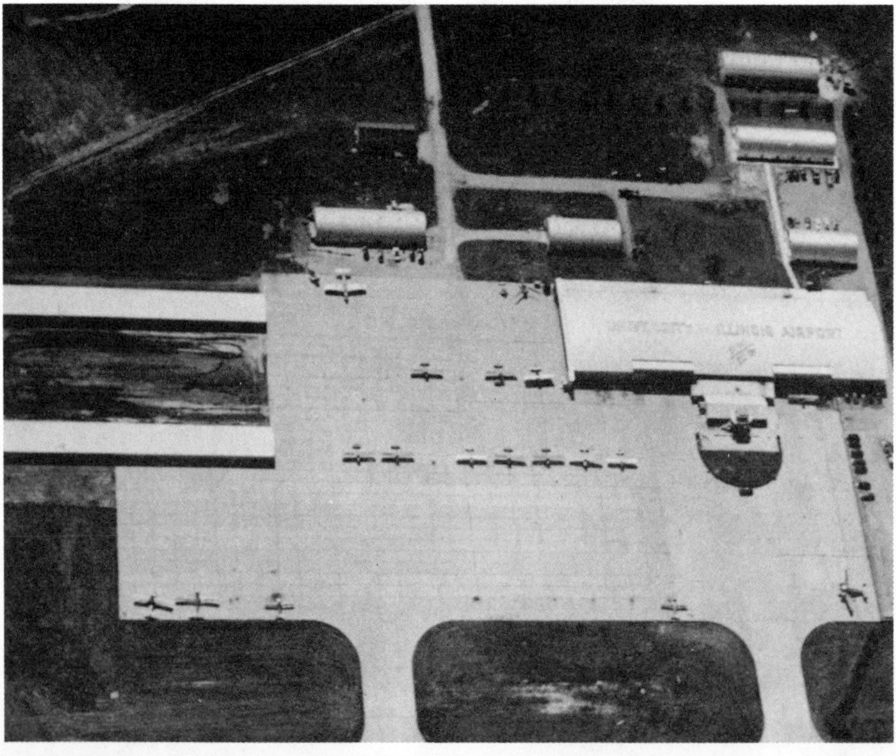

after 1927, the Pacific remained unconquered by air until 1931. In June, 1927, Lieutenants Lester J. Maitland and Albert F. Hagenberger crossed from the mainland of the United States to Hawaii for the first time by air, but a flight on to Japan was not possible at that time because no airplanes then available could carry the huge quantity of gasoline needed for so long a nonstop flight. Flights between the United States and other countries of the Far East were not completed until Pan-American Airways reached Manila and other cities in the Orient in the mid-1930's, and, even then, flights were made by stages from island to island.

The long flight from Japan to the United States became a challenge to flyers in 1929 when two different Japanese newspapers offered prizes of $25,000 for a nonstop flight. Flyers from the United States and Japan made several attempts, but none succeeded prior to 1931. Harold Bromley and Harold Gatty failed in 1930 because they could not carry sufficient fuel. Shorter flights to the North American mainland were completed as early as 1927, from eastern Siberia to western Alaska, a relatively short distance compared to a flight from Japan to the United States. Finally, in July, 1931, Clyde E. Pangborn and Hugh Herndon completed the long flight on a round-the-world tour, which they had started with the hope of eclipsing the record set by Wiley Post and Gatty earlier the same summer. A long delay interrupted their flight in Japan when government officials arrested them as spies on the charge of flying over restricted territory and taking pictures of fortifications. Even though they were released after several days, there was no chance of setting a new record for global flight. At that point, Pangborn recalled that a Tokyo newspaper had offered a prize two years earlier for a nonstop flight from Japan to the United States; an investigation revealed that the offer was still valid. Consequently, Pangborn and Herndon began preparations for the flight. On October 4, they departed from Sabushiro, 300 miles south of Tokyo, on a flight that ended 41 hours and 4,465 miles later at Wenatchee, Washington. Their attempt to break the round-the-world flight record had failed, but they were $25,000 richer when they landed in the United States.

Several attempts were made to blaze an air route to Europe from the Middle West over northern Canada, Greenland, and Iceland to Scandinavia prior to 1931. Three different flights, from Rockford, Chicago, and Detroit, ended in failure between 1928 and 1931. One man, Parker D. ("Shorty") Cramer, of Lancaster, Pennsylvania, figured in all three flights: on the first, from Rockford, as co-pilot for Bert R. J. Hassell; on the second from Chicago, as co-pilot for Robert Gast; and on the last, as pilot, with Oliver Pacquett as radio operator. The flight from Rockford, which started August 16, 1928, ended in near tragedy when Hassell and Parker crashed and were lost in Greenland for nearly two weeks before being rescued by a field team of weather observers from the University of Michigan. On the second attempt, sponsored by the *Chicago Tribune*, Gast and Cramer lost their Sikorsky amphibian near Port Burrell, Labrador, on July 14, 1929, when it was carried out to sea and wrecked by floating ice. Fortunately, neither Gast nor Cramer was in the ship at the time. On the third attempt, Cramer and Pacquett, a radio operator loaned especially for the flight by the Canadian government, were blazing an airmail route to Europe for Trans-American Airways, a subsidiary of Thompson Aeronautical Corporation of Cleveland. Leaving Detroit July 27, 1931, Cramer and Pacquett proceeded as far as the Faroe Islands by easy stages in 13 days before disaster struck. On the final portion of the long flight, between the Faroe Islands and Copenhagen, they were apparently forced down in the North Sea during a sudden storm and perished. Wreckage thought to be from their plane was later recovered by a Dutch fishing trawler, but the bodies of Cramer and Pacquett were never found.

Many other famous transoceanic flights were in some way related to aviation in Illinois. If space allowed, it would be appropriate to tell in detail the story of such great flights as the round-the-world trip of Post and Gatty in 1931, Post's solo record-breaking global flight two years later, and the global flights of Jimmy Mattern, who, with Lieutenant Bennett Griffin, attempted to duplicate Post and Gatty's triumph in 1932. In 1933, Mattern started again on a solo flight in an effort to beat Post's record set the same year. Mattern's solo flight around the world was financed by two Chicago-area men as publicity for the spectacular Chicago World's Fair of 1933–1934; his plane bore the name *Century of Progress.* Mention should also be made of the flights of Charles and Anne Morrow Lindbergh, while carrying out surveys for Pan-American Airways in the Pacific, and the achievements of George Haldeman, Russell N. Boardman, Stephen Darius and Stanley Girenan, Thor Solberg, Harry T. ("Dick") Merrill, Harry Richman, Amelia Earhart, Ruth Elder—all outstanding pilots of the 1930's.

Transoceanic flights often monopolized the headlines of American newspapers, but other outstanding performances also contributed to the progress of aviation. Transcontinental and intercity flights, air races and record-breaking flights for speed, altitude, and endurance focused public attention on the development of safer, more efficient airplanes for private and commercial flying. Roscoe Turner, Frank M. Hawks, Jimmy Wedell, Jimmy Haizlip, Charles W. ("Speed") Holman, and Howard Hughes established speed records for closed course and intercity flights between 1925 and 1940. Pilots of the best racing planes of their day, these men made a habit of setting new records in rapid succession; speeds rose higher and higher with new improvements in the design and construction of airplanes, first to 200 miles per hour, then 250, and finally above 300 in 1939. Then the perfection of jet-powered planes during World War II sent the record beyond the speed of sound. The achievement of supersonic speed after a century of flight in Illinois completed the advance of aeronautics from balloons to jets.

Meets and air shows which featured races, acrobatics, stunt flying, and other entertaining events were a significant part of aviation in Illinois between 1919 and 1940. Hundreds of local air meets were staged in the state; the number cannot be determined exactly. For the most part, they were organized and financed by airport operators, sometimes with financial assistance from groups or organizations that hoped to benefit from greater flying activity in the community. Almost without exception, the dedication of a new airport was the occasion for an air meet or show, with local flyers furnishing the talent for races and stunts. If prizes were offered, flyers from other communities, even one or two of great reputation, would invariably enter the contests. In many of the larger meets held in the Chicago area, well-known professional racing and acrobatic pilots from the Midwest often appeared. The National Air Races of 1930 and the International Air Races of 1933, both sanctioned by the National Aeronautical Association, and the American Air Races of 1933 drew to Chicago outstanding pilots from all parts of the United States.

An excellent example of the type of air show given by airport operators in an effort to stimulate business can be seen in the activities of David L. Behncke at Checkerboard Field, Maywood, in the early 1920's. Behncke and his partners, Bert Blair and Lutz Meyers, presented air shows frequently on Sundays and holidays in order to draw local residents to the flying field; once the crowds appeared, the proprietors hoped to sell passenger rides and refreshments from concession stands. At the same time, they hoped to encourage more people to take up flying for pleasure or business, for, as operators of Illinois Aero Sales Company, they wanted to sell planes. The shows were generally widely publicized and consisted of a few stunts, perhaps formation flying and a parachute jump; the latter was always the big attraction. But as long as the business in passenger rides and refreshments held up, the main attraction was delayed. Eventually, when the patience of the crowd was exhausted, the big event was held, after which the concession stands and passenger planes quickly went out of business, for there was nothing more to hold the crowd. The financial difficulties of most airport operators at that time seemed to justify schemes that would stimulate business, regardless of ethical considerations. Behncke's methods were not unique, for others resorted to similar schemes in order to operate their businesses at a profit.

Other local air shows and meets provided competitive races and events which tested the flying skill of the entrants. In many instances, as at the Monmouth Aero Club air meet in June, 1922, winners received trophies; on a few occasions, modest cash prizes were awarded. The Monmouth meet is interesting because it was one of the first of its type in Illinois and set the pattern followed by air show promoters throughout the state during the next twenty years.

The Monmouth Aero Club, in conjunction with the Curtiss-Iowa Aircraft Corporation of Fort Dodge, Iowa, operators of a branch recently established in Monmouth, presented a three-day program of races and other competitive events on June 15-17, 1922. The novelty of competing in air races, which were virtually unknown in the Midwest at that time, attracted aviators from all parts of Illinois and Iowa as well as local flyers associated with the Curtiss-Iowa branch at the Monmouth field. The meet fulfilled the ambitions of the promoters who had hoped to present "the biggest event of its kind in Illinois outside of Chicago."

The three-day program included free-for-all races around a closed course, climbing, altitude, gliding, acrobatic, and spot-landing contests, for which the winners received trophies provided by local business houses and groups. Participants included four airmail pilots, three of whom were engaged in flying between Chicago and Monmouth over a special route created by the Post Office Department for the duration of the air meet. These flyers, E. Hamilton Lee, Ira O. Biffle, and Shirley J. Short, took part in the contests between flights. Another airmail pilot, Harry G. Smith, who was normally stationed in Cheyenne, Wyoming, appeared in the contests as the pilot of a new biplane developed by airplane designer Giuseppe M. Bellanca. Other contestants included Emil M. ("Matty") Laird and Walter Beech of the E. M. Laird Company of Wichita, manufacturers of the Swallow biplane; George B. Post, who flew a Petrol biplane manufactured by T. H. Huff of Ogdensburg, New York; James Curran, of Chicago, pilot of an S.V.A. pursuit plane owned by Ralph C. Diggins; and several local pilots, among whom John H. Livingston and Ed Kohlstedt were most conspicuous. The Lincoln Standard Aircraft Corporation of Lincoln, Nebraska, entered a biplane that was flown by Biffle in several races, and the Yackey Aircraft Company of Forest Park entered a Curtiss Oriole flown by Short.

The four airmail and two Laird flyers won a majority of the

contests at Monmouth. Under the watchful eye of R. W. Schroeder, official judge and starter of all events, the program began on the afternoon of June 15 with a parade through Monmouth and around the local airfield. Speed races, climbing, acrobatic, gliding, and spot-landing contests followed, with separate events for different sizes of planes in the speed and climbing races. In almost all contests, a battle developed between Smith in a powerful Bellanca and Laird and Beech in Swallows. When the races ended, Smith walked off with top honors in one of the three speed races, both climbing contests, and the gliding event; Beech won trophies in one speed race and the acrobatic contest. Other trophies were won by Lee, in one speed race; Kohlstedt, in the spot-landing contest; and Short, in the altitude contest. In addition to the competitive contests, thousands of spectators enjoyed daily acrobatics and stunt-flying exhibitions, wing-walking demonstrations, and parachute jumps.

One of the largest of the local air meets in Illinois occurred at Sky Harbor Airport, Northbrook, on September 11, 1932. It was sponsored by the American Legion to raise money for charity. Nearly two dozen flyers, including many from other states, participated in the one-day program of races and competitive events for trophies offered by Chicago newspapers and business firms. The speed events attracted such well-known racing stars as John H. Livingston, of Aurora; William A. Ong, of Kansas City, Missouri; Roger Don Rae, of East Lansing, Michigan; Roy Liggett, of Wichita, Kansas; and Bob Clampett, of San Francisco. Local racing pilots who participated were Emil M. Laird and Herman Hamer. Two races for sportsmen-pilots drew the largest number of contestants, mostly from the Chicago area. In all, six speed races were held; one other, a novelty event called an African Pursuit race, was held for the amusement of the 50,000 spectators who turned out for the program.

The races for professional pilots were the big attractions. In the two feature races of the afternoon, Livingston twice shot across the finish line a few seconds ahead of Ong. In the *Chicago Tribune* Trophy Race, a 10-lap, 50-mile contest, Livingston in a Monocoupe won first place honors over Ong by a close margin. He repeated his victory in the *Chicago Daily News* Trophy Race for the same distance, even though Ong posted the fastest speed of the day in one lap. In other races for professional race pilots, Rae won the Henry Horner Trophy in an event for planes of less than 350-cubic-inch displacement, and James Mattern, of Oklahoma City, won the L. B. Manning Trophy in a 15-mile race for Stinson planes. The *Chicago Daily Times* and Lear Radioaire trophies for the sportsmen-pilots' race were won by Eldon Cessna of Wichita, who flew a speedy Cessna stock-model airplane. First place in the African Pursuit Race, a three-lap, 15-mile race in which each contestant had to land and blow up a balloon after completing each circuit, went to Victor Lindemann of Chicago.

Chicago aviation boosters first succeeded in obtaining a nationally sanctioned air race for Illinois in 1930, when the National Air Races were held at Curtiss-Reynolds Airport, Glenview. From August 23 to September 1 of that year, Chicago was the center of aviation activity as hundreds of pilots from all over the United States gathered to watch the country's top flyers compete for $100,000 in prizes. Closed-course races, air derbies from distant cities, acrobatics, dead-stick landings, and balloon-bursting contests for men and women were the main attractions of the ten-day program. Stunt flying by a team of foreign pilots, formation flying by squadrons from the military service, parachute jumps, and glider contests supplemented the main program and entertained an average of 50,000 spectators during lulls in the daily racing program.

The National Air Races presented the greatest array of professional flyers ever seen in Chicago at one time. Five intercity air derbies, all timed races of three or more days' duration with prescribed refueling and overnight stops, were launched from different points in the United States, timed to end in Chicago after the official opening of the races on August 23. Another air derby, a nonstop race from Los Angeles, was held August 25. For men there were two Class A derbies—from Seattle and Miami—and two Class B events, from Brownsville, Texas, and Hartford, Connecticut. In the women's division there was a

Class A event from Long Beach, California, and a Class B race from Washington, D.C.

All these derbies presented fine examples of dependable airplane performance and pilot skill. Mrs. Gladys O'Donnell, of Long Beach, California, in a Waco 10-T, easily won top honors in the women's Class A derby over Mildred Morgan, of Beverly Hills, California, and Jean La Rene, of Kansas City. Mrs. Phoebe F. Omlie, of Memphis, Tennessee, placed first in the Washington-to-Chicago race, defeating Martie Bowman, of Hempstead, New York, and three other contestants. Among the male participants, John Blum, of Seattle, in a speedy Lockheed Vega, nosed out Nick Mamer, of Spokane, in the Seattle-Chicago race by less than 23 minutes. In the other Class A derby, from Miami, Arthur W. Killips, of La Grange, Illinois, fought a close battle with Arthur J. Davis, of East Lansing, Michigan, winning in the final day by less than three minutes in total flying time. George T. Burrell, of La Grange, was the only other contestant. Both of the Class B derbies were close races. In the dash from Brownsville, John H. Livingston, of Aurora, in a Lambert-powered Monocoupe, finished more than an hour ahead of Wilfred G. Moore, of Kansas City. Although the rules called for at least five contestants, Livingston and Moore were allowed to compete for the $4,000 in prizes set aside for that event. Two Philadelphia flyers, J. Wesley Smith and H. H. Little, Jr., turned the race from Hartford into a two-man competition. The outcome remained in doubt until both flyers reached Curtiss-Reynolds Airport. Final official statistics showed that Smith had won by five minutes. C. W. Meyers, of Cleveland, and Leslie Bowman, of Hempstead, New York, finished third and fourth respectively.

The National Air Races opened with speed races, acrobatic and stunting events, and other types of flying demonstrations. Interest focused on the speed events in which the best professional racing pilots in the country vied for prize money and honors around a five-mile closed course. In the men's events, entrants were classified according to the size of their planes, with races for each category based on the piston displacement of engines. Only in the famous Thompson Trophy Race were racers of unlimited size permitted to enter, and even then they had to qualify at a speed that eliminated all but the fastest of the smaller racers. Special races were also held for certain types of planes—such as those powered with OX engines, cabin planes, and multi-engine transports—and six events were scheduled for sportsmen-pilots; all but two of the latter were eventually canceled for lack of contestants.

Only the faster racing planes and the best of the racing pilots participated in the 28 closed-course events of the 1930 air races. Among consistent winners were several pilots from Illinois: Charles W. Holman, who made his residence in Minneapolis but flew regularly out of Chicago; Arthur C. Chester, airport operator from Joliet; John H. Livingston, manager of the Mid-West Airways of Aurora; Art Killips, of La Grange; R. T. ("Stub") Quimby and Vern Roberts, of Moline; and Edward B. Heath and Herman Hamer, of Chicago. Other Illinois pilots entered speed events, but Holman, Chester, Livingston, and Roberts were by far the finest performers, competing against such outstanding racing stars as Arthur J. Davis, Ben O. Howard, James R. Wedell, and Erett Williams.

In the Thompson Trophy Race, Holman upset all predictions by dashing across the finish line ahead of the entire field. Jimmy Haizlip, Frank Hawks, or Captain Arthur H. Page had been favored to win. But Holman, originally not even scheduled to enter, piloted Laird's "Solution" racer to victory after Lee Shoenhair of Los Angeles was unable to fly it. The new racer left the factory the morning of the race, Holman put it through brief trial flights, then flew it that afternoon in the speed classic of American aviation. After the first few laps, the race settled down to a three-way fight between Holman, Haizlip, and Page. The latter, in a "souped-up" Curtiss "Hawk" pursuit plane modified by the Marine Corps especially for the race, gradually pulled out ahead of his rivals and held his lead for 16 laps; then his fast ship suddenly plunged to the ground out of control at a speed of more than 200 miles per hour. Hawks, in a Travel Air racer, dropped out in the fourth lap, and Williams, in a Cessna, quit after the eighth, leaving only Ben Howard and Paul T. Adams to trail the leaders. Nearly 60,000 spectators stood throughout the last part of the race, watching Haizlip and Holman jockey for position; both racers displayed breathtaking speed but lost ground on the turns around the short triangular course. By the last lap, Holman gained a slight lead and held on to finish 18 seconds ahead of his rival. After landing, Holman had to be helped from his racer; exhaust fumes had flooded the cockpit throughout the race, making him terribly sick.

The unqualified success of the National Air Races of 1930 should have assured their return to Chicago in the near future, but since that date they have almost always been held in Cleveland. For a time, the favorable public response to the American Legion Air Races at Sky Harbor Airport in 1932 gave Chicago hopes of obtaining the national races during the Century of Progress Exposition in 1933, but they were held in Los Angeles in spite of Chicago's bid. However, two big air races, one of them sanctioned by the National Aeronautical Association, did take place in Chicago during the fair. The first was held at Municipal Airport, July 1-5, under the sponsorship of the *Chicago Tribune;* the other, at Curtiss-Reynolds Airport, September 1-4, under the joint sponsorship of the *Chicago Daily News* and the National Aeronautical Association.

Chicago's first big air-racing program of 1933, the American Air Races, was held on the same days the National Air Races were going on in Los Angeles; consequently, it failed to draw many of the top stars who might otherwise have appeared. The outstanding performers and leading money-winners were John H. Livingston and Arthur J. Davis, who thrilled the spectators with their keen rivalry in the two feature speed events. Since both men flew Warner-powered Cessnas of essentially the same design and speed, experience and skill were the deciding factors in determining the outcome of the events in which they appeared. On July 3, in the 50-mile Baby Ruth Trophy Race for 500-cubic-inch planes, Livingston flashed across the finish line only a few seconds ahead of Davis, the difference in their average speeds being less than one mile per hour. Other money-winners placed far behind the two rivals: Harold Neumann, of Elmhurst, finished third; Jack Wright, of Utica, New York, fourth; and Joe Jacobson, of Kansas City, fifth. Before renewing their rivalry in the Aero Digest Trophy Race the following day, both Livingston and Davis made changes in their planes which increased their speeds slightly over the 200-mile-per-hour mark. But on the afternoon of July 4, Livingston, cutting pylons by the narrowest margins, again raced home ahead of Davis to win the 25-mile race. On the final day of the program, Livingston proved that his racer was the fastest ship in the meet by setting an unofficial speed record for planes of 500-cubic-inch displacement. On July 5, he pushed the small yellow and red Cessna around four laps of a measured course at an average speed of 237.4 miles per hour, exceeding the record of 213.8 set by Ben Howard at the Cleveland National Air Races in 1932.

In speed events for smaller planes, Jack Wright and Neumann were the outstanding performers. Helen MacCloskey, of Pittsburgh, the only woman who participated in speed races, finished among the money-winners in two events. Top money-winners, in the order of their total earnings, were Livingston, Davis, Neumann, and Wright. Art Carnahan, of Bloomington, Walter Franklin, of Kankakee, and David H. Bishop, of Chicago, were also notably successful. Carnahan, for many years manager of Bloomington Municipal Airport and operator of Carnahan Flying Service, flew a Tilbury-Fundy Flash, a midget racer designed by Owen Tilbury and built by Tilbury, Carnahan, and Clarence Fundy, all of Bloomington. The diminutive racer was completed in 1932 but failed to fly until modified the following year.

The second big air-racing program of 1933 opened at Curtiss-Reynolds Airport September 1, with many of the headliners of the previous National Air Races as contestants. Frank Hawks, Roscoe Turner, and James R. Wedell headed the list of distinguished participants. Among the pilots of small racing planes, Art Chester, of Joliet, Illinois; Steve J. Wittmann, of Oshkosh, Wisconsin; Gordon Israel, of St. Louis; George O. Hague, Leland S. Miles, and Roy Minor, of Los Angeles; and Roy T. Liggett, of Omaha, Nebraska, were the principal stars. Women contestants included Mae Haizlip, holder of the world's speed record for women, Florence Klingensmith, of Minneapolis, Martie Bowman, of Burbank, California, and Henrietta Lantz, of Los Angeles. These and other contestants, aided by flying units of the military services, parachute jumpers, and the Gordon-Bennett Cup balloonists, who started from Glenview field September 2, entertained Chicago-area residents and visitors to the World's Fair with the finest exhibition of air-racing events seen in Chicago since 1930.

The International Air Races were filled with thrilling races, spectacular acrobatic and stunting exhibitions, and tragedy. Frank Hawks set the stage for the four-day program of outstanding events by racing from Chicago to Los Angeles, on to Seattle, and back to Chicago, a total distance of 4,500 miles, in 24 hours and 25 minutes of flying time. On the following day, James R. Wedell, a designer, builder, and flyer of racing planes from Patterson, Louisiana, diverted attention from Hawks's remarkable intercity record flight by setting an unofficial world's speed record of 294.8 miles per hour for land planes in one of his own Wasp-powered Wedell-Williams Special racers. Because he completed only two legs of the measured course, instead of four, and failed to carry a sealed barograph, Wedell's flight could not be recognized by the National Aeronautical Association. Undaunted, however, he exceeded this unofficial record and set a new world's speed record in the Shell Straightaway Speed Dashes on September 4. In competition with Lee Gahlback and Roscoe Turner, Wedell thundered along a three-kilometer course four times, twice in each direction, at an average speed of 305.33 miles per hour—a new record for land planes. On one downwind flight, he pushed his big red and black racer to a speed of 316.55 miles per hour, probably the fastest speed achieved in level flight to that date. Later the same afternoon, Wedell flew the same ship to victory in the feature 100-mile, free-for-all race.

In the races for smaller planes, Chester, Wittmann, Miles, and Minor dueled with one another for top honors. The first three men piloted speedy racers of their own design and construction, while Minor flew a compact racer designed and built by Ben Howard. In race after race, Minor's ship showed greater speed, though the others frequently overcame that disadvantage with greater skill and daring in rounding the pylons. In the official standings of contestants, Minor, Chester, Miles, and Wittmann appeared in that order. All four flyers continued at the International Races a keen rivalry that had first appeared at the Los Angeles races, where Minor in the Howard racer had consistently beaten the other three.

Even though big air races were seldom held in Illinois, a large number of pilots from the state were consistent performers elsewhere. For many years, Charles Holman, Ed Ballough, Jimmy Doolittle, and Roscoe Turner—to name only the top pilots—flew Laird racers built in Chicago by Matty Laird and the E. M. Laird Airplane Company. Besides the Thompson Trophy Race of 1930, Holman won many other national honors in Laird ships, including the New York-Spokane race in 1927 and the Gardner Trophy Race in 1929. Ballough, a Chicago flyer, placed second behind Holman in the New York-Spokane race and won many other honors in air races in the late 1920's. Turner, one of the greatest racing pilots of all time, won the Thompson Trophy Race of 1939 in a big racer that had been redesigned and modified by Laird. Outside of Chicago, Illinois had many well-known professional racing pilots, of whom the most outstanding were John H. Livingston, of Aurora; Harold Neumann, of Moline; Rudy Kling, of Lemont; and Art Chester, of Joliet. In six years of professional racing, beginning in 1928, Livingston earned more than $60,000 and a reputation as the most consistent winner in the game. Another consistent winner, Neumann earned national recognition when the National Aeronautical Association selected him as "pilot of of the year" in 1935 after he captured that year's Thompson Trophy Race at Cleveland. Two years later, Kling, a garage proprietor as well as a professional race pilot, won the Thompson Trophy, the high point of his career, which ended tragically at the Miami Air Maneuvers in January, 1938.

One of the greatest professional racing pilots in Illinois and the United States during the past three decades was Arthur C. Chester, for many years operator of Wilhelmi Airport near Joliet. As a designer, builder, and flyer of racing planes, Chester displayed extraordinary ability and consistently won top honors in national races against any and all competition. His uncanny ability in an all-around way put him in a class almost by himself; few racing figures of recent time could equal the sweep of his talent.

In 1921, when 22 years of age, Chester learned to fly at the Aurora Aviation Company, not far from his home in Downers Grove. Thereafter, he devoted his life to aviation, particularly airplane races. After becoming a pilot, he worked one season with Anna's Flying Circus, one of many which toured the Midwest in the early 1920's. He spent the next four years making charter and passenger flights and, in 1927, joined the Yackey Aircraft Company as a design engineer, chief pilot, and instructor. Two years with the Yackey firm gave Chester a thorough knowledge of airplane design and construction, and, in a sense, made possible his future success as a designer, builder, and flyer of racing airplanes. In 1929, after Yackey Aircraft went out of business, Chester moved to Joliet to take over the management of Wilhelmi Airport, where, in his spare time, he built his first racing plane.

Beginning with the National Air Races in Cleveland in 1929, Chester appeared in every one of the annual events during the next twenty years. However, he was not especially conspicuous until 1933, when he first entered a racer of his own design, a small midwing monoplane called *Jeep,* which won numerous honors during the next five years. At first, the little plane barely exceeded 150 miles per hour, but further refinements, including a gradual increase in the power of the engine from 190 to 300 horsepower between 1933 and 1937, resulted in additional speed, surpassing 220 miles per hour in some races.

At the close of the 1937 season, Chester realized that he must have a more powerful plane to compete against newer models if he hoped to win the Louis M. Greve and Charles E. Thompson Trophy races, feature speed events in the National Air Races. For months preceding the 1938 races, he worked on a new racer which he called the *Goon.* Pressed for time as the date of the races approached, he literally threw the small plane together before entering it in the speed events. Even though the *Goon* lacked the refinements Chester would have provided with more time, he flew it in the Greve Trophy race for planes of less than 500-cubic-inch displacement and finished a close second behind Tony Le Vier in a Monasco-powered Schoenfeldt Special. The race was a grueling one in which the outcome remained in doubt until the final lap. For 200 miles, Le Vier and Chester fought a close battle, with the lead changing several times but as the two racers flashed across the finish line, Le Vier was in front by a slight margin. Chester's speed for the race was only a fraction slower than Le Vier's winning 250.46 miles per hour.

The disappointment of losing the Greve race by so narrow a margin induced Chester to completely overhaul the *Goon* in preparation for the same event the following year, which he intended to win. When the National Air Races opened in Cleveland in September, 1939, Chester's *Goon* gave the appearance of speed from nose to tail; not a ripple could be seen in the tapered cantilever wings or streamlined body. With methodical care, Chester had tuned the small racer for the two big events, and, because of his recognized ability, the sleek *Goon* was favored to win the Thompson Trophy and place high in the Greve race. Though it proved to be a speedy racer, it failed to fulfill all the predictions of the forecasters. In the Greve Trophy Race, where Earl Ortman, in a Monasco-powered Marcoux-Bomberg racer, was favored to run away from all contestants, Chester won easily; but in the Thompson classic, Roscoe Turner's big twin-Wasp-powered Turner-Laird racer outdistanced all competition.

The mobilization of the aviation industry for production of war planes in 1940 ended all national racing competition, and former racing plane designers and flyers turned to important posts in the expanding industry. During the next six years, Chester devoted his time to the design and manufacture of airplanes, but his real interest remained in racing competition. When drastic cutbacks in the aviation industry followed the surrender of Japan, Chester and other professional racing pilots lost little time in returning to the highly competitive business of racing. At the opening of the National Air Races in Cleveland in 1946, Chester and Steve J. Wittmann, the two outstanding designers and flyers of the prewar years, were on hand with new racers to compete with a new generation of racing enthusiasts.

Wartime developments produced noticeable changes in the first postwar National Air Races. Unlike the races of previous years, in which small planes were often the fastest, the postwar events featured many larger planes that could easily outdistance the smaller racers. To meet the new conditions, the races were rigidly divided into classes for small and large planes, with no overlapping of entrants. Chester and other professional racing pilots had watched with apprehension the conversion of fast military pursuit planes into racing models, for they feared that air races of the future might be dominated completely by military designs unless something were done to save air races for "backyard inventors" and designers of home-built racers. Consequently, a group of pilots, at Chester's suggestion, organized the Professional Race Pilots' Association to encourage the design and construction of small racing planes for national competition. Through the efforts of the Association, of which Chester was president, the Goodyear Tire & Rubber Company, of Akron, Ohio, and the Continental Motor Company sponsored special small-plane trophy races at the Cleveland National Air Races and at the Miami All-American Air Maneuvers. Small racers were classified as those with less than 190-cubic-inch displacement.

Chester's 20-year career as a professional racing pilot came to a close in April, 1949, when he crashed and died during the American Gold Cup Races at San Diego. While rounding a pylon in his *Swee' Pea,* the 1948 version of the racer with which he had entered postwar competition, Chester apparently lost control and crashed. His death was a tragic blow to the racing profession that he had welded into a respected and valuable organization. His contribution to aviation is signalized in a tribute from the National Aeronautical Association, which had awarded him an honorary life membership "for the design, construction, and piloting of light-weight high-speed racing aircraft and the direction of safe air race competition."

Closely rivaling transoceanic flights and national air races in popular appeal were attempts to establish endurance flight records. Until the late 1920's, endurance records attracted little attention outside aviation circles, primarily because until that time the number of hours an airplane could remain in the air was not particularly impressive. Even though the technique of refueling airplanes in flight had been developed as early as 1923, there were only a few attempts to use that method in establishing endurance records before January, 1929. On that date, Major Carl Spaatz and a crew of four in the Air Corps tri-motor Fokker transport *Question Mark* set a record of 150 hours, 40 minutes, 15 seconds, circling over Los Angeles Airport. After that, new records appeared in rapid succession as the number of hours of continuous flight went up steadily—it is now more than 1,000 hours. In the past 30 years, two endurance records were established in Illinois, and many more were attempted.

Two brothers from Sparta, Illinois, John and Kenneth Hunter, set a new endurance record in the summer of 1930. Circling over Sky Harbor Airport, Northbrook, in a second-hand Stinson-Detroiter named the *City of Chicago,* the brothers remained aloft 23 days, from June 11 to July 4, pushing the record to a new high of 553 hours, 41 minutes, 30 seconds. The Hunters turned their record-making endurance flight into a family affair. While John and Kenneth circled Sky Harbor, two other brothers, Walter and Albert, manned a second plane to carry aloft fuel and provisions. On July 4, when it seemed that the flight might continue several more days, John and Kenneth landed unexpectedly because of trouble with oil pressure and an overheated engine. Earlier that same day, the flight had nearly ended when an oil feed-line broke, but the trouble was quickly repaired before the engine was damaged. The Hunters' remarkable flight shattered the old record of 420 hours set the previous year by Dale Jackson and Forest O'Brien in St. Louis, but five weeks later Jackson and O'Brien regained the title by staying in the air 627 hours.

Between July 23 and August 6, 1939, two brothers from Dalton City, Hunter and Humphrey Moody, established a new endurance record for light planes. Circling above Springfield Municipal Airport, the Moody brothers remained in the air 343 hours, 47 minutes, 30 seconds, surpassing the old record of 218 hours set in Long Beach, California, in 1938. The flight proceeded without incident until August 5, when the effects of over 300 hours of continuous operation of the 55-horsepower engine of their Taylorcraft began to appear; only four of eight cylinders were firing at one point, and one generator completely failed. However, hope brightened the following morning when their engine "took a new lease on life." A "secret" mixture invented by Le Roy Murphy, chief mechanic and manager of the flight, cleaned the spark plugs and all but one began firing in order. Later the same night, however, the threat of a severe electrical storm forced the brothers to land, for it was feared their balky engine would not stand the exertion of flying above the disturbance. At 10:46 P.M., as light rain and high winds swept across the airport, the small plane rolled to a stop, ending a flight which had covered nearly 27,000 miles, all within a 100-mile radius of Springfield.

At least two other attempts were made to set endurance records during the 1930's, but both were unsuccessful. In August and September, 1934, Jean La Rene and Mary Owens, both of Texas, made three unsuccessful attempts to set new endurance records from Sky Harbor Airport. The last attempt ended September 3, after 19 hours in the air, because of murky weather. In-flight refueling operations on all three flights were handled by Kenneth Hunter and Leo Sauerborn. Less than a year later, another endurance flight began at Peoria with the financial backing of the Peoria Air Associates. The flight started August 19 with Kenneth Ringel, operator of Mt. Hawley Airport, as pilot and Ellis Friedrich as radio operator and technical adviser. But what started out to be a 30-day flight ended after only 42 hours because of motor trouble.

For more than a decade prior to World War II, the Illinois Chamber of Commerce, the Illinois Aeronautics Commission, and the State Board of Agriculture stimulated interest in private flying by sponsoring frequent air tours and efficiency flight contests for operators of small pleasure aircraft. In 1928, and again in 1930, the Aviation Committee of the Illinois Chamber of Commerce sponsored what were to have been annual air tours to arouse interest in municipal airport construction and in the operation of private airplanes for both pleasure and business flights. The former objective, however, far outweighed the latter, since aviation enthusiasts of that time realized that any significant increase in the use of airplanes, whether for private or commercial purposes, would have to be preceded by a sizable airport construction program throughout the state.

The first air tour sponsored by the Aviation Committee visited 15 communities in three days. Sixteen airplanes, carrying 20 passengers in addition to pilots, departed from Chicago Municipal Airport, June 20, 1928, led by a Ford tri-motor. The tour included stops at Rockford, Sterling, Moline, and Monmouth the first day. At each stop, officials of the city and local chamber of commerce welcomed the air travelers in brief official ceremonies, and dignitaries accompanying the flight responded with praise for the local flying field and the community's concern for the prosperous growth of civil aviation. Following an overnight stop in Monmouth, the tour continued on to Peoria, Bloomington, Decatur, and Springfield, with a repetition of the same type of ceremony at each stop. On the third day, the itinerary included stops at East St. Louis, Belleville (Scott Field), Carbondale, Marion, Champaign, Danville, and Kankakee before returning to Chicago.

Participants in the Illinois Chamber of Commerce air tours were for the most part companies and business firms that operated airplanes for the transport of personnel or freight. Three firms entered two planes each: Standard Oil Company (Indiana) of Chicago, a Ford tri-motor flown by Rodney S. Lamont and a Laird biplane piloted by John Porter; Airads, Inc., of Chicago, two International cabin planes operated by Walter Vaughan and George Brew; and Mid-West Airways Corporation of Monmouth, a Waco biplane flown by Oren P. Harwood and a Ryan Brougham, by John H. Livingston, president and general manager of the company. Nine other companies or individuals also entered planes in the tour. A plane from the Aeronautics Branch of the Department of Commerce took part, with

Assistant Secretary of Commerce William P. MacCracken, Jr., as passenger and George Gardner as pilot. Fred J. Burchard and Murvin D. Actor, of Chicago, Elwood C. Cole, of Peoria, and Basil Sims, of Kankakee, also piloted planes in the tour.

The Chamber of Commerce air tour of 1930 immediately preceded the opening of the National Air Races at Glenview and sought to advertise that event throughout the state in addition to stimulating interest in civil aviation and airport construction. On the first day of a four-day tour, 15 planes visited seven northern Illinois communities: Elgin, DeKalb, Rockford, Dixon, Sterling, Kewanee, and Moline. At each stop, prominent business, civic, and chamber of commerce officials greeted the tourists as before, and at several stops Merrill C. Meigs, chairman of the Chicago Aero Commission and director of the tour, inspected local airport facilities. On the second day, the tourists visited Monmouth, La Salle (where a plane carrying Wayne Hammer, president of the Illinois Chamber of Commerce, L. V. Orsinger, and Walter Duncan joined the group for the remainder of the day), Streator, Peoria, Bloomington, and Decatur; on the third, Springfield, East St. Louis, Belleville (Scott Field), Marion, Centralia, and Mattoon; and on the fourth and final day, Champaign, Danville, Kankakee, and Aurora, returning to Curtiss-Reynolds Airport where the National Air Races were in progress.

This was the last Illinois Chamber of Commerce air tour. There was little reason for trying to stimulate interest in aviation at a time when airports were rapidly going out of business, when private pilots were giving up flying and commercial flyers were seeking work elsewhere. Apparently nothing could be done to prevent the decline of civil aviation in Illinois during the early years of the depression decade. The use of airplanes for either private or business travel was considered at best an expensive luxury that could be dispensed with in a period of financial distress.

By the mid-1930's, however, when civil aviation had recovered somewhat, the need for stimulating interest in it on a state-wide scale induced the Illinois Aeronautics Commission and the State Board of Agriculture to sponsor an annual efficiency flight contest in conjunction with the State Fair. At first, these contests were limited in scope: each year, on opening day of the Fair, aviators from all parts of the state were invited to participate in an efficiency flight in which contestants were judged for ability to handle a plane; landing technique; observance of state, federal, and special rules; and compliance with flight plans during a brief flight over a prescribed course. However, after a few years, in response to a demand for a larger program, the sponsoring agencies made the efficiency flight a contest over an irregular course approximately 150 miles in length, ending in Springfield. The State Board of Agriculture offered prizes to participants in the event.

A total of 20 private and commercial pilots took part in the 1938 Illinois Pilots' Air Tour and Efficiency Flight Contest. On the first day of the tour, 24 planes carrying 47 passengers visited several northern Illinois communities: a group of the larger planes flew from Springfield to Danville, Joliet, Rockford, and Moline, stopping briefly at each point, while a group of smaller planes went from Springfield to Bloomington, Joliet, and Dixon, joining the first group in Moline, the overnight stop. On the second day, the tour continued to Quincy and East St. Louis and, after visiting Parks Air College, flew on to Marion, where the efficiency flight contest was to start the next morning.

On the morning of August 13, a total of 20 planes, some with passengers, flew to Springfield. A few of the smaller planes landed en route at St. Elmo, a check point on the irregular course; the others circled the airport and continued on to Springfield Municipal Airport, where all the contestants arrived between 10:30 and 11:30 A.M. At noon, an escort of motorcycle policemen led a motor caravan of flyers to the State Fairgrounds where the pilots were the honor guests of the day. Lawrence F. Zyzmunt, of Chicago, received the Governor's Trophy for recording the highest score among all contestants.

The success of the tour-contest in 1938 led to its continuance as an annual affair until World War II. The program was exceedingly popular with Illinois flyers, and the number of participants increased year after year. Between 1938 and 1941, the number of pilots entering rose from 20 to 40, and the last year more would have participated if they had been permitted to do so. William A. Thatcher, of Aurora, was the only flyer who took part in all four tours, but several participated three times —Fred S. Disosway, of Sheldon; R. A. Teutsch, of Bloomington; H. E. Horner, of Peoria; and Adelaide O'Brien, Fred C. Smith, and Nelson Weber, of Springfield.

In the 1939 program, 35 airplanes made a two-day tour of 12 airports. Four of the participating planes were escort craft which carried contest officials and observers. The planes left Springfield in one group on August 10, flying to Decatur, St. Elmo, East St. Louis, Quincy, and Peoria on the first day and to Bloomington, Kankakee, Aurora, Glenview, Dixon, Sterling, and Galesburg, the next. On the third day, contestants in the efficiency flight from Galesburg to Springfield were delayed for several hours by heavy fog that blanketed most of northern and central Illinois. The seven ships permitted to start when the fog temporarily lifted early in the morning were soon grounded; only Adelaide O'Brien proceeded as far as Peoria, where she too was forced to land because of poor visibility. Shortly before noon, however, all contestants started or renewed their flights when the fog lifted. Miss O'Brien, the first to get away at Galesburg, was also the first to arrive at the Springfield airport. Speed alone, however, did not determine the winner. R. A. Teutsch took top honors and the Governor's Trophy in the contest and also won $100 first-prize money in the sportsmen's division. The largest money winner was Fred Disosway, who not only captured first place in the commercial division but also won additional prizes for flying the greatest distance to take part in the contest and for carrying the largest number of passengers to the State Fair. In all, the State Board of Agriculture awarded prizes totaling $1,000; each contestant received a $10 participation prize for each day he took part in the tour or contest.

The 1940 tour penetrated less deeply into southern Illinois than the previous ones. Forty-five planes, including eight escort ships, left Springfield on August 15, for a two-day tour of airports at Salem, Greenville, Champaign, Bloomington, Lockport, Sterling, Moline, Monmouth, and Quincy, where they stopped at the end of the second day and started the efficiency flight contest. This was the first tour in which two women took part: Adelaide O'Brien, for the third straight year, and Genevieve Waples, of Decatur, in her first appearance, with Edwina Moody, of Dalton City (sister of the flying Moody brothers), as a passenger in her yellow and red Cub.

In the 1941 program, 40 pilots and 46 passengers covered an 850-mile air tour without a single accident and with only one instance of motor trouble. The air tourists left Springfield on August 7 and proceeded to Alton, Du Quoin, Marion, Mt. Vernon, Charleston, and Danville before tying down their planes for the night. The next day, the tour continued on to Bloomington, Kankakee, Lansing, Dixon, and Galesburg.

As was customary, the efficiency contest started out from the last city on the morning of the third day. Paul D. Fulk of Bethany registered the highest efficiency point score in his Taylorcraft, winning the Governor's Trophy and first-prize money in the sportsmen's division. Art Curry, operator of an airport at Galesburg, won first place in the commercial division, while in a new division, created especially for women pilots, Irene Crane Gaby, of Springfield, won the prize for commercial pilots, and Janet Mayhercy, of Wilmette, the prize for private flyers.

The prewar Illinois Pilots' Air Tour and Efficiency Flight Contest served a twofold objective. In the first place, the programs brought together many of the most active pilots in the state and gave them an opportunity to talk over their mutual problems. In the second place, and probably more important, the programs stimulated public interest in civil aviation and encouraged flyers to broaden the scope of their activities by flying to other portions of the state.

After World War II, these needs were amply fulfilled through the activities of flying clubs, the Illinois Flying Farmers, and the Civil Air Patrol; consequently, the postwar revival of the air tours and efficiency flights was of short duration. The 1955 air tour, sponsored by the Illinois Department of Aeronautics and other organizations, had little similarity to the earlier programs; it was, in fact, little more than a mass flight of vacationers from all parts of Illinois to a vacation spot in Wisconsin. The absence of a promotional tour to various communities and of prizes for participants indicated the tremendous strides made in Illinois aviation in the decade following World War II.

11

REGULATION OF AERONAUTICS: STATE AND FEDERAL, 1926–1955

Until the mid-1920's, the aviation industry in the United States experienced an unrestricted growth, free from virtually any form of regulation. There had been attempts to regulate the use of aircraft, particularly over heavily populated areas, but they were made several years before most people were willing to concede their practical value. The first effective, constructive legislation was the federal Air Commerce Act of 1926.

Agitation for regulation gained momentum in the years immediately following World War I as a result of the sudden expansion of aeronautical activity. The release of surplus military aircraft in vast numbers at relatively low prices had provided the impetus for this expansion and the war-surplus Curtiss Jenny, Standard, or any one of a dozen models, became the basis for a new type of professional aviator known as an itinerant flyer or "gypsy." At one time their number was possibly as high as 1,000, but in 1922, and for the next few years, there were probably between 500 and 600. Though not numerous by today's standards, when approximately 17,000 private pilots in Illinois hold federal licenses, they seemed dangerously so in the early 1920's.

In 1925, many private, civic, and governmental organizations aroused public sentiment for regulation and control of civil aeronautics by the state and federal governments. Such agitation had occurred sporadically since 1919 but never with sufficient force to produce lasting results. In five years from 1919 through 1923, Congress acted upon 24 different bills designed to impose some degree of regulation and control. The first was introduced, July 23, 1919, by Senator Lawrence Y. Sherman, of Springfield, Illinois. On the floor of the Senate, he stated that the bill was motivated by a recent tragic airship crash in Chicago that might have been averted if federal regulation of air navigation had been in force. The tragedy referred to was the crash of the Goodyear Tire & Rubber Company's blimp *Wing-Foot* through the skylight of the Illinois Trust and Savings Bank on the afternoon of July 21, 1919. The crash killed one crew member and twelve bank employees and seriously injured many others. Sherman's bill failed to pass, as did others introduced in the next four years. Senator Harry S. New, later Postmaster General under President Coolidge and a stanch supporter of airline transportation, introduced two bills in 1919 to create a federal Department of Aeronautics. Representative Julius Kahn of California twice attempted to win the approval of the House for bills to create a Bureau of Air Navigation with authority to regulate aviation; both were rejected by the 67th Congress. Senator James W. Wadsworth, Jr., of New York, sponsored six bills: one in 1920, two in 1921, one in 1922, and two in 1923. Two passed in the Senate but failed in the House of Representatives.

When Congress failed to act, many states, alarmed by the sudden expansion of civil aviation and the high accident rate among itinerant flyers, attempted to establish laws that would curb the apparently hazardous practices followed by a small group of irresponsible aviators. Some cities considered ordinances to prevent particular acts by aviators, and in a few instances such laws were enacted. The *Wing-Foot* disaster prompted the Chicago City Council to consider ordinances governing aircraft navigation above the city. Elsewhere in Illinois, the need for regulation became increasingly apparent as the state led the nation in aircraft accidents and fatalities year after year.

Advocates of state regulation continued to introduce regulatory legislation in the General Assembly during the 1920's. On March 9, 1921, Representative Charles W. Baldwin, of Chicago, introduced H.B. 325, an act to regulate the operation of aircraft over cities and villages; the measure died in the Committee on Judiciary. In the next regular session, three more efforts were made to secure similar legislation without success. Senator William S. Jewell, of Lewistown, sponsored, on March 7, 1923, S.B. 162, a uniform aeronautics law defining sovereignty and ownership of the air and the rights and liabilities of owners and operators of aircraft. The Senate passed the bill, but opponents brought about its defeat in the lower chamber. They argued that regulation was a federal rather than a state function and that the General Assembly need not consider such action since regulatory legislation was then pending in Congress. They maintained further that civil aviation was vital to defense; therefore, any attempt by the states to regulate, or restrict, its natural growth would constitute a serious blow to the nation's ability to fend off aggression by a foreign power. These arguments, though too illogical to withstand critical analysis, impressed the House; the bill was voted down by a nearly two-to-one majority.

In spite of opposition, particularly from pilots and aviation enthusiasts in and around Chicago, the agitation for legislation persisted. While the fate of the Jewell bill was still in the balance, Representative John Paul, of Chicago, sponsored two bills providing for a mild, almost indirect type of control. On April 4, 1923, he introduced an act providing for the licensing of aircraft and motor vehicle repairmen. This was followed by another that provided for an amendment to the state civil administrative code permitting the creation of a five-member board to supervise the licensing of all aircraft and motor vehicle mechanics. Both bills were tabled before the House had a chance to vote on them.

Four separate, similar measures were introduced in the 54th General Assembly. On March 29, 1925, Representative Sidney Lyon, of Chicago, introduced an act to create a uniform aviation law. Lyon's bill was tabled, but by that time another proposal had been introduced by Representative James A. Reeves, of Champaign, on May 14, providing for the licensing of aircraft operators and the bonding of owners by the Secretary of State. Reeves pushed the bill through the House, but the Senate tabled it after a second reading. Meanwhile, in the Senate, John S. Brown, of Monmouth, had introduced, on April 2, an act providing for the appointment by the governor of a three-member "Air Commission of Illinois," with authority to license aircraft after January 1, 1926, and to create and enforce rules and regulations governing the operation of aircraft. This won the overwhelming approval of the Senate; in the House, the bill was tabled, though it received favorable consideration from the Committee on Appropriations. Even while the Senate deliberated on the Brown bill, another proposal, introduced on May 26 by Lowell D. Mason, of Oak Park, provided for the creation of a committee of operators to supervise the licensing of all aircraft in Illinois. Though its aim was the removal of unsafe aircraft from the airways—a commendable objective in that era when a large percentage of the itinerant flyers operated antiquated, unsafe airplanes—this bill, too, was tabled by the Senate.

On the national level, demands for federal regulation of civil aeronautics resulted in the passage of the Air Commerce Act of 1926. Over the preceding two-year period, there had been numerous investigations of various aspects of aviation by government and private agencies, each urging the enactment of regulatory legislation. Among these were (1) the Lampert-Perkins Committee, known officially as the Select Committee of Inquiry into the Operations of the United States Air Services; (2) a joint committee created under the auspices of the Department of Commerce and the American Engineering Council, commonly known as the Hoover Committee; and (3) the President's Aircraft Committee, known more familiarly as the Morrow Committee. The Lampert-Perkins Committee, headed by Representatives Florian Lampert, of Wisconsin, and Randolph Perkins, of New Jersey, began its investigations in March, 1924. The Hoover Committee, appointed by Secretary of Commerce Herbert Hoover and headed by Assistant Secretary J. Walter

Drake, began its review of the economic aspects of the aviation industry in June, 1925. The Morrow Committee, so named in honor of its chairman, Dwight W. Morrow, began in September, 1925, a study of every phase of aviation, primarily military, to determine the most practical and efficient means of developing and applying aircraft to national defense. The appointment of all three committees was largely the result of General William Mitchell's one-man crusade to awaken the administration, the commands of the military services, and the American people to the importance of maintaining a strong, effective air arm as the first line of defense.

Each of the investigating committees pointed to the need for effective, constructive regulation of civil aeronautics in order to insure the creation of a large pool of trained aviators for the military air fleets in the event of a national emergency. They also recommended specific legislation for civil aeronautics. In a report filed December 14, 1925, the Lampert-Perkins Committee recommended that Congress "provide by law for the regulation and encouragement of commercial flying through the creation of a bureau of air navigation in the Department of Commerce," that provisions be made to chart airways, to establish emergency fields and air navigation facilities, to light the airways for night flying and to make available a specialized Weather Bureau service for air travelers. The Hoover Committee, in a report filed November 26, 1925, urged Congress to enact a civil aeronautics law providing for the creation of a bureau of civil aeronautics within the Department of Commerce. This bureau should be given authority to regulate civil aviation, license pilots, inspect and register aircraft, establish and maintain airways and air navigation facilities, administer relevant international aviation regulations, and encourage and promote the aircraft industry and air transport. The Morrow Committee recommended the creation of a Bureau of Air Navigation within the Department of Commerce, the extension of airmail service through the use of contracts with private operators, and government aid in establishing airways and air navigation facilities, including an adequate weather service maintained at government expense and suited to the special needs of air commerce.

Soon after the Morrow report was released, two members of the committee, Senator Hiram Bingham, of Connecticut, and Representative James S. Parker, of New York, introduced in their respective chambers bills embodying the recommendations of the Morrow, Lampert-Perkins, and Hoover committees. On December 14, 1925, in the recently convened 69th Congress, Bingham introduced a bill drawn up by the Committee on Commerce, of which he was chairman. Later, in the House of Representatives, the Bingham bill, with amendments devised by Representative Parker, was approved and emerged from conference committee to receive President Calvin Coolidge's signature on May 20, 1926.

This bill, known as the Air Commerce Act of 1926, created a framework within which the industry prospered and developed in a constructive, orderly fashion for more than a decade. The administration of the act was placed in the hands of a newly created Assistant Secretary of Commerce. The act asserted the constitutional right of the federal government to regulate interstate commerce; to assert its sovereignty in the air, to the exclusion of foreign powers, over lands and waters of the United States; to establish airways and compel adherence to prescribed flying rules on the part of all who used those airways, whether engaged in interstate or intrastate travel; and to establish and maintain lighting systems and emergency fields along federal airways. Other provisions empowered the Aeronautics Branch of the Department of Commerce to compel registration of all aircraft engaged in interstate travel; the registration of aircraft used solely for intrastate travel remained optional. Pilots were to be given periodic examinations upon which ratings were to be issued. Until the new agency was established, existing regulatory facilities, meager though they were, continued in operation.

President Coolidge hastened the establishment of the Aeronautics Branch of the Department of Commerce and the implementation of the Air Commerce Act by nominating, on August 11, William J. McCracken, Jr., as Assistant Secretary of Commerce for Aeronautics. McCracken was a prominent Chicago lawyer who had shown an intense interest in aviation. He served as a flying instructor in the Army Air Service during World War I and, for some time previous to his appointment, had been chairman of the Committee on the Law of Aeronautics of the American Bar Association. Even before the appointment was announced, the Department of Commerce began reorganizing in preparation for assuming the administration of the Air Commerce Act. The department thoroughly studied the problem of regulations in an effort to allay the criticism of those who feared over-regulation as much as no regulation. The rules and regulations placed in effect as of December 13, 1926, consisted of two main categories: (1) those dealing with licensing of aircraft, aviators, and aircraft mechanics, and requirements governing the operation of aircraft engaged in interstate commerce and (2) air traffic rules for all aircraft operations along federal airways—whether civilian or military, interstate or intrastate, or commercial or noncommercial.

The 1926 act, and subsequent rules and regulations promulgated by the Aeronautics Branch, provided effective, constructive regulation of airplanes engaged in interstate travel, but only indirect and generally ineffective controls over private and commercial aircraft operations that were purely intrastate in character. The effective administration of the Air Commerce Act, particularly the pilot-licensing and aircraft-registration programs, convinced many aviation enthusiasts that state legislation should extend the principles of the law to that portion of civil aeronautics outside the federal police power.

The apparent need for regulation in Illinois led to the consideration of a state aeronautics law by the 55th General Assembly. On May 3, 1927, Senator Rodney B. Swift, of Lake Forest, introduced an act providing for the creation of a one-man "Air Commission of Illinois," authorized to classify, certify, issue, and revoke licenses for aircraft, aviators, and landing facilities, and to draw up and promulgate rules and regulations for civil aviation in the state. Eight days after its introduction, the bill received the unanimous approval of the Senate and was forwarded to the House, where for lack of time it was tabled on the final day of the session. Although not enacted, the Swift bill served a year later as the model for the first Illinois aeronautics law.

After the adjournment of the General Assembly, numerous meetings were held to win public support for state aviation regulation. Representatives of seventeen municipalities formed an association to work for legislation permitting the acquisition and operation of airports outside municipal limits. This agitation bore fruit in the second special session of the 55th General Assembly, May 15–June 6, 1928. Senator Edward J. Hughes introduced and guided to a favorable vote in the upper chamber an act to regulate aeronautics, by which federal aeronautics laws were extended to cover the operation of commercial aircraft. The Aeronautics Act approved June 8, with amendments effective July 1, 1929, stipulated that the licensing and registration clauses of the federal law were to be extended and applied to all airmen and aircraft engaged in commercial air operation, whether or not in interstate travel. Amendments approved June 26, 1929, stipulated specific types of licenses that were to be in the possession of airmen flying under certain conditions, and prohibited the operations of aircraft over congested cities and towns except at prescribed altitudes. Violations were punishable as misdemeanors, by fines, imprisonment, or both. This law, in spite of its basically constructive features, was almost totally ineffective because the legislature neglected to provide either appropriations or provisions for enforcement.

Within less than a year, steps were taken to correct these defects. A joint legislative resolution, adopted May 28, 1929, created a six-member Aerial Navigation Commission vested with authority to investigate state-wide aviation conditions, to prepare legislation essential to effective, constructive regulation of all phases of the industry, and to report its findings and recommendations to the 57th General Assembly. Two members from each chamber of the legislature and two licensed transport pilots were to constitute the commission. Reed G. Landis, of Chicago, and Howard C. Knotts, of Springfield, were the nonpolitical appointees. Senators Lowell B. Mason and Richard R. Meents and Representatives Elmer C. Wilson and Charles

H. Weber were selected to represent the legislature. Landis was chosen chairman, and Knotts, secretary.

The commission's report, filed with the House of Representatives on January 14, 1931, recommended the creation of a permanent five-member aeronautics commission, whose members were to be appointed by the governor for four-year terms. It should have authority to define and enforce rules and regulations designed to promote public safety. Its rules should apply to all aviation facilities in the state, including airports, flight schools, and owners of operating beacons and other air navigation aids.

On the day the report was read and accepted in the General Assembly, bills embodying its recommendations were introduced in each chamber by former members of the commission. In the Senate, Meents introduced S.B. 9, and in the House Wilson introduced H.B. 42. The Meents bill, with amendments, was approved by both chambers, and signed by Governor Louis L. Emmerson on July 9, 1931.

The Illinois Aeronautics Commission, appointed by Governor Emmerson in August, 1931, immediately opened offices in Springfield and Chicago from which to carry out its statutory responsibilities and duties. The aeronautics act stipulated that at least two members of the commission should be, or have been, experienced pilots with at least 200 hours of solo time and at least three years of practical experience in aeronautics. Actually four of the five commissioners were former military pilots, but only one held a pilot's license in 1931. Landis served as chairman of the first commission; the other members were Roger Humphreys, of Bloomington; Wallace Wright, of East St. Louis; Fred D. Fagg, Jr., of Evanston; and Fred E. Gardner, of Rochelle. Elwood C. Cole, formerly an operator of a flying service and school in Peoria, became the secretary. Legislation in 1933 repealed the flight qualifications for commission membership; therefore, from that date until another amendment eight years later, experienced pilots on the commission were generally in a minority.

The duties of the commission, as set forth by statute, were designed simultaneously to regulate and promote the growth and development of civil aeronautics. Its regulatory functions included state registration of federal airman's licenses and aircraft certificates; licensing of airports, flight schools, and operators of air navigation facilities; investigation of aircraft accidents; and promulgation of rules and regulations governing the operation of aircraft and activities of pilots in Illinois. The commission did not license airmen or register aircraft since this was already a federal function, but it required that all airmen and aircraft engaged in commercial air travel in Illinois be registered with the federal agency and that their certificates be recorded with the state. State licenses for airports, flight schools, and beacons cost $25 during the first two years; in 1933, they were reduced to $2 in response to pleas for relief during the depression years. The depression and reduced appropriations forced the commission to curtail activities that year by closing its Chicago office.

An amendment to the Aeronautics Act of 1931 terminated the services of all members of the commission as of July 1, 1933, that body remaining inoperative until new members were appointed by Governor Horner on September 7. The new commissioners were Lawrence P. Bonfoey, of Quincy, chairman; Fred D. Fagg, Jr., of Evanston; Edward J. Lorenz, of Belleville; Eugene F. McDonald, of Chicago; and Carl P. Slane, of Peoria. Maurice D. Horner, Jr., of Chicago, became executive secretary, and Cole remained as secretary.

Through the 1930's, the commission, in addition to its purely regulatory functions, carried on a variety of programs designed to stimulate the growth and development of aviation. Through the Civil Works Administration and later federal emergency relief agencies, it obtained funds for local airport construction and improvement projects. Its engineering facilities, though limited, were frequently utilized by communities seeking advice and guidance in the selection and layout of new airports. The Works Progress Administration, with the cooperation of the commission, completed improvements at Chicago Municipal, Moline, Galesburg, and Camp Grant (Rockford) airports, and in other communities throughout the state.

Through its dual function of regulating and promoting state-wide civil aeronautics, the commission guided the development of aviation through the lean depression years of the 1930's and the war years that followed. Even though deprived of compensation during twelve of those years, many prominent leaders in business and industry welcomed the opportunity to serve on the commission. Merrill C. Meigs, Chicago newspaper publisher, was appointed December 31, 1936, to succeed Fagg, who had resigned. On May 18, 1937, the office of executive secretary was abolished, and Maurice L. Horner, Jr., was appointed to the vacancy created by the resignation of McDonald. Four years later, Governor Dwight H. Green appointed a new commission made up of Ben Regan, of Chicago, chairman; Horner; Slane; Lyman W. Sherwood, of Chicago; and C. W. Chiles, of Springfield. Except for the appointment of Harold Stickler, of Chicago, on February 8, 1943, to succeed Horner (who resigned to accept a commission in the Navy), this commission continued to function until superseded by the Department of Aeronautics. Most of its administrative tasks were handled by the secretary and a small clerical staff. Cole was secretary until May, 1937, when he resigned to become a technical adviser to the Bureau of Air Commerce; George C. Roberts served in that post for the next eight years.

The commission was represented in local communities by nonpaid inspectors, who were available in case of an emergency and were used, in the absence of the secretary, to investigate minor accidents, supervise air meets, inspect airports, and report violations of rules and regulations. Although the inspectors served without pay, they were allowed expenses for their services. Their number increased from 25 in 1935 to 47 in 1941, and to 99 in 1943. To facilitate administration, the state was divided into four districts with two commissioners for the Chicago and one for each of three downstate areas; each commissioner appointed five (later more) inspectors to assist with the work in his district.

On the national level, regulation of civil aeronautics was under the Aeronautics Branch of the Department of Commerce until July 1, 1934. On that date, the original agency became the Bureau of Air Commerce, but its functions were unchanged.

The Civil Aeronautics Authority Act, signed June 23, 1938, by President Franklin D. Roosevelt, completely reorganized federal regulation of civil aeronautics by vesting regulatory functions in a nonpolitical agency known as the Civil Aeronautics Authority. In addition to the five-member Authority, the act created the office of Civil Aeronautics Administrator and an Air Safety Board. On August 22, 1938, these agencies took over the personnel and responsibilities of the Bureau of Air Commerce of the Department of Commerce and assumed, in addition, numerous complex responsibilities prescribed in the new law.

Members of the Authority, appointed for six-year terms by the President, were empowered by statute to regulate commercial air transport companies, including economic regulation of business practices. Under its searching eye, airlines were permitted to continue operations designed to serve the public with adequate transportation at reasonable rates. At the same time, the airlines were assured of permanent routes, freedom from costly duplication of services, and protection against unfair business practices by competitors.

The administrator, appointed without definite term by the President, was empowered and directed to encourage and foster the development of civil aeronautics and air commerce. Specific provisions directed him to encourage the establishment of civil airways, airports and landing fields, and other air navigation facilities. It was also his duty to co-operate with the Air Safety Board in the administration and enforcement of the act. Through the administrator, the Civil Aeronautics Authority was to make a survey of all existing airports and report to Congress eight months later with recommendations for federal participation in a nation-wide airport construction and improvement program.

A three-member Air Safety Board, appointed for six-year terms, was charged with the responsibility for investigating accidents, assisting the Authority in studying matters relating to air safety, and making recommendations designed to promote safety. The reports of the Air Safety Board and studies of the Authority's Bureau of Safety Regulation became the basis for developing air safety practices to a remarkably high level of effectiveness during the late 1930's.

Within less than two years, at the insistence of President Roosevelt, Congress approved a reorganization plan containing the recommendations of the so-called Brownlow Committee. By the provisions of the new act, effective June 30, 1940, the Authority, the office of the administrator, and their functions were transferred to the Department of Commerce. The Air Safety Board was abolished; its functions were combined with those of the Civil Aeronautics Authority and given to a new agency, the Civil Aeronautics Board. The functions of the office of the administrator were taken over by the Civil Aeronautics Administration, which operated under the direction of the Civil Aeronautics Board and the Department of Commerce. A Bureau of Air Safety operated within the Civil Aeronautics Board with virtually the same tasks as the former Air Safety Board, but without its independence or authority. One of the additional changes sanctioned by the same reorganization plan was the transfer of the Weather Bureau from the Department of Agriculture to Commerce, where, because of its importance to civil aviation, it could be smoothly co-ordinated with the Civil Aeronautics Administration.

The reorganization, and the apparent subjection of the Civil Aeronautics Administration to political influences because of its dependent position within the Department of Commerce, had no visible effect upon aviation regulation. Critics claimed that the new agency would exert a less constructive influence, but this prophecy failed to materialize in the next fifteen years. David L. Behncke, founder and president of the Air Line Pilots' Association, pointed out that the original authority had amply fulfilled its twofold objective of destroying the fear of air travel and replacing that fear with confidence. These objectives had been accomplished primarily through safety programs and regulations devised by the Air Safety Board and enforced with the co-operation of the Civil Aeronautics Authority and the air transport industry. They could not be maintained by the new agency, Behncke charged, because of its subordinate position within an executive department. At the time, the charge seemed well founded, but critics and proponents alike soon discovered that the Civil Aeronautics Board and the Civil Aeronautics Administration had sufficient independence and authority to improve upon the work of their predecessors.

Federal regulation and promotion of civil aeronautics, since the adoption of the reorganization plan in June, 1940, has been the responsibility of the Civil Aeronautics Administration and the Civil Aeronautics Board. The former licenses pilots and aircraft, enforces safety regulations, builds and operates federal airways and air navigation facilities, and fosters the development of a national airport system under the provisions of the Federal Airport Act of 1946. The Administration conducts its activities as an operating agency of the Department of Commerce and under the direction of an Administrator of Civil Aeronautics appointed by the President. The Civil Aeronautics Board, unlike its companion agency, is virtually independent of the Department of Commerce and concerns itself principally with the regulation and promotion of the air transport industry. It regulates the activities of airlines engaged in the transport of passengers, mail, and freight through its authority to issue certificates of convenience and necessity, to formulate safety regulations, and to investigate accidents.

Even though federal regulation of civil aeronautics had achieved a satisfactory status by the late 1930's, regulation on the state level gave evidence of need for reorganization. In spite of its shortcomings, the Illinois Aeronautics Commission sought to foster civil aviation as an industry and as an adjunct of national defense. From the date of its inception, the commission was active in the National Association of State Aviation Officials, an organization dedicated to the promotion of aeronautics through the co-operation of state and federal agencies, and to the encouragement of co-operation among states, particularly in the development of uniform aviation laws and regulations. Informing the public of the importance of aviation constituted another aspect of the commission's work and entailed numerous addresses before civic clubs, schools, and similar groups.

Agitation for the reorganization of the Illinois agency reappeared sporadically throughout the late 1930's and the war years. The only concerted effort in this direction was stimulated by the Illinois Aviation Conference, an organization created originally from the aviation committee of the Illinois Chamber of Commerce. This group was a rallying point for all persons interested in the constructive growth and development of civil aviation throughout the state. Its principal efforts consisted of conducting state-wide meetings in which laws and regulations and state support of aviation comprised the major topics for discussion. However, before the agitation for more up-to-date state regulation of civil aeronautics could gain momentum, the entry of the United States into World War II diverted attention to the mobilization of civilian aircraft and pilots into voluntary organizations as supplementary wings of Army and Navy air fleets.

In time, the prewar campaign for more effective state regulation and promotion of civil aviation yielded limited results. On May 15, 1941, Senator Earle B. Searcy, of Springfield, introduced in the 62d General Assembly a bill amending the Illinois Aeronautics Act of 1931. It contained eight amendments to the earlier act, many of which added to the effectiveness of the commission. In addition to clarifying the definition of the term "airport" to include landing fields, and substituting the term "certificate" for "license" with reference to aircraft and airmen, it provided that two of the five members of the commission should be experienced pilots with 200 hours of solo flying and at least three years of practical experience. The bill also restored the commissioner's $15 per diem expense allowance that had been repealed eight years earlier, and conferred general police powers on the commission to facilitate enforcement of the act. The final amendment designated the commission as the sole state agency, except for municipal corporations of more than 500,000 inhabitants, to receive federal aid for airports and the promotion of aeronautics. After passage by both chambers of the General Assembly, the bill became a law without the Governor's signature, on July 29, 1941.

The wartime emphasis on air power and the resulting prestige for air travel gave promise of a bright future for aviation in the postwar years. Consequently, the agitation for a reorganization of the commission was taken up with renewed vigor. The Illinois Chamber of Commerce, the Governor, and prominent figures in civil affairs, business, industry, and the press, added their voices to the demand for new legislation. By 1945, even the commission, recognizing its own inadequate powers, joined in the sponsorship of new laws.

Victory came within the grasp of the reformers in the spring of 1945 when the General Assembly took up consideration of a new aeronautics law. At that time, Congress seemed likely to adopt a national airport plan embodying a Civil Aeronautics Administration proposal to spend billions of dollars on the construction of airports throughout the several states in proportion to their population. The prospect of obtaining approximately $40,000,000 prompted many legislators and aviation enthusiasts to seek legislation that would create effective state machinery for handling the federal and state funds for construction and improvements. Therefore, several important bills were introduced in the General Assembly. H.B. 518 provided for the creation of a code Department of Aeronautics to take the place of the ineffective Illinois Aeronautics Commission. Four Senate bills—S.B. 459, the Illinois Aeronautics Act; S.B. 443, the Country Airports Act; S.B. 10, the Municipal Airport Authority Act; and S.B. 445, the Airport Zoning Act—provided the future Department of Aeronautics, municipalities, and counties with adequate powers to utilize federal and state funds for construction and improvements.

The original reorganization bill, S.B. 342, was introduced April 12, 1945, by Senators Everett R. Peters and Edward R. Laughlin. It provided for the repeal of antecedent legislation and stipulated new laws which assured the proposed Department of Aeronautics sufficient powers to carry out its statutory duties. In reference committee, the bill encountered unexpected opposition. After nearly a month, Peters, a member of the Committee on Aeronautics and Military Affairs, recommended that S.B. 342 be tabled and a new bill substituted. On motion by Laughlin, the recommendation carried. The new bill, S.B. 459, cleared the legislature on June 29 and was signed by Governor Green on July 24.

The act gave the Department of Aeronautics ample authority for regulating and supervising civil aviation in those areas where federal law was ineffective. It was authorized to carry out multiple duties affecting every aspect of civil flying in Illinois. The act directed the department to co-operate with the federal government and municipalities in the regulation, promotion, and development of aviation and to render financial assistance to communities in the planning, construction, development, and improvement of airports and navigation facilities. It was authorized to receive federal funds for and in behalf of the state, municipalities, or political subdivisions and to enter into contracts for the construction and development of aviation facilities. Regulatory duties included registration of federal certificates of aircraft, pilots, and instructors; classification and approval of airports and their operation; and the preparation of zoning plans for publicly owned airports.

The administrative machinery of the Department of Aeronautics took shape in August and September, 1945. The act creating the code department contained the outline for its organization: the executive and administrative officers were the director and assistant director appointed by the governor. A nonexecutive or advisory board of nine members, including the director and assistant director, who served respectively as chairman and vice-chairman, formed a Board of Aeronautical Advisors. Though appointed at the pleasure of the governor, the advisory board had to include persons "interested" in specific areas: air commerce, commercial flying, and schools having a comprehensive curriculum for instruction in the operation, repair, and maintenance of aircraft.

In addition to the executive officers and advisory board prescribed by law, there quickly appeared four distinct sections—administrative, engineering, safety, and information—assigned specific functions and maintained by trained personnel under the direction of a section chief. Under the general supervision of the director, assistant director, and the respective section chiefs, and with the counsel of the advisory board, the department promulgated and enforced rules and regulations conforming to the general provisions of the aeronautics act. Effective, constructive regulations and strict enforcement, coupled with policies and programs designed to stimulate and nourish the aviation industry, led in time to its prosperous, healthy development and growth. Slowly at first, and then at a quickened tempo, Illinois climbed to a place of prominence in aeronautics. In number of licensed pilots, registered aircraft, and approved airports and landing fields, it contended for recognition among the leading states, ranking no lower than fifth in any category. To a large degree, this remarkable record reflects the outstanding work of the Department of Aeronautics. For this reason, a detailed examination of its work is an essential element of the history of aviation in the past decade.

The administrative section, with finance and legal divisions, took charge of the general administration of the department, including in time the administration of the Aircraft Financial Responsibility Law and matters pertaining to civil defense, public education, airport surveys, and similar functions.

The legal division was given the responsibility for conducting administrative hearings regarding violations of the Illinois Aeronautics Act with reference to personal and property rights. Hearings could also be conducted on violations of air safety rules, though normally these were given to the safety section.

The engineering section assumed the responsibility for carrying out the state airport improvement plan. Section 31 of the Aeronautics Act empowered the department to "designate, design, and establish, expand or modify a state airport plan and a state airways system which will best serve the interest of the State," both in the present and the future. The department's engineering section, headed by Norman C. Bird, consequently instituted and carried out an improvement program for a statewide system of publicly owned public-use airports. In addition, air-marking and airport-zoning programs have been handled by the engineering section.

The safety section approved and inspected continually, from a safety point of view, all commercial airports, restricted landing areas, and G.I. flight training schools. Accident investigation and enforcement of air traffic regulations were other important functions of the section. All enforcement measures were co-ordinated with the Civil Aeronautics Administration. Investigations of accidents were designed to determine whether or not infractions of air safety regulations were involved and to determine the cause of the accident in order to institute remedial and preventive action. In this, the department has co-operated with the Flight Safety Foundation and the Crash Injury Research Division of the Cornell University Medical College. Representatives of the safety section traveled extensively throughout the state to investigate and enforce air safety regulations, assisting complainants and law enforcement agencies in apprehending violators and instigating proceedings against violators of state air safety laws.

The general services section served primarily to register Federal Airmen and Airworthiness Certificates, to record violations, suspensions, and revocations, and to prepare and distribute informative charts, directories, bulletins, and other publications. In 1955, approximately 11,000 copies of *Illinois Aviation* were prepared and mailed quarterly to all pilots, airport managers, flight schools, and other interested persons. Special bulletins were mailed twice monthly to all airport operators, restricted landing-area owners, and fixed-base operators to keep them informed of state and federal aviation developments.

Since 1945, three men have held the position of director. The first, Robert Dewey, was appointed by Governor Green on September 15, 1945. During the next four years, Dewey guided the department through the difficult task of implementing the Illinois Aeronautics Act of 1945 and of establishing the programs and policies upon which the future of civil aeronautics in Illinois was to be founded. A bomber pilot and flight commander with 28 combat missions during World War II, Dewey assumed the directorship only ten days after his discharge from the Air Corps. His interest in the development of civil aviation fitted him for the active role he played in the National Association of State Aviation Officials, which he served as vice-president in 1946. In September, 1949, Governor Adlai E. Stevenson appointed Joseph K. McLaughlin to succeed Dewey. McLaughlin brought to the directorship a background that included aviation experience in private flying dating back to 1931, service in navy aviation as a lieutenant commander, and work as legal adviser for the Civil Aeronautics Administration. Following the resignation of McLaughlin on September 6, 1954, Governor William G. Stratton named Arthur E. Abney to the post. Abney had been assistant director since 1950. A native of Harco, Illinois, he served as a navy pilot in World War II and with the Aircraft Traffic Control Division of the Civil Aeronautics Administration before joining the Department of Aeronautics as a safety representative in 1948.

The excellent work of the department in the past ten years reflects not only the administrative ability of successive directors but also that of the various section chiefs and their personnel. Norman C. Bird, a veteran employee of the Illinois Aeronautics Commission, has served as chief engineer of the department's vital engineering section since 1945. William T. Thatcher, long a pilot and fixed-base operator, was chief inspector of the safety section between 1945 and 1947, while Kenneth W. Lawver was head of the section. Lawver became a special administrative assistant in 1947 and was succeeded by Mark A. Cooper as chief of safety. An information service, operated for several years under the direction of Malden Jones, later became a part of the general services section, Al Kaszynski, chief. More recently, the information section was re-created and placed under Robert Keller.

In order to provide close co-operation between the state government and private aviation interests, the Board of Aeronautics Advisors represents various phases of aviation activity. It consists of the executive officers of the department and seven other persons active in flying, either for business or pleasure. The first board, made up of Director Dewey, Assistant Director George C. Roberts, Lieutenant Colonel Henry Crown, Arthur Curry, A. H. Luke, W. A. Patterson, Fred C. Parks, Andrew P. Reboric, and Ben Regan, played an important part in revising the rules and regulations promulgated by the department. Since that time, the membership of the Board has been increased to nine. Dr. Leslie A. Bryan, director of the Institute of Aviation of the University of Illinois, and Leslie C. Johnson, of Rock Island, have served since 1949. The six other members appointed in 1949 served two consecutive two-year terms. They were N. Y. Alvis, of Salem; Norman D. McCoy, of Blue Mound; Q. Don Baily, of Table Grove; Gail Borden, of Chicago; Alvin W. Ahrens, of Lincoln; and William Burry, of Lake Forest. The present advisory board is made up of Bryan; Johnson; Director Abney; Assistant Director James D. Summers; George P. Johns, of Decatur; Louis Leverone, of Chicago; Milton J. Reed, of Champaign; Hal Roberts, of Dixon; and Bernard Roos, of Hinsdale.

The duties of the department, though already tremendously vast in scope, were broadened in the postwar years to include activities that were at one time within the sphere of federal agencies. These included maintenance and operation of certain types of air navigation facilities previously maintained and operated by the Civil Aeronautics Administration and its predecessors. The outlook for the future points to ever greater activity by the state agency in areas traditionally thought of as federal responsibilities. In the late 1940's, the Civil Aeronautics Administration announced that a number of airway facilities would be decommissioned and that henceforth only those facilities able to conform to instrument flight rules would be maintained at public expense; in other words, they would be maintained only for the airlines, the military, and large professionally piloted aircraft. This policy not only ignored the contribution of visual-type markers, guides, and certain other types of aids to nonscheduled flyers, including thousands of private pilots, but left their maintenance and operation up to private or state agencies. In the interests of nonscheduled flying the Illinois Department of Aeronautics assumed the responsibility for these airway facilities wherever possible. The department also maintains rooftop markers in some 500 communities. This service is financed by a special aeronautics fund, derived from the $1.00 annual fees for the registration of federal certificates.

In addition to the numerous functions cited in the preceding paragraphs, there are various areas of aeronautical regulation and supervision in which the federal government exercises no authority or only partial authority, leaving state agencies to do the necessary policing. Many of these duties actually fall within the sphere of federal regulations, as in the case of airport certification and zoning and the supervision of agricultural aviation and soil conservation and aircraft financial responsibility laws. The Civil Aeronautics Administration, however, requires only certain standards of airports in connection with certification of air carrier operating permits and, beyond this, views certification as an area for state action. The effectiveness of the department in this respect is indicated by the testimony of a national aviation underwriting firm attributing the small loss-ratio in Illinois to high standards for certification of airports, to periodic follow-up checks, to a vigorous safety enforcement program, and a continuous safety education program.

INDEX

INDEX

HOWARD L. SCAMEHORN is a professor emeritus in history at the University of Colorado. *Balloons to Jets* is the first of the seven books that Scamehorn has authored or coauthored in the course of his academic career. Among them are *The University of Colorado, 1876–1976; The Buckeye Rovers in the Gold Rush: An Edition of Two Diaries;* and *Albert Eugene Reynolds: Colorado's Mining King.*